Preface

Barely more than twenty years ago the inquiry into the nature and implications of the psychophysiologic stress response seemed to be restricted to laboratory animals. Today, however, scientists from a wide range of disciplines are studying stress and its implications for human health and disease. This may be because our technical ability actually to measure the phenomenon has increased, as has our understanding of human psychophysiology. Just as important, however, may be the fact that we have entered a new era of disease.

According to Kenneth Pelletier, we have entered upon an era in which stress plays a dominant role in the determination of human disease. Pelletier has stated that up to 90% of all disease may be stress-related. Whether this estimation seems inflated or not, the fact remains that clinicians of all kinds, including physicians, psychologists, physical therapists, social workers, and counselors, are daily being confronted with clients suffering from excessive psychophysiologic stress arousal. This fact has created a need to know more about the stress response and its treatment.

Although more and more health-care professionals are directly or indirectly working with clients who manifest excessive stress, there has been no text previously written which attempted to condense between the covers of a single volume a practical, clinically comprehensive discussion of what stress is (as best we currently understand it) and how to treat it when it becomes excessive.

This book was created to serve two basic functions: first, as a reference for practicing clinicians—whether they be physicians, psychologists, nurses, physical therapists, social workers, counselors, or health educators of any type; second, as a textbook for the growing number of courses which deal with the management or treatment of excessive stress. Our intent is not to present the final, definitive word on the subject but to offer the first practical digest of clinical interventions into the problem of excessive psychophysiological stress arousal. We must be quick to add that, in writing such a condensed text, the need arises to take a generic view of many topics. On the one hand, this can be a refreshing presentation of old issues that may yield new insight; on the other, in condensing material as must be done to create such a text, occasional omissions are inevitable. Therefore, wherever useful, we have chosen to cite primary sources, more elaborate discussions, or complete reviews in order to give the reader the advantage of access to more detailed information as it pertains to the issues discussed herein.

Because clinical practice is sometimes an art as well as a science, we have chosen occasionally to include our own "useful clinical perspectives," sometimes known as biases. However, when such perspectives are based on a wide range of clinical experience, they may prove of some value to the less experienced clinician.

This text, then, represents a digest covering many of the most commonly used, and a few relatively new, clinical interventions into the problem of excessive psychophysiologic stress arousal. Our main purpose is to provide an up-to-date, practical, and clinically useful guide to the nature and treatment of the stress response.

George S. Everly, Jr., Ph.D.
Robert Rosenfeld, M.D.

Washington, D.C.

The Nature and Treatment of the Stress Response

A Practical Guide for Clinicians

The Nature and Treatment of the Stress Response

A Practical Guide for Clinicians

George S. Everly, Jr.
University of Maryland
College Park, Maryland

and

Robert Rosenfeld
Walter Reed Army Medical Center
Washington, D.C.

with

Roger J. Allen
Lora C. Brown
Steven A. Sobelman
Harold J. Wain

PLENUM PRESS • NEW YORK AND LONDON

Library of Congress Cataloging in Publication Data

Everly, George S 1950-
The nature and treatment of the stress response.

Includes index.
1. Stress (Psychology) 2. Stress (Physiology)I. Rosenfeld, Robert, 1945- joint author. II. Title. [DNLM: 1. Stress, Psychological. 2. Stress, Psychological—Therapy. WM 172 E93n]
BF575.S75E88 616'.001'9 80-28550
ISBN 0-306-40677-2

First Printing—March 1981
Second Printing—February 1983

A Division of Plenum Publishing Corporation
233 Spring Street, New York, N.Y. 10013

Printed in the United States of America

To MARIDETH ROSE EVERLY, the new love in our lives
and to BECKY and JESSICA

Acknowledgments

We should like to thank the following individuals for their help in making this book possible: Betty Donovan, for meeting the unrealistic deadlines we placed on her typing skills, and for keeping a smile on her face through the entire process; Dr. Daniel Stern, for reviewing a portion of the manuscript; Flora Beaudet, for the illustrations in Chapters 1 and 2; Henry Schoebel, for the illustrations in Chapter 10; Jim Donnelly, for his technical assistance; Leonard R. Pace, our friend at Plenum, for his encouragement and support, as well as his professional insight; and finally our families, for their understanding and support.

Contents

PART ONE

THE STRESS RESPONSE AND ITS TREATMENT

In this first of three parts we shall present a basic introduction to the nature of the psychophysiological phenomenon generally referred to as stress. In addition, because the major focus of this text is on clinical intervention, we shall present seven fundamental concepts which are designed to facilitate the treatment of excessive stress.

CHAPTER 1

What Is Stress?

The focus of this text is on the treatment of excessive stress. Yet before the clinician can effectively intervene, he or she must thoroughly comprehend the nature of the clinical problem to be faced. In this first chapter the reader will be introduced to some of the basic considerations or foundations on which the treatment of the stress response is inevitably based.

DEFINING STRESS

It seems appropriate to begin a text on stress with a basic definition of the stress response. Later we shall examine what stress is from a far more detailed perspective, but for now let us start with the basics.

The term "stress" comes originally from the field of physics, where it refers to any strain, pressure, or force applied to a system. The term was first introduced into the allied health fields in 1926 by Hans Selye. As a second-year medical student at the University of Prague, he noted that individuals suffering from a wide range of physical ailments all seemed to have a constellation of common symptoms. These included loss of appetite, decreased muscular strength, elevated blood pressure, and loss of ambition to accomplish anything (Selye, 1974). Wondering why these symptoms seemed to appear commonly, regardless of the nature of the somatic disorder, led Selye to label this condition the "syndrome of just being sick" (Selye,

1956). In his early writings Selye used the term "stress" to describe "the sum of all nonspecific changes (within an organism) caused by function or damage," or more simply "the rate of wear and tear in the body." In a more recent definition the Selyean concept of stress is "the nonspecific response of the body to any demand" (Selye, 1974, p. 14).

Although widely accepted by many, the Selyean definition of stress has not gone unchallenged. The aspect of this definition to be most questioned is the degree of "nonspecificity" inherent in the stress response. Selye (1956, 1974) has argued that the stress response represents, for the most part, a highly nonspecific array of psychophysiological alternations independent of the nature of the precipitating stimulus. Other researchers have argued that there may exist varying degrees of specificity in the psychophysiological response patterns which emerge after stimulation. Such patterns may be a function of stimulus and individual organism predispositions (Everly, 1978a; Humphrey & Everly, in press; Mason, 1971; Mason, Maher, Hartley, Mougey, Perlow, & Jones, 1976; Sternbach, 1966). As to this point, this issue remains unresolved.

TREATING EXCESSIVE STRESS—CLINICAL ASSUMPTIONS

The focus of this text is primarily on the treatment of stress. Therefore, rather than offer our own definition of the stress response, it may be of far more utility to the clinician for us simply to summarize some of the key concepts that we consider to underlie the treatment of the stress response. Where necessary, these points will receive further elaboration later in the text.

1. Stress is a reaction to some stimulus.

2. The stress response represents a psychophysiological reaction. That is, the stress response involves complex mind/body interrelationships (Cannon, 1914; Mason, 1972; Selye, 1956).

3. The stress response is characterized by a potentially wide constellation of reactions which entail psychophysiological arousal (Cannon, 1953; Mason, 1972; Selye, 1956). These potential response mechanisms will be detailed in Chapter 2. Although the manifestations of the stress response are usually indicative of arousal, the stress response has been noted as entailing such extreme forms of arousal as to cause an actual slowing, inhibition, or complete stoppage of the

systems affected (Engle, 1971; Gellhorn, 1968, 1969; Selye, 1956, 1974). This depressive effect may be owing to the fact that the stress response has triggered inhibitory neurons or the secretion of inhibitory hormones, or simply aroused the affected end-organ to a point of creating a nonfunctional state (as in cardiac fibrillation). This seemingly paradoxical nature of the stress response is often a point of confusion for the beginning clinician.

4. The stimulus that evokes a stress response is called a stressor. A stimulus becomes a stressor by virtue of the cognitive interpretation, or meaning, that the individual assigns to the stimulus (see Ellis, 1973; Kirtz & Moos, 1974; Lazarus, 1966, 1976; Malmo, 1972); or by virtue of the fact that the stimulus affects the individual by way of some sensory or metabolic process which is in itself inherently stressful (see Cutting, 1972; Greden, 1974). For example, if an individual interprets some stimulus in his or her environment as being somehow challenging or aversive, then the stress response will most likely result. On the other hand, some stimuli, sometimes called sympathomimetics, are inherently capable of causing a stress response merely by sufficient exposure to the stimulus. These stimuli evoke a stress response without involving the higher interpretive mechanisms in the brain. They affect the individual via lower brain sensory mechanisms (as with extreme heat, cold, or noise intensities in excess of 85 decibels), digestive and metabolic mechanisms (as with caffeine, theobromine, theophylline, nicotine, and amphetamines), and via strenuous motor activity (such as heavy exercise or exertion). For technical elaboration of the mechanisms involved in these processes, see Selye (1976).

It is important for the clinician to understand that by far the greater part of the excessive stress in the client's life is self-initiated and self-propagated. This is owing to the fact that it is the client who interprets an otherwise neutral stimulus as possessing stress-evoking characteristics. Kirtz and Moos (1974) suggest that social stimuli do not directly affect the individual. Rather, the individual reacts to the environment in accordance with his or her interpretations of the environmental stimuli. These interpretations are affected by such variables as personality components, status and social-role behaviors, etc. As Hans Selye has stated, "It is not what happens to you that matters, but how you take it." These congitive-affective reactions are subject to exacerbation through usually self-initiated exposures to sympathomimetic stimuli, such as excessive caffeine consumption, etc.

Having the client realize and accept responsibility for the cause and reduction of excessive stress can be a major point in the therapeutic intervention. Therefore, we shall discuss this issue in greater detail in a later chapter.

5. In many individuals the chronic elicitation of the stress response can result in end-organ (the organ which manifests the clinical signs of excessive stress) dysfunctions or end-organ pathologies, characterized by structural changes in the end-organ tissue and structural system. When such change occurs because of stress, the disease bears the generic label of psychosomatic or psychophysiological disease.

Psychophysiological disorders are often confused with what has been formally termed hysterical neurosis, conversion type. The psychophysiological disorders, then called psychosomatic, were first described by Felix Deutsch in 1927 (see Shontz, 1975), in his examination of mind–body interaction in disease. However, it was Helen Dunbar (1935) who published the first major work on the phenomenon. At the present time, psychophysiological disorders are considered to be physical alterations in the body which are psychogenically induced (i.e., psychological in origin). If the tissue alterations are significant enough, and if the organ system being affected is essential to life, then the psychophysiological disorder may lead to exhaustion of the entire organism and ultimately death. Conversion reactions, on the other hand, involve functional impairments of sensory or motor systems, for example, hysterical blindness or hysterical paralysis. Like the psychophysiological disorder, the conversion reaction is psychogenic; unlike the psychophysiological disorder, the conversion reaction involves no direct tissue destruction. Therefore, the conversion reaction cannot lead directly to death.

Confusion between the two disorders can easily lead both the clinician and the client to underestimate the potential severity of the psychophysiological disorder. Similarly, client motivation to affect a remedy for the problem may be jeopardized. Therefore, it appears important not only for the clinician to understand the true nature of the psychophysiological disorder but for the client to do so as well.

6. Although recent reports concerning stress have emphasized its negative characteristics, stress arousal does have positive aspects as well.

Previous writers have viewed the stress response as an innate preservation mechanism, which in earlier periods of evolutionary development allowed man to endure the primitive challenges to his survival. Numerous researchers (Cannon, 1953; Chavat, Dell, & Folkow, 1964; also see Henry & Stephens, 1977 for a brief review) have concluded, and we shall see in later chapters, that the nature of the psychophysiological stress response is that of apparent preparatory arousal—arousal in preparation for physical exertion. When used in such a way, it is easy to see the adaptive utility of the stress response. Yet stress arousal in modern man under circumstances of strictly psychosocial stimulation might be viewed as inappropriate arousal of primitive survival mechanisms, in that the organism is aroused for physical activity, but seldom is such activity truly warranted and therefore seldom does it follow (see Benson, 1975).

Selye (1956, 1974) further distinguishes constructive from destructive stress, clearly pointing out that not all stress is deleterious. He argues that stress arousal can be a positive, motivating force which improves the quality of life. He calls such positive stress "eustress" (prefix *eu* from the Greek meaning "good"), and debilitating, excessive stress "distress." Figure 1 depicts the relationship between stress and health/performance. As Figure 1 indicates, as stress increases so does health/performance and general well-being. However, as stress continues to increase, a point of maximal return is reached. This point may be called the optimal stress level, because as stress continues to

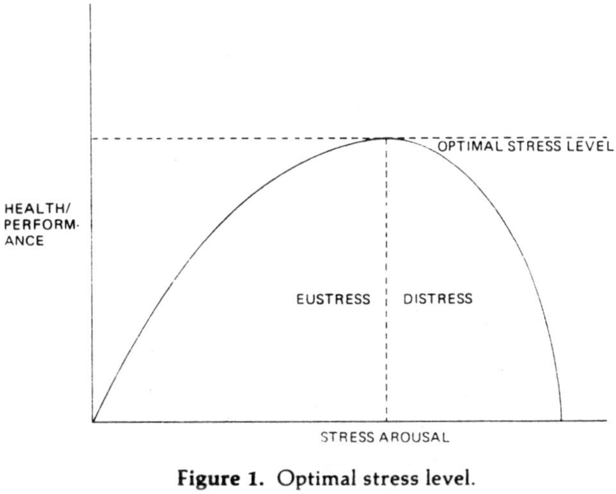

Figure 1. Optimal stress level.

increase, it becomes deleterious to the organism. The point at which an individual's optimal stress level is reached, that is, the apex of one's tolerance for stress as a productive force, seems to be a function of genetic biological, acquired physiological, and behavioral factors.

7. Last in this series of assumptions about what stress is and what it is not, there is common confusion as to the role of the nonmedical clinician in the treatment of the stress response. This confusion exists primarily because the end-organ effects or pathologies that result from excessive stress are mistakenly thought of as the psychophysiological stress response itself. It is important to remember the distinction that stress is a process of psychophysiological arousal (as detailed in Chapter 2), whereas the end-organ effects and pathologies (such as migraine headache, peptic ulcers, etc.) are the manifestations of chronically repeated and/or intense triggerings of the psychophysiological stress response (see Chapter 3). Treating the end-organ pathologies is clearly within the realm of the physician or specialist in behavioral medicine. However, the traditional psychologist, counselor, physical therapist, social worker, or health educator can effectively intervene in the stress-response process. This includes treating the excessive stress/anxiety that accompanies, and often exacerbates, chronic infectious and degenerative diseases (see Basmajian & Hatch, 1979).

It is important for the reader to understand that this text addresses the clinical problem of excessive psychophysiological arousal—that is, the excessive stress-response process itself. This text is not a detailed guide for psychotherapeutic intervention in the psychological trauma or conflict which may be at the root of the arousal (although we do feel that such intervention can play a useful role and we shall address this point later in the text). Nor is this a text which addresses the direct treatment of the end-organ pathologies which might arise as a result of excessive stress. We shall limit ourselves to a discussion of the clinical treatment of the psychophysiological stress-response process itself.

Based on a reivew of the literature, our conclusion is that treatment of the process of excessive psychophysiological stress arousal may take the form of three discrete interventions (see Girdano & Everly, 1979):

1. Helping the client develop and implement strategies by which to avoid/minimize/modify exposure to stressors, thus reducing

the client's tendency to experience the stress response (Ellis, 1973; Lazarus, 1966; Meichenbaum & Novaco, 1978).

2. Helping the client develop and implement skills which reduce excessive psychophysiological functioning and reactivity (Benson, 1975; Gellhorn & Kiely, 1972; Jacobson, 1938, 1970, 1978; Stoyva, 1976, 1977; Stoyva & Budzynski, 1974).
3. Helping the client develop and implement techniques for the healthful expression, or utilization, of the stress response (see Chavat *et al.*, 1964; Gevarter, 1978; Kraus & Raab, 1961).

Finally, it has been suggested that the clinicians who are the most successful in treating the stress response are those who have training not only in the psychology of human behavior, but in medical physiology as well (Miller, 1978; Miller & Dworkin, 1977). Our own teaching and clinical observations support this conclusion. If indeed accurate, this conclusion may be owing to the fact that stress represents the epitome of mind–body interaction. As Miller (1979) suggests, mere knowledge of therapeutic techniques is not enough. The clinician must understand the nature of the clinical problem as well. Therefore, the reader will find the treatment section of this text preceded by a basic discussion of the functional anatomy and physiology of the stress response.

PLAN OF THE BOOK

The purpose of the text is to provide a basic framework for the understanding and treatment of the stress response. With this goal in mind, we shall address the practical foundations of primary interest to the clinician. Therefore, we shall not attempt to provide exhaustive reviews of theoretical or esoteric research issues. At appropriate points, however, we shall reference more elaborate theoretical and research discussions for the interested reader.

In essence then, the first half of this text is really to serve as a foundation which the reader may use to place the treatment section in a better perspective. We will focus on as much theory as is necessary for understanding the rationale and techniques for therapeutic intervention. This is in no way diminishing the importance of basic theory in stress and its treatment, however. Similarly, we shall focus on functional anatomy and physiology as it relates to the stress response and its treatment. We do this because we feel that such a basic understanding is imperative for the development of effective clinical skills, yet we are also aware that far more exhaustive discussions of anatomy and physiology are available elsewhere (see Guyton, 1976; Mountcastle, 1974; Selye, 1976; Weil, 1974).

Finally, it is hoped that we will provide an appropriate mix of theory, research, and practical clinical considerations that the reader can use eventually to evolve clinical knowledge and skills far beyond the scope of this text.

PART TWO

THE NATURE OF THE STRESS RESPONSE

In this second part of the text we shall describe the nature of the stress response. In Chapter 2 we shall present a detailed model of the psychophysiological nature of the stress response. This model is unique in that it attempts to integrate the numerous and complex potential stress-response mechanisms. It must be mentioned in preface, however, that the precise nature of the human stress response has yet to be unquestionably defined. The model that we shall present is based on human research, animal research, and theory as well. Its intent is not to be complete in every finite detail, but to offer the clinican an integrated "global" perspective of the psychophysiological nature of stress which will hopefully add to clinical insight. Chapter 3 takes the logical extension from Chapter 2 and reviews how stress may lead to disease. We shall also briefly overview some of the more commonly proposed stress-related disorders. Finally, Chapter 4 addresses the measurement of the stress response.

CHAPTER 2

The Nervous Systems and the Stress Response

So intimately interwoven are mind and body that it has been said that there can be no psychological event without a resulting somatic (bodily) event, and no somatic event without a psychological event.

The stress response represents the epitome of mind–body interrelationships. Indeed, to understand the stress response one must possess a fundamental understanding not only of psychology but of physiology as well.

The purpose of this chapter is twofold: (1) to describe the neurological foundations of the stress response, and (2) to trace sequentially the active involvement of the psychophysiological mechanisms which represent the stress-response process.

In writing this chapter we have attemped to avoid needless complexity, yet elected to include information which may, at this point, seem excessively detailed or peripheral to the thrust of the chapter. Our rationale for including such information is simply the observation that some points, now seemingly irrelevant, will provide useful insight when later combined with clinical experience treating the stress response.

THE ORGANIZATION OF THE HUMAN NERVOUS SYSTEMS

In order to understand the stress response, we must first understand its foundations, which reside in the fundamental anatomy and physiology of the human nervous systems.

The basic anatomical unit which constitutes the nervous systems is the *neuron* (see Figure 2). The function of the neuron is to conduct sensory, motor, or regulatory signals throughout the body. The neuron consists of three basic functional subunits: the *dendrites*, which receive incoming signals; the *neural cell body*, or soma, which contains the nucleus of the cell; and the *axon*, which conducts signal impulses away from the cell body and relays the signal to another dendrite or to a target organ. Before this relay occurs, however, the impulse must be transmitted across a space called a *synapse*. To accomplish this crossing, the impulse utilizes various neurotransmitters, which are nothing more than chemical substances released from storage at the terminal branches (called *telodendria*) of the axon. The neurotransmitting substances cross the synaptic gap and allow the impulse to continue its transmission. The neurotransmitters of primary interest in the study of stress are noradrenalin (norepinephrine) and acetylcholine.

The actual transmission of the impulses along the neuron is based on a complex process of electrochemical conduction. This electrochemical activity occurs by the movement of ions across the membrane of the axon (see Figure 3). The conduction of impulses yields a measurable electrical event, seen as the increase in voltage occurring in the action-potential spike during depolarization. The measurable

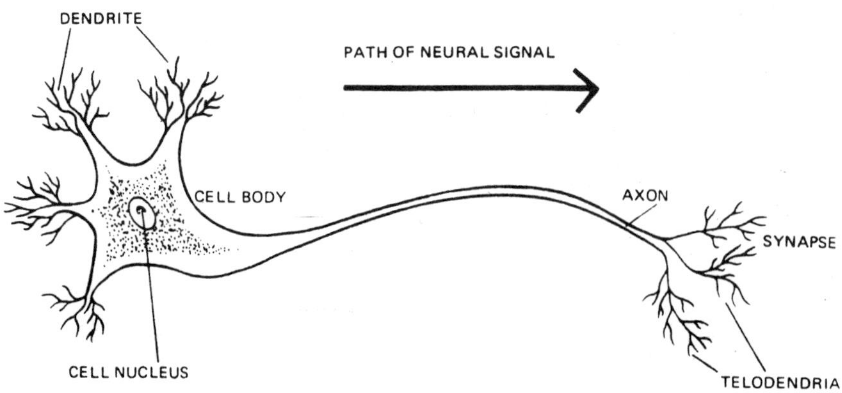

Figure 2. A typical neuron.

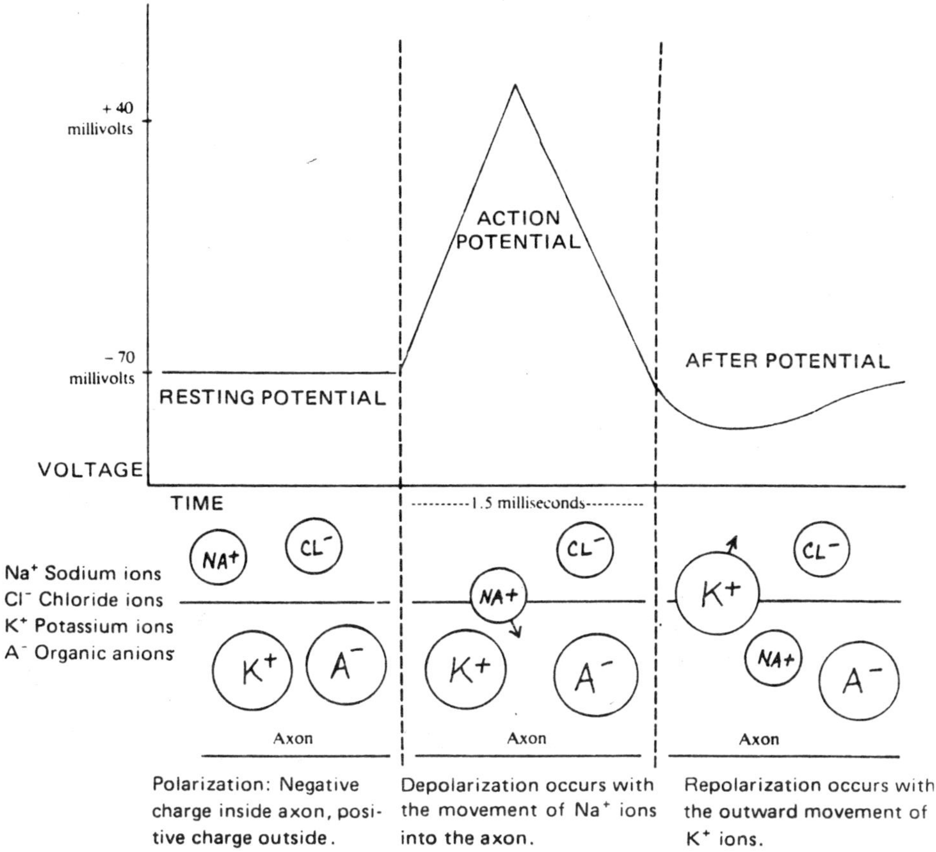

Figure 3. The electrochemical neural impulse.

electrical event acts as the basis for electrophysiological measurement processes, such as electromyography, electrocardiography, etc.

From the neuron, we may now progress into a discussion of the major nervous systems in which neurons reside. These systems may be classified from a "functional" viewpoint, or from an "anatomical" viewpoint. For the sake of parsimony, we shall choose the latter. Therefore, from an anatomical perspective there exist two fundamental nervous systems: the *central nervous system* (CNS) and the *peripheral nervous system* (PNS). (See Figure 4.)

The CNS consists of the brain and the spinal chord (see Figure 5).

Paul MacLean (1975) has called the human brain the "triune brain," because of its three functional levels.

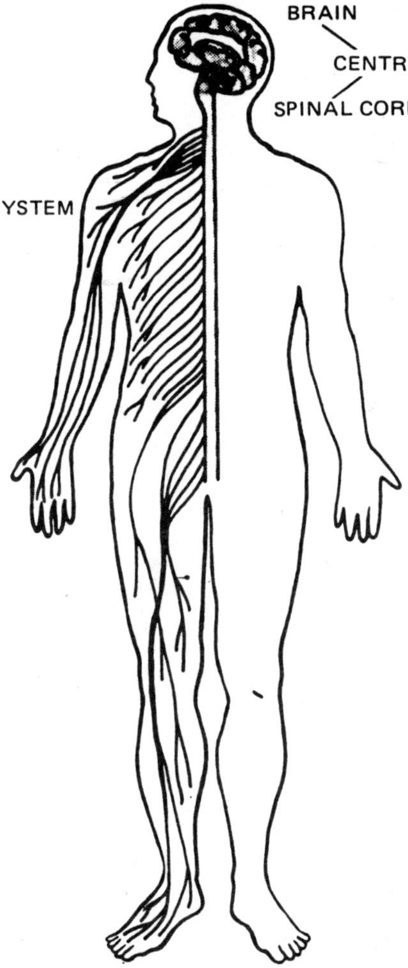

Figure 4. Nervous systems (adapted from Lachman, 1972).

The *neocortex* represents the highest level of the triune brain and is the most sophisticated component of the human brain. Among other functions, such as the decoding and interpretation of sensory signals, communications, and gross control of motor (musculoskeletal) behaviors, the neocortex (primarily the *frontal lobe*) presides over imagination, logic, decision making, memory, problem solving, planning, and apprehension.

The *limbic system* represents the major component of the second level of the triune brain. The limbic brain is of interest in the discussion of stress because of its role as the emotional (affective) control center for the human brain. The limbic system is believed to be just that, that is, a *system*, consisting of numerous neural structures, for example, the *hypothalamus, hippocampus, septum, cingulate gyrus,* and *amygdala.* The *pituitary gland* plays a major functional role in this system in that it is the master endocrine gland.

The *reticular formation* and the *brain stem* represent the lowest level of the triune brain. The major functions of this level are the maintenance of vegetative functions (heart beat, respiration, vasomotor activity) and the conduction of impulses through the reticular formation and relay centers of the *thalamus* en route to the higher levels of the triune brain.

As for the spinal cord, it represents the central pathway for neurons as they conduct signals to and from the brain. It is also involved in some autonomically regulated reflexes.

The PNS consists of all neurons in the body exclusive of the CNS. Anatomically, the PNS may be thought of as an extension of the CNS in that the functional control centers for the PNS lie in the CNS. The

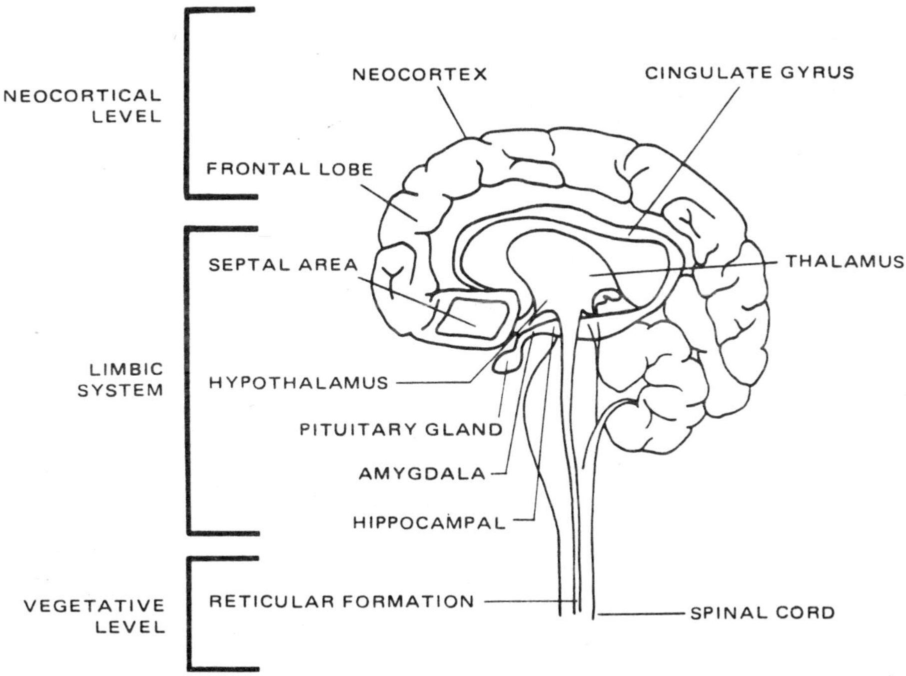

Figure 5. The human brain.

PNS may be divided in two networks: the somatic and the autonomic.

The somatic network carries sensory and motor signals to and from the CNS. Thus it innervates sensory mechanisms and striate muscles.

The autonomic network carries impulses which are concerned with the regulation of the body's internal environment and the maintenance of homeostasis (balance). The autonomic network,

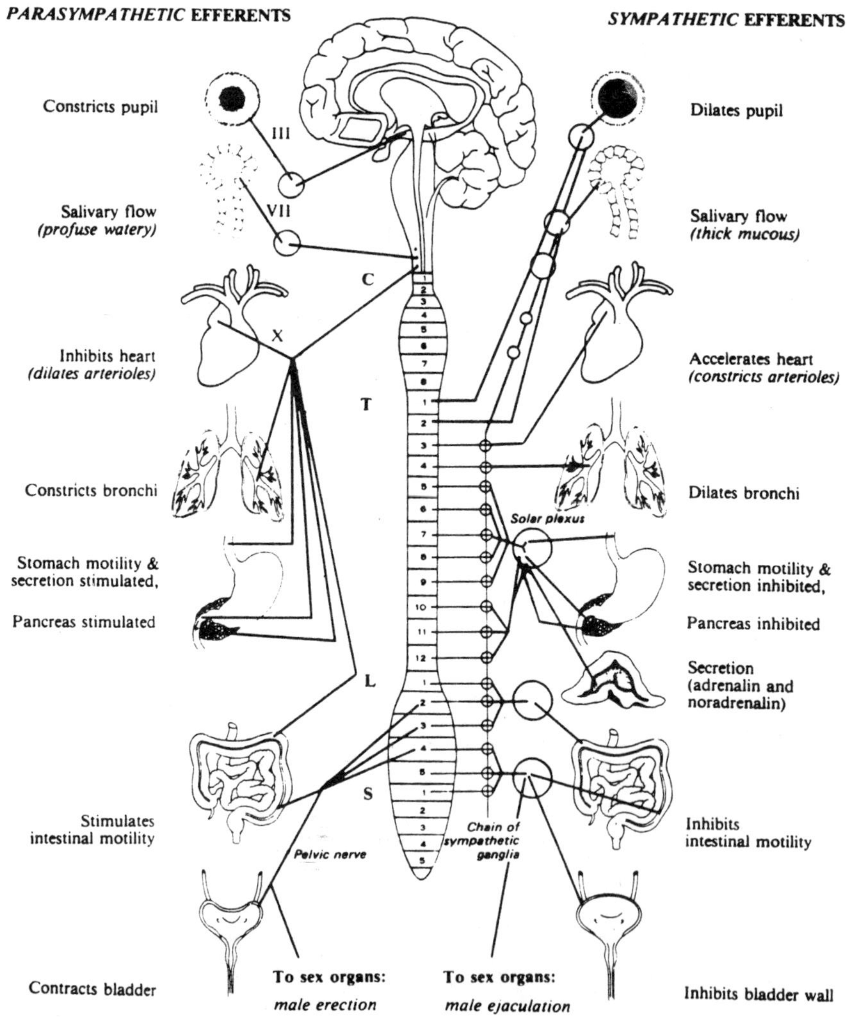

Figure 6. Efferent autonomic pathways.

therefore, innervates the heart, the smooth muscles, and the glands.

The autonomic nervous system can be further subdivided into two branches, the sympathetic and the parasympathetic (see Figure 6 for details of autonomic innervation). The sympathetic branch of the autonomic nervous system is concerned with preparing the body for action. Its effect on the organs it innervates is that of generalized arousal. The parasympathetic branch of the autonomic nervous system is concerned with restorative functions and the relaxation of the body. Its general effects are those of slowing and maintenance of basic bodily requirements. The specific effects of sympathetic and parasympathetic activation on end-organs are summarized later in this chapter (see Table I).

To this point we have briefly described the most basic of the anatomical and functional aspects of the human nervous system. We are now ready to see how these elements become interrelated as constituents of the human stress-response process.

INTRODUCTION TO THE STRESS RESPONSE

The stress response is perhaps best described in the context of the "process" it appears to be. Therefore our description of the stress response will focus, in order, on the sequence of events which collectively define the stress-response process.

The following, sometimes oversimplified, description is used to illustrate the stress response as a reaction to an external psychosocial stimulus.

The Initiation of the Stress Response—CNS Mechanisms

If any given, otherwise neutral, stimulus is to evoke a stress response, it must first be received by the sensory receptors of the PNS. Once stimulated, the sensory receptors send impulses along the sensory pathways of the PNS toward the brain. According to Snyder (1974) and Penfield (1975), once in the CNS, collateral nerves from the sensory pathways diverge from the main ascending pathways to the neocortex and innervate the reticular formation. Snyder (1974) argues that "Via these collaterals, events perceived in the environment may be integrated with . . . emotional states encoded in the hypothalamus and limbic system" (p. 221).

Table I. Responses of Effector Organs to Autonomic Nervous System Impulses

	SNS	PNS
Function:	ergotropic; catabolism	trophotropic; anabolism
Activity:	diffuse	discrete
Anatomy:		
emerges from spinal cord	thoracolumbar	craniosacral
location of ganglia	close to spinal cord	close to target organ
postganglionic neurotransmitter	noradrenalin[a] (adrenergic)	acetylcholine (cholinergic)
Specific actions:		
pupil of the eye	dilates	constricts
lacrimal gland	—	stimulates secretion
salivary glands	scanty, thick secretion	profuse, water secretion
heart	increases heart rate increases contractility increases rate of idiopathic pacemakers in ventricles	decreases heart rate decreases metabolism
blood vessels		
skin and mucosa	constricts	—
skeletal muscles	dilates	—
cerebral	constricts	dilates
renal	constricts	—
abdominal viscera	mostly constricts	—
lungs		
bronchial tubes	dilates	constricts
sweat glands	stimulates[a]	—
liver	glycogenolysis for release of glucose	expels bile
spleen	contracts to release blood high in erythrocytes	—
adrenal medulla	secretes adrenaline (epinephrine) and noradrenaline (norepinephrine)[a]	—
gastrointestinal tract	inhibits digestion	increases digestion

Table I. (*cont.*)

	SNS	PNS
	decreases peristalsis and tone	increases peristalsis and tone
kidney	decreases output of urine	?
hair follicles	piloerection	—
male sex organ	ejaculation	erection

[a] Postganglionic SNS neurotransmitter is acetylcholine for most sweat glands and some blood vessels in skeletal muscles. Adrenal medulla is innervated by preganglionic cholinergic sympathetic neurons. Partially adapted from Hassett, 1978.

These divergent pathways ultimately reunite with the main ascending pathways and innervate the neocortex where interpretive analysis of the stimulus is undertaken. In addition to the "orienting response," Snyder (1974) and Gevarter (1978) conclude that the collaterals which diverge into the reticular formation may then account for the emotional "gut reaction" which we sometimes experience in response to psychosocial stimuli.

The "emotionally-colored" (Gevarter, 1978) neocortical interpretations are then fed back to the limbic system. If the neocortical-limbic interpretation of the psychosocial stimulus yields a perception of a threat or a challenge, or is otherwise aversive, then emotional arousal will most likely result.

In most individuals the activation of emotional mechanisms stimulates one or more of the three major psychosomatic stress axes (see Figure 7).* Therefore we see that in the final analysis stress reactions to psychosocial stimuli result from the cognitive interpretation of the stimuli and the emotional arousal (see Lazarus, 1966, 1976; Malmo, 1972; Stoyva, 1976), rather than from the stimuli themselves.

Neural Axes—Stress Response via Direct Neural Innervation of End-Organs

The first major pathways which will make their activation manifest somatically during the stress response are the sympathetic

*In cases where the stressor stimulus is internally initiated (e.g., imagined or recalled), the incoming functions of the PNS are bypassed. In cases where the stressor is a sympathomimetic, the neocortical and limbic CNS centers are not required to initiate a stress reaction.

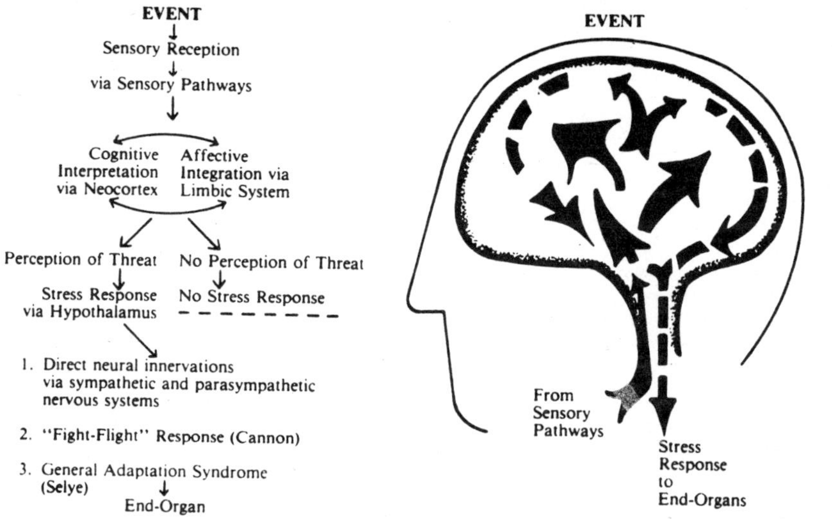

Figure 7. The stress response.

and the parasympathetic branches of the autonomic nervous system. This is because their pathways to affect somatic end-organs are completely neural and therefore quickest.

It is clear that autonomic nervous system activation occurs during states of emotional arousal in human beings (Duffy, 1962; Johnson & Spalding, 1974; Lindsley, 1951). These neural axes are the most direct of all stress pathways. Following the complex neocortical and limbic integrations which occur in the interpretation of a stimulus as "threatening," neural impulses descend to the posterior hypothalamus (in the case of a sympathetic activation) and the anterior hypothalamus (in the case of a parasympathetic activation). From here sympathetic neural pathways descend from the posterior hypothalamus through the thoracic and lumbar regions of the spinal cord. Having passed through the sympathetic chain of ganglia, the sympathetic nerves then innervate the end-organs. Parasympathetic pathways descend from the anterior hypothalamus through the cranial and sacral spinal-cord regions. Parasympathetic nerves then innervate the end-organs (Guyton, 1976).

Generally speaking, the release of the neurotransmitter norepinephrine from the sympathetic telodendria is responsible for changes in end-organ activity. Acetylcholine is the neurotransmitter in the remaining cases, and for the parasympathetic postganglionic transmissions as well.

The effects of neural activation via the sympathetic system are those of generalized arousal within the end-organ—what Hess (1957) referred to as an "ergotropic" response. The effects of activation via the parasympathetic system are inhibition, slowing, and "restorative" functions—what Hess called a "trophotropic" response. The specific end-organ effects of the sympathetic and the parasympathetic nervous systems are summarized in Table I.

Although the most common form of neural autonomic stress responsiveness in human beings is in the form of the ergotropic response (Johnson & Spalding, 1974), simultaneous trophotropic responses have been observed in human beings as well (Gellhorn, 1969). The trophotropic stress response may be perceived by some clinicians as paradoxical, owing to the expectation of manifestations of somatic "arousal." However, the important work of Gellhorn (1968, 1969) in addition to the clinical observations of Karasarsky (1969), Engle (1971), and Carruthers and Taggart (1973), have demonstrated that sympathetic stress arousal can be accompanied by parasympathetic trophotropic activation.

The major effects of autonomic neural activation on end-organs during the stress response are immediate, but not potentially chronic. This is because of the limited ability of the sympathetic telodendria to continue constantly to release neurotransmitters under chronically high stimulation (LeBlanc, 1976). Therefore, in order to maintain high levels of stress arousal for a longer time, an additional psychophysiological axis must be activated for participation in the stress response. This axis has been called the "fight or flight" response.

"Fight or Flight" Response—The Neuroendocrine Axis

In the same year that Selye first described the "syndrome of just being sick," 1926, Walter Cannon first wrote about a phenomenon that he termed homeostasis. Homeostasis was described as the effort of the physiological systems within the body actively to maintain a level of functioning, within the limits of tolerance of the systems, in the face of ever changing conditions. Homeostasis was the adaptational effort of the body to stay in balance. From his early efforts, it was clear that the work of Cannon was to parallel and augment that of Selye in terms of understanding the psychophysiological stress response.

Cannon wrote extensively on one particular aspect of the autonomic nervous system's role in the stress response—the neuroendocrine process. He researched what he termed the "fight or flight" response. The pivotal organ in this response is the adrenal medulla—thus giving this response both neural ANS characteristics and endocrine characteristics (Cannon 1914, 1953; Cannon & Paz, 1911).

The "fight or flight" response is thought to be a mobilization of the body to prepare for muscular activity in response to a perceived threat. This mechanism allows the organism either to fight or to flee from the perceived threat (Cannon, 1953).

Research has demonstrated that the homeostatic, neuroendocrine "fight or flight" response can be activated in human beings by numerous and diverse psychologic influences, including varied psychosocial stimuli (Fröberg, Karlsson, Levi, & Lidberg, 1971; Levi, 1972; Mason, 1968a, 1972; Roessler & Greenfield, 1962).

The dorsomedial-amygdalar complex appears to represent the highest point of origination for the "fight or flight" response as a functionally discrete psychophysiological axis (Lang, 1975; Röldan, Alvarez-Pelnez, & de Molina, 1974). From that point, the downward flow of neural impulses passes to the lateral and posterior hypothalamic regions (Röldan *et al.*, 1974). From here neural impulses continue to descend through the thoracic spinal cord, converging at the celiac ganglion, then innervating the adrenal medulla (Guyton, 1976).

Adrenal medullary stimulation results in the release of adrenalin and noradrenalin into the systemic circulation.

The effects of these medullary catecholamines are to create an increase in generalized adrenergic somatic activity in human beings (Folkow & Neil, 1971; Marañon, 1924; Wenger, Clemens, Coleman, Cullan, & Engel, 1960). Their effects, therefore, are functionally identical to direct sympathetic innervation (see Table I), except that they require a twenty- to thirty-second delay of onset for measurable effects and display a tenfold increase in effect duration (Usdin, Kretnansky, & Kopin, 1976). Also, the catecholamines only prolong the adrenergic sympathetic response. Cholinergic responses, such as increased electrodermal activity and bronchiole effects, are unaffected by medullary catecholamine release (Guyton, 1976; Usdin *et al.*, 1976).

Specific somatic effects which have been observed in human

beings as an apparent result of activation of the amygdalar-posterior hypothalamic-adrenal medullary axis in response to psychosocial stimuli are summarized in Table II.

Although the effects of the adrenal medullary catecholamines far outlast the effects of the neural ANS axes, there is an even more chronic phase in the stress response. These most chronic of stress mechanisms result from activation of the endocrine stress axes.

Endocrine Axes and the "General Adaptation Syndrome"

The most chronic and prolonged somatic responses to stress are the result of the endocrine axes (Mason, 1968b). There exist three basic endocrine axes which have been implicated in the stress response of human beings: the adrenal cortical axis, the somatotropic axis, and the thyroid axis. These axes not only represent the most chronic aspects of the stress response, but also require greater intensity stimulation to activate (Levi, 1972).

Reviews by Mason (1968c, 1972), Selye (1976) and Levi (1972) conclude that the three endocrine axes can be activated in human beings by numerous and diverse psychological influences, including varied psychosocial stimuli.

The Adrenal Cortical Axis

The septal-hippocampal complex appears to represent the highest point of origination for the adrenal cortical axis as a physiologically

Table II. Effects of Adrenal Medullary Axis Stimulation[a]

Increased arterial blood pressure
Increased cardiac output
Decreased amount of blood flow to the kidneys
Decreased size of the arterial lumen at the vascular bed levels in skin (vasoconstriction)
Increased plasma levels of free fatty acids
Increased muscle tension (contraction of muscle fibers)
Increased plasma triglyceride levels
Increased plasma cholesterol levels

[a] See Brod, 1959, 1971; Froberg, Karlsson, & Lidberg, 1971; and Henry & Stephens, 1977, for reviews.

discrete mechanism (Henry & Ely, 1976; Henry & Stephens, 1977). From these points, neural impulses descend to the median eminence of the hypothalamus. The neurosecretory cells in the median eminence release corticotropin releasing factor (CRF) into the hypothalamic-hypophyseal portal system (Rochefort *et al.*, 1959). The CRF descends the infundibular stalk to the cells of the anterior pituitary. The chemophobes of the anterior pituitary are sensitive to the presence of CRF and respond by releasing adrenocorticotropic hormone (ACTH) into the systemic circulation (Guyton, 1976). Ultimately, the ACTH finds its way to the adrenal cortex.

ACTH appears to act upon three discrete layers, or zona, of the adrenal cortex. ACTH stimulates the cells of the zona reticularis and zona fasciculata to release the glucocorticoids cortisol and corticosterone into the systemic circulation. The effects of the glucocorticoids in apparent response to stressful stimuli are summarized in Table III.

Similarly, ACTH allows the zona glomerulosa to secrete the mineralocorticoids aldosterone and deoxycorticosterone into the systemic circulation. These hormones are primarily concerned with regulating electrolytes and blood pressure through volumetric adjustments: primarily sodium reabsorption (Guyton, 1976).

Excessive activation of mineralocorticoid secretion in human beings has been implicated in the development of Cushing's Syndrome (hyperadrenocorticism) by Gifford and Gunderson (1970), and in high blood pressure and myocardial necrosis by Selye (1976).

The Somatotropic Axis

The somatotropic axis appears to share the same basic physiological mechanisms from the septal-hippocampal complex through the hypothalamic-hypophyseal portal system as the previous axis, with the exception that somatotropin releasing factor (SRF) stimulates the anterior pituitary within this axis. The anterior pituitary responds to the SRF by releasing growth hormone (somatotropic hormone) into the systemic circulation (see Selye, 1976).

The role of growth hormone in stress is somewhat less clearly understood than that of the adrenal cortical axis. However, research has documented its release in response to psychological stimuli in human beings (Selye, 1976), and certain effects are suspected. Selye (1956) has stated that growth hormone stimulates the release of the mineralocorticoids. Yuwiler (1976) in his review of stress and endo-

Table III. The Effects of the Glucocorticoid Hormones[a]

Increased glucose production (gluconeogenesis)
Increased urea production
Increased free fatty acid release into systemic circulation
Increased susceptibility to nonthrombotic myocardial necrosis
Thymicolymphatic atrophy (demonstrated in animals only)
Potential of supression of the immune mechanisms
Exacerbation of herpes simplex
Increased ketone body production

[a] See Henry & Stephens, 1977; Selye, 1976; Yates & Maran, 1972; and Yuwiler, 1976, for reviews.

crine function suggests that growth hormone produces a diabeticlike insulin-resistant effect, as well as a mobilization of fats stored in the body. The effect is to increase the concentration of free fatty acids and glucose in the blood.

The Thyroid Axis

The thyroid axis is the least understood of the stress-response endocrine axes. Although known to be vulnerable to psychological activation (Levi, 1972; Yuwiler, 1976), its specific role is unclear, and some research evidence is clearly conflicting (see Selye, 1976).

It appears to be safe to conclude at this time that the thyroid axis shares the septal-hippocampal complex and median eminence with the two previous axes. However, from the median eminence thyrotropin releasing factor (TRF) is sent through the portal system to the anterior pituitary. From the anterior pituitary, thyroid-stimulating hormone (TSH) is released into the systemic circulation. TSH stimulates the thyroid gland to release the hormone thyroxine into the systemic circulation.

In human beings, psychosocial stimuli have generally led to an increase in thyroidal activity (Levi, 1972; Yuwiler, 1976). Levi (1972) has stated that the thyroid hormones have been shown to increase general metabolism, heart rate, heart contractility, peripheral vascular resistance (thereby increasing blood pressure), and the sensitivity of some tissues to catecholamines. Levi therefore concludes that the thyroid axis could play a significant role as a response axis in human stress.

The "General Adaptation Syndrome"

Hans Selye (1956) has developed a theoretical framework within which to structure the collective role of the endocrine response axes during *chronic* stress. The framework is called the "General Adaptation Syndrome" (GAS).

The GAS is a triphasic phenomenon. The first phase he calls the *alarm* phase. This reaction represents a generalized somatic shock, or "call to arms" of the body's defensive mechanisms. During this phase the endocrine system responds with activation of the three endocrine axes detailed earlier. The primary emphasis appears to be on the adrenal cortical system. The next phase is called the *stage of resistance*. In this phase there is a dramatic reduction in most *alarm*-phase processes. Localized somatic resistance is high during this phase. This is the body's attempt to maintain homeostasis in the presence of the stressor which initiated the *alarm* phase. Should the stressor persist, eventually the "adaptive energy," that is, the adaptive mechanisms involved in supporting the *stage of resistance*, will become depleted. At this point the body enters its final phase, the *stage of exhaustion*. Here the body once again triggers a generalized somatic alarm. The three endocrine axes are once again highly activated. In some cases the actual survival of the organism may be at stake (see Selye, 1976, for a more detailed discussion of GAS).

The GAS represents a further extension of the temporal perspective that we have attempted to show as being inherent in the stress response. However, the GAS sequence appears to pertain primarily to the role of the endocrine axes in stress.

Posterior Pituitary Axis

Since the early 1930s there has been speculation on the role of the posterior pituitary in the stress response.

The posterior pituitary (neurohypophysis) receives neural impulses from the supraoptico nuclei of the hypothalamus. Stimulation from these nuclei results in the release of the hormones vasopressin (antidiuretic hormone, sometimes shortened to ADH) and oxytocin into the systemic circulation.

ADH affects the human organism by increasing the permeability of the collecting ducts which lie subsequent to the distal ascending tubules within the glomerular structures of the kidneys. The end result is a retention of water.

Corson and Corson (1971) in their review of psychosocial influences on renal function note several studies which report significant amounts of water retention in apparent response to psychological influences in human beings.

Although there seems to be agreement that water retention can be psychogenically induced, there is little agreement on what the specific mechanism is. Corson and Corson (1971) report studies which point to the release of elevated amounts of ADH in response to stressful episodes. On the other hand, some studies conclude that the antidiuretic effect is due to decreased renal blood flow. Some human subjects even responded with a diuretic response to psychosocial stimuli.

At this time the data on ADH as a stress-responsive hormone are inconclusive.

As for oxytocin, there exists no current evidence to suggest a psychogenic role in the stress response.

SUMMARY—THE STRESS RESPONSE

In this chapter we have presented a unifying perspective from which to view the complex psychophysiological processes that have come to be known as the stress response. Clearly, some aspects of this model are theoretical or based on limited research. Our intention was merely to provide the clinician with an understandable interpretation of the complexities of the stress response process which he or she will often find him- or herself treating. Since effective treatment of the stress phenomenon is related to comprehension of the nature of the problem (Miller, 1978, 1979), it is hoped that this discussion will prove of some utility for the clinician.

The unifying thread throughout this discussion has been the temporal sequencing of the stress-response process. We have shown that the most immediate response to a stressful stimulus occurs via the direct neural innervations of end-organs. The intermediate stress effects are due to the neuroendocrine "fight or flight" axis. The reaction time of this axis is reduced by its utilization of systemic circulation as a transport mechanism. However, its effects range from intermediate to chronic in duration and may overlap with the last stress-response system to respond to a stimulus—the endocrine axes. The endocrine axes are the final pathways to react to stressful stimuli. This is primarily owing to the almost total reliance on the circulatory system for transportation, as well as the fact that a higher intensity stimulus is needed to activate this axis. The GAS provides an additional schema to extend the endocrine response axis in the adaptation of the organism to the presence of a chronic stressor (see Selye, 1956, for a discussion of diseases of adaptation). Figure 8 summarizes the sequential activation of the stress-response axes.

It is important to understand that there is a potential for the

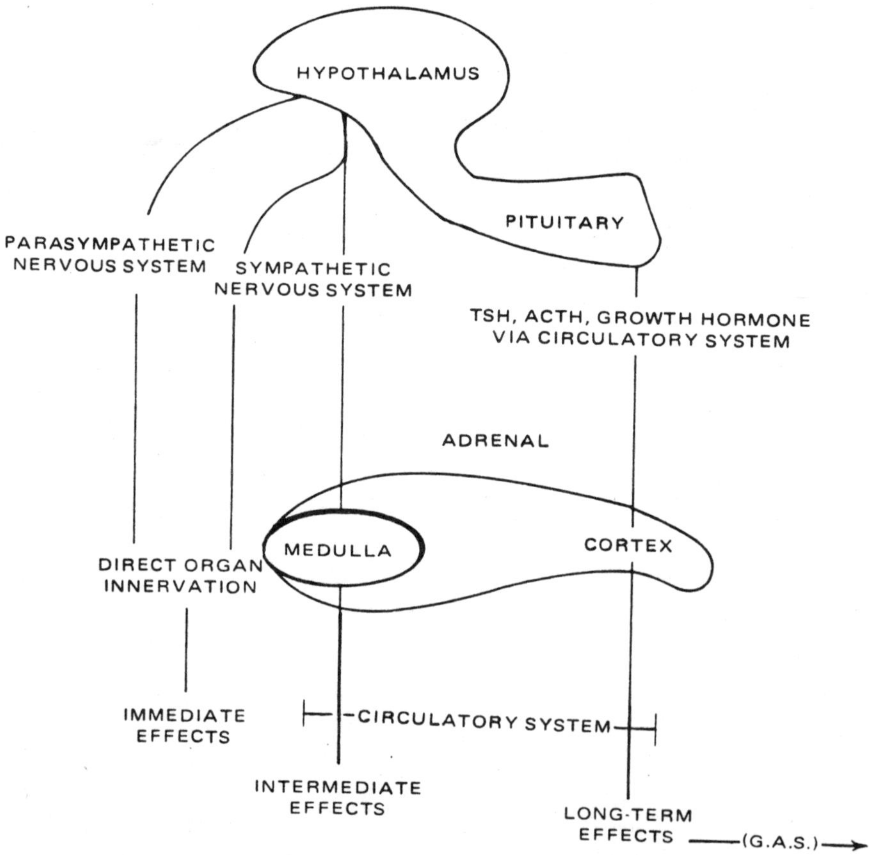

Figure 8. Cognitive and affective arousal. Temporal relationships between stress pathways.

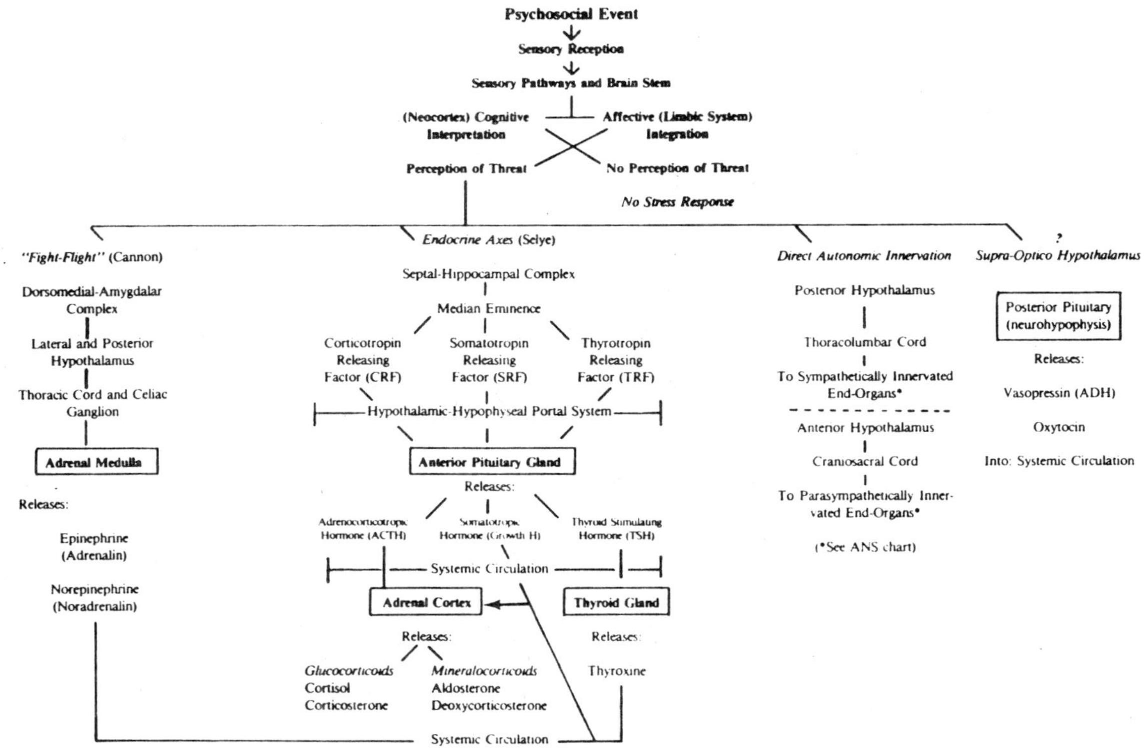

Figure 9. A model of potential pathways for stress reactivity to psychosocial stimuli.

activation of each of these axes to overlap into one another. The most common axes to be simultaneously active are the neuroendocrine and endocrine axes—both of which have potential for chronic responsivity (Mason, 1968a,c).

On the other hand, it is clear that all mechanisms and all axes which we have detailed cannot possibly discharge each and every time a person is faced with a stressor. Perhaps clearest of all is the fact that each sympathetic and parasympathetic effect is not manifest to all stressors. Therefore, what determines which stress-reponse mechanisms will be activated by which stressors in which individuals? The answer to this question is currently unknown. However, there is some evidence to suggest the existence of a psychophysiological predisposition for some individuals to undergo stress-response pattern specificity (see Sternbach, 1966). We will expand on this topic in Chapter 3.

These, then, are the stress-response axes and the various mechanisms that work within each. They represent the response patterns that can potentially result each time the human organism is exposed to a stressor. As to when each responds and why, we are unsure at this time. Current speculations will be reviewed in a later chapter. Despite this uncertainty, the clinician should gain useful insight into the treatment of the stress response by understanding the psychophysiological processes involved once the stress response becomes activated. To assist the reader in putting the picture together, we have provided a unique "global" perspective (Figure 9) into the nature of psychophysiological stress.

The next chapter takes the logical extension of the stress response and follows it into the potential effects that stress can have on the major organ systems in the human body. This chapter will be of value in providing the clinician with biomedical insight into excessive stress by examining its potential adverse reactions on end-organ systems—and these end-organ pathologies are typically the motivating force which drives the client to seek professional assistance. For the internist or behavioral-medicine practitioner, they may be the target problems; for the psychologist and psychiatrist they will be merely the manifestations of the pathological stress response. In either case, an understanding of their psychophysiological origins and signs will be of value in their ultimate treatment (Miller, 1978, 1979; Miller & Dworkin, 1977).

CHAPTER 3

From Stress to Disease

In Chapter 2 we reviewed the literature and proposed a model which may be used as a basis for understanding stress as a psychophysiological response process. In Chapter 3 we shall take the logical extension from the psychophysiological stress response itself and discuss how stress may lead to disease. Also in this chapter we shall briefly mention the stress-related disorders which are most commonly encountered by the clinician.

THEORETICAL BASES FOR THE DEVELOPMENT OF STRESS-RELATED DISEASES

As noted in the previous chapter, all the potential stress-response axes detailed earlier cannot become active at once within the same individual. Nor can all of the potential end-organ systems be affected within the same individual during a single stress response. However, the method by which the human body specifically selects which end-organ system to affect and via which stress response axis to do so is currently open to speculation. As a result, there has been considerable theory formulation and research as to the nature of the link between stress and disease.

Lachman's Model

In a "behavioral interpretation" of psychosomatic disease, Lachman (1972) proposes the following model to explain the stress-to-disease phenomenon: "In order for emotional reactions to assume pathological significance such reactions must be intense or chronic or both" (p. 70). He goes on to state that which end-organ structure will be affected pathologically depends on:

1. Genetic factors which biologically predispose the organ to harm from psychophysiological arousal.
2. Environmental factors which predispose the organ to harm from psychophysiological arousal. These would include such things as nutritional influences, infectious disease influences, physical trauma influences, etc.
3. The specific structures involved in the physiological reactivity.
4. The magnitude of involvement during the physiological response, which he has defined in terms of intensity, frequency, and duration of involvement of the organ.

Lachman (1972) concludes that the determination of which structure is ultimately affected in the psychosomatic reaction depends on "the biological condition of the structure," (whether a function of genetic or environmental influences), "on the initial reactivity threshold of the organ, and on . . . learning factors" which affect the activation of the organ. He goes on to note that the "magnitude of the psychosomatic phenomenon" appears to be a function of the frequency, intensity, and chronicity of the organ's activation.

Sternbach's Model

In a somewhat more psychophysiologically oriented model, Sternbach (1966) provides another perspective on the stress-to-disease issue.

The first step in Sternbach's model is *response stereotypy*. This term generally refers to the tendency of an individual to exhibit characteristically similar patterns of psychophysiological reactivity to a variety of stressful stimuli. Sternbach views it as a "predisposed response set." That such a response stereotypy phenomenon does indeed exist has been clearly demonstrated in patient and normal populations (Lacey & Lacey, 1958, 1962; Malmo & Shagass, 1949; Moos & Engel, 1962; Schnore, 1959).

Response stereotypy may be generally thought of as a form of the "weak-link" or "weak-organ" theory of psychosomatic disease.

Whether the weak organ is genetically determined, a function of conditioning, or acquired through disease or physical trauma is unclear.

The second step in the Sternbach model entails the frequent activation of the psychophysiological stress response within the stereotypic organ. As Stoyva (1977) notes, the mere existence of response stereotypy is not enough to cause disease. It is obvious that the organ must be involved in frequent activation in order to be adversely affected.

Finally, Sternbach's model includes the requirement that homeostatic mechanisms fail; that is, once the stereotypic organ has undergone psychophysiological arousal, that stress-responsive organ must now be slow to return to its baseline level of activity. In effect, a slow recovery to baseline is evidenced. Such homeostatic failure has been implicated in the onset of disease since the work of Freeman (1939). Freeman advanced the theory that autonomic excitation which is slow to deactivate from an organ system does increase the strain on that system. Malmo, Shagass, and Davis (1950) empirically demonstrated such a phenomenon to exist. Lader's (1969) review on this issue implicates it as a potential precursor to disease.

Sternbach (1966) has then put forward these conditions as prerequisites for the development of a stress-related disorder. The reader is referred to the work of Stoyva for further commentary on the Sternbach model, as well as other theories of psychosomatic illness (Stoyva, 1976, 1977; Stoyva & Budzynski, 1974).

Clearly, there exist other theoretical mechanisms for the development of stress-related disorders. The theories of personality type as a predictor of specific stress-related illnesses (Dunbar, 1935; see Graham, 1972, for a review) have yet to generate sufficient empirical support to be widely accepted. The one exception would clearly be the Type A personality as a predictor of premature coronary heart disease (see Friedman & Rosenman, 1974; and Glass, 1977, for more recent research). There also exists the notion that specific emotions generate specific types of stress reactivity (Lang, Rice, & Sternbach, 1972). Henry and Stephens (1977) have suggested that during aggression the sympathetic-adrenal medullary stress response is activated, whereas during depression or withdrawal the anterior pituitary-adrenal cortical system is activated. Finally, the "hypokinetic disease" theory of Kraus and Raab (1961) states that stress arousal coupled with suppressed physical activity leads to psychosomatic diseases (see also Chavat *et al.*, 1964).

Several different theories have been advanced to explain how psychophysiological arousal can be channeled to affect end-organs adversely. Despite the disparity between the theories mentioned, there does appear to be one element, either directly stated or implied, which is common to all. That commonality pertains to how the end-organs ultimately become dysfunctional or pathological—simply stated, if any given end-organ is subjected to psychophysiological overload (overstimulation) for a long enough period, that organ will eventually manifest symptoms of dysfunction or pathology. According to Stoyva (1976) in his review of stress-related disorders, "A number of investigators have hypothesized that if the stress response is evoked too often, or sustained for too long, then disorders are likely to develop" (p. 370). In a "behavioristic interpretation" of psychosomatic disorders, Lachman (1972) states, "The longer a given structure is involved in an on-going emotional reaction pattern, the greater is the likelihood of it being involved in a psychosomatic disorder" (pp. 69–70). Lachman (1972) concludes "Theoretically, any bodily structure or function can become the end focus of psychosomatic phenomena—but especially those directly innervated and regulated by the autonomic nervous system" (p. 71).

Perhaps of greater interest to the clinician than the theory concerning what causes an end-organ symptom to be overloaded is what appears to be the widely accepted hypothesis that end-organ diseases result from excessively frequent, intense, and/or prolonged activation (see Lachman, 1972; Sternbach, 1966; Stoyva, 1976; Stoyva & Budzynski, 1974).

Let us now briefly mention some of the generally accepted stress-related diseases that the clinician will most commonly encounter.

GASTROINTESTINAL DISORDERS

Excessive stress and the diseases of the gastrointestinal system have been thought to be related for decades. The two gastrointestinal disorders most often linked to excessive stress are peptic ulcers and ulcerative colitis.

Peptic Ulcers

Peptic ulcers are usually further classified by their location in the gastrointestinal system: gastric, or stomach, ulcers, and duodenal ulcers. It was demonstrated many years ago that emotions of anger and rage were related to increased secretion of acid and pepsin by the stomach, and that this secretion decreased with depression (Mahl & Brody, 1954; Mittelman & Wolff, 1942; Wolf & Glass, 1950). Although it might be concluded that what one sees in gastric ulcer, that is, an erosion of the wall of the stomach by the acid and enzyme it produces, is simply an exaggeration of a normal physiological response, actually, it is not quite so simple. Certainly emotions can raise gastric acid secretion and exacerbate an already existing ulcer, but normally the stomach wall is protected from the acid within it by a lining of mucus secreted by other cells in its wall. How this protective system breaks down and what predisposes a person to such an event are facts which remain elusive. There seems to be a combination of emotional and genetic factors involved in the pathogenesis of gastric ulcer, and such studies as that of Weiner, Thaler, Reiser, and Mirsky (1957) have demonstrated this quite well. They were able to predict in a group of recruits in basic training in the army which ones would develop gastric ulcers on the basis of serum pepsinogen levels—a genetic trait which is apparently a necessary but not sufficient factor in the formation of gastric ulcers. Gastric ulcer was also of interest to Selye (1951), who described ulcers apparently in response to chronic arousal of the endrocrine stress axes in the General Adaptation Sydrome. One could thus conceive of a mechanism whereby stress through the intermediation of neural or hormonal mechanisms could result in significant irritation. In individuals who are so predisposed, ulceration of the stomach would occur given sufficient time and continued exposure to the stress. The picture is less clearcut, however, in that it has been suggested that the duodenal ulcer results from changes in the mucosal wall "associated with sustained activation and a feeling of being deprived" (Backus & Dudley, 1977, p. 199).

Therefore, though strongly implicated in the stress response, the specific causal mechanisms involved in peptic-ulcer formation are currently unknown. Vagus-stimulated gastric hypersecretion as well as glucocorticoid anti-inflammatory activity on the mucous lining have been implicated. Yet conclusive data are lacking at present with regard to the selective activation of each mechanism.

Ulcerative Colitis

Ulcerative colitis is an inflammation and ulceration of the lining of the colon. Research by Grace, Seton, Wolf, and Wolff (1949), Almy, Kern, and Tulin (1949), and Grace, Wolf, and Wolff (1950) produced evidence that the colon becomes hyperactive and hyperemic with an increase in lysozyme levels (a proteolytic enzyme which can dissolve mucus) under stress. The emotions of anger and resentment are reported to create observable ulcerations of the bowel (Grace, Wolf, & Wolff, 1950). "Sustained feelings of this sort might be sufficient to produce enough reduction in bowel wall defenses to the point that the condition becomes self-sustaining" (Backus & Dudley, 1977, p. 199).

CARDIOVASCULAR DISORDERS

The cardiovascular system is thought by many researchers and clinicians to be the prime target end-organ for the stress response. The cardiovascular disorders most often associated with excessive stress are essential hypertension, arrhythmias, migraine headache, and Raynaud's phenomenon. Though all these disorders are generally accepted as being stress-related, the pathophysiology is less clear.

In a review of the pathophysiology of hypertension, Eliot (1979) states that in less than 10% of the cases can organic disorders be found to explain hypertension. However, he suggests that both the sympathetic-adrenal medullary and the anterior pituitary-adrenal cortical stress axes are capable of increasing blood pressure. This may occur through a wide range of diverse mechanisms (see also Selye, 1976). With chronic activation, he concludes, the deterioration of the cardiovascular system may be irreversible.

Henry and Stephens (1977), in a useful review of psychosocial stimulation and hypertension, present evidence similar to that of Eliot. In their review of animal and human studies, they point to the ability of the psychophysiological stress mechanisms to effect an increase in blood pressure. They point to the role of medullary norepinephrine as a vasoconstrictive force capable of increasing blood pressure. In addition, they point to the notion that increased sympathetic tonus (apparently regardless of origin) will lead to further increased sympathetic discharge. The end result may well be the tendency for the carotid sinus and aortic baroreceptors to "reset" themselves at a higher level of blood pressure. The normal effect of the baroreceptors is to act to moderate blood-pressure elevations. However, if they are reset at higher levels, they will tolerate greater blood pressure before intervening. Therefore, resting blood pressure may be allowed to rise slowly over time. Finally, these authors point to the role of the adrenal cortical response in the elevation of blood pressure, perhaps through some arterial narrowing or sodium-retaining mechanism. They suggest that psychosocial disturbance can play a major role in blood-pressure elevations that could become chronic in nature.

Weiner (1977), however, states that "Psychosocial factors do not by themselves 'cause' essential hypertension" (p. 183). They do, however, "interact with other predispositions" to produce high blood pressure (p. 185). He concludes that the available data point toward the conclusion that essential hypertension can be caused by a wide variety of influences, and that psychological and sociological factors "may play a different etiological, pathogenetic, and sustaining role in its different forms" (p. 185).

The etiology of arrhythmias may relate to conduction disturbances caused by small blood vessel obstruction or sympathetic dysfunction. Both can result from excessive stress arousal (Duncan, Stevenson, & Ripley, 1950; Lipowski, 1974; Selye, 1976).

Finally, both migraine and Raynaud's phenomena appear to be vasospastic disorders with a high potential to be caused or exacerbated by the stress response. In the case of migraine, cranial vasoconstriction precedes the pain. The vasoconstriction of the cranial blood supply may produce an "aura" (visual disturbance) if the retinal artery is involved. When the vasoconstriction finally ceases (relaxation), blood vessels dilate beyond their normal size. When this occurs the pain is experienced. It is unclear whether the pain results from biochemical or mechanical events (see Wolff, 1963, for a discussion of this process). In the case of Raynaud's, exposure to cold or emotional distress can initiate a vasoconstrictive phenomenon in the hands, fingers, feet, or toes (Taub & Stroebel, 1978). Excessive sympathetic tone is implicated in both migraine and Raynaud's disorders.

RESPIRATORY DISORDERS

Allergy

An allergy is a hypersensitivity that some people have to a particular agent. Their bodies react with exaggerated defensive responses when an agent to which they are allergic is encountered.

One of the most familiar forms of allergy is hay fever. In this condition, the individual is sensitive to some forms of plant pollen, and when these are inhaled in the air, mucous membranes swell, nasal secretion becomes excessive, and nasal obstruction can occur. Since other particles in the air do not seem to elicit such a response, this is clearly an overreaction to a stimulus. However, this has been generally thought to be a phenomenon related only to the body, as opposed to the mind. Yet the mind–body dualism is once again challenged by the finding that a subject with hay fever will respond minimally, if at all, when challenged with the allergenic substance in an environment in which he feels secure and comfortable, whereas in other, more stressful situations, the same challenge is met with by the usual nasal hypersecretion, congestion, etc. (Holmes, Trenting, & Wolff, 1951).

Bronchial Asthma

Although sharing some similarities with allergy, asthma is a more complex and potentially serious disorder. In these patients, bronchial secretions increase, mucosal swelling takes place, and finally smooth muscle surrounding the bronchioles contracts, leading to a great difficulty in expiring air from the lungs. This "inability to breath" is, of course, anxiety-producing, and this stress itself leads to a need for more oxygen, thus exacerbating the stress response caused by the original stimulus no matter what its nature. That bronchial asthmatic attacks can be caused by or at least exacerbated by psychosocial stimulation is no longer in question. Research reviewed by Lachman (1972) warrants such a conclusion.

Hyperventilation

Hyperventilation may be considered an example of an acute stress response. However, episodic hyperventilation can become a long-standing problem which goes undiagnosed for long periods of time in patients presenting vague problems that do not fit any particular pattern, such as vague aches and pains, nausea, vomiting, chest pains, etc. The clinician must be on his guard for this particular manifestation of the stress response, in order to protect the individual from unnecessary suffering and expense while searching for the cause. This, again, is a part of the fight–flight response in which the body is readied for action by increasing O_2 and decreasing CO_2; however, no action takes place (see Chapter 11 for the signs and symptoms of hyperventilation). It has been suggested that any time a patient presents such vague problems that seem elusive to the clinician, he or she should maintain a high degree of suspicion regarding hyperventilation and consider asking the patient to hyperventilate in the office. If his symptoms are reproduced, much time and effort of both physician and patient may be saved. For methods and cautions, refer to articles by Campernolle, Kees, and Leen (1979), and Lum (1975).

MUSCULOSKELETAL DISORDERS

This system comprises, as its name implies, all the body's muscles and bony support. It is thus the system which is responsible for the body's mobility, and therefore plays one of the more obvious roles in a fight-or-flight type of response. At such a time, the muscles tense, blood flow is increased to them, and the very word "tension" associated with emotions such as anger or anxiety relates to this state of the musculoskeletal system.

The stress-related disorders here are quite predictable. Low back pain may often be produced in a situation in which there is contraction of the back muscles as if to keep the body erect for fleeing a situation. If the contraction continues but there is no associated action (and therefore the stress situation remains), blood flow to the muscles decreases, metabolites increase, and pain is produced (Dorpat & Holmes, 1955; Holmes & Wolff, 1952).

Tension headache is a situation similar to that above, the muscles of the head and neck being kept in prolonged contraction, resulting in pain by the same mechanism. This is to be differentiated from the pain of vascular headaches which seems to begin in periods *following* tension, when muscles have already relaxed (Simons, Goodell, & Wolff, 1943).

There have even been some studies which indicate a possible role for stress in the development or influence of the course of the inflammatory joint disease, rheumatoid arthritis (Amkraut & Solomon, 1974; Heisel, 1972; Selye, 1956).

SKIN DISORDERS

The skin is thought to be a common target end-organ for excessive arousal (Musaph, 1977). Common stress-related disorders include eczema, acne, urticaria, and psoriasis according to Lachman (1972). The mechanisms of involvement are not clearly understood at this time. However, neurodermatological syndromes have been initiated and exacerbated through the manipulation of psychosocial stimuli. Yet the conclusion that the skin is a prime target organ for excessive stress still rests on clinical case reports.

THE IMMUNE SYSTEM

Before leaving the topic of organic manifestations of excessive stress, mention should be made of the effects of excessive stress on the immunological system. Selye (1976) and Amkraut and Solomon (1974) present impressive reviews that support the conclusion that excessive stress can exert a generalized immunosuppressive effect. The mechanism of action is not clear at this point. However, Selye (1976) states, "The immunosuppressive effect of stress and glucocorticoids is probably one of the characteristic consequences of thymicolymphatic involution and lymphopenia which have long been recognized as typical stress effects" (p. 712). If, indeed, excessive stress can exert generalized immunosuppresive effects, then it must be considered as a potential influence in the initiation and propagation, not only of psychosomatic diseases, but of infectious and degenerative diseases as well. More research on this important topic is obviously needed in order to determine the degree to which immunosuppression may indeed occur in human beings, and the degree of significance such immunosuppression may have for the initiation and/or propagation of disease. A review of the immunosuppressive effects of psychosocial stimulation in animals (Henry & Stephens, 1977) points to generalized systemic immunosuppression as well as tumor formation as resultant phenomena.

PSYCHOLOGICAL MANIFESTATIONS OF THE STRESS RESPONSE

The final category of disease that we shall discuss in this chapter is the psychological manifestations of the stress response. The psychological disturbances most associated with excessive stress are diffuse anxiety, manic behavior patterns, insomnia, depression, and finally schizophrenia.

Acute and chronic stress episodes are both implicated in the development of diffuse anxiety, as well as in that of manic behavior patterns which are without defined direction or purpose. Gellhorn (1969) argues that high levels of sympathetic activity can result in anxiety reactions. This anxiety may occur as a result of sympathetic nervous system and proprioceptive discharges at the cerebral cortical level. Thus generalized ergotropic tone may then lead to conditions of chronic and diffuse anxiety. Guyton (1976), in apparent agreement with Gellhorn, notes that general sympathetic discharge and proprioceptive feedback may contribute to arousal states such as mania, anxiety, and insomnia. Greden (1974) and Stephenson (1977) have both found that the consumption of methylated xanthines (primarily caffeine) can create signs of diffuse anxiety as well as insomnia, and may lead to a diagnosis of anxiety neurosis. The action of the methylated xanthines rests on their ability to stimulate a psychophysiological stress response primarily through sympathetic activation. Finally, Jacobson (1938, 1978) has argued that proprioceptive impulses as such would be found in conditions of high musculoskeletal tension and can contribute to anxiety reactions.

Physiologically, in each of the cases just cited, it may be suggested that an ascending neural overload via the reticular activating system to the limbic and neocortical areas may be responsible for creating unorganized and dysfunctional discharges of neural activity which is manifested in the client's presenting symptoms of insomnia, undefined anxiety, and in some cases manic behavior patterns which lack direction or apparent purpose (see Guyton , 1976).

In each of the three examples cited, activation of the psychophysiological stress response preceded the manifestation of diffuse, undefined anxiety.

It is interesting to note that one link between anxiety and sympathetic stress arousal, specifically striate muscle tension, (Gellhorn, 1969; Jacobson, 1938, 1978) has prompted the development of techniques designed to reduce anxiety through the reduction of muscle tension. We shall discuss such techniques later in this text.

Another psychological manifestation of excessive stress is thought to be depressive reactions. Stressor events which lead the client to the interpretation that his or her efforts are useless, that is, that he or she is in a helpless situation, are clearly associated with arousal of the psychophysiological stress response (Henry & Stephens, 1977). The affective manifestation which typically follows is that of depression. Henry and Stephens have compiled an impressive review that points to the reactivity of the anterior pituitary-adrenal cortical axis during depressive episodes. In addition to physiological evidence, there is psychological evidence to support the notion that excessive stress can precipitate a depressive reaction. Sociobehavioral research with depressed patients (see Brown, 1972; Paykel, Myers, Dienelt, Klerman, Lindenthal, & Pepper, 1969) produced somewhat similar evidence that social stressors can lead to a depressive breakdown. Evidence supports a link between stress and schizophrenia as well. One behavioral interpretation of schizophrenia views the illness as a maladaptive avoidance mechanism in the face of an anxiety-producing environment (Epstein & Coleman, 1970). Serban (1975) found in a study of 125 acute and 516 chronic schizophrenics that excessive stress did play a role in the precipitation of hospital readmission. A more far-reaching view of psychopathology and stress is presented by Eisler and Polak (1971). In a study of 172 psychiatric patients, they concluded that excessive stress could contribute to a wide range of psychiatric disorders, including depression and schizophrenia, as well as personality disturbances—depending on the predisposing characteristics of the individual. The nature of the predisposing characteristics is unknown at this time.

SUMMARY

In this chapter we have attempted to provide a logical extension of the preceding chapter, that is, we have attempted to provide a basic discussion of the implications of the psychophysiological stress response for the ultimate development of disease. Our purpose has been simply to provide the clinician with a basic awareness of the possible clinical manifestations of excessive stress that he or she may encounter. Far more in depth discussions of psychosomatic manifestations are available (see Eliot, 1979; Henry & Stephens, 1977; Lachman, 1972; Weiner, 1977; Wittkower & Warnes, 1977).

The reader should understand that much of what we know about the so-called psychosomatic diseases in human beings is based on anecdotal and clinical case reports. This condition is slowly changing as new insights are gained every year. And yet the lack of reliable empirical data has compromised the "credibility" of psychosomatic phenomena in the eyes of many professionals. This condition will be slow to change, owing to the complexities of psychosomatic phenomena as well as the limitations of conducting such research with human beings. However, these facts in no way diminish the reality of the psychosomatic disease state in the eyes of the clinicians who are faced with finding viable clinical solutions to what most of them perceive as very real clinical problems in need of very real and effective clinical interventions. The major thrust of this text is toward introducing the clinician to viable clinical tools that may be used to combat the condition of excessive psychophysiological stress arousal which is thought to underlie many of the disorders mentioned above.

In conclusion to the preceding two chapters we feel that the summary of Henry and Stephens (1977) is worthy of consideration:

> There has been skepticism that emotions aroused in a social context can so seriously affect the body as to lead to long-term disease or death. But the work, such as that of Wolf, shows that machinery of the human body is very much at the disposal of the higher centers of the brain. . . . Given the right circumstances, these higher controls can drive it mercilessly, often without awareness on the part of the individual of how close he is to the fine edge. (p. 11)

CHAPTER 4

The Measurement of the Stress Response

The previous chapters of this text have described the nature of the stress response. However, no discussion of the nature of any given phenomenon is complete without describing how to identify or measure the phenomenon of interest. The purpose of this chapter is briefly to introduce the reader to the most commonly used criteria for the measurement of the stress response in human beings. Our discussion will entail the most commonly used physiological and psychological criteria.

CHEMICAL MEASUREMENT

According to Selye (1976) the most commonly used "indicators" of the stress response are the plasma and/or urinary levels of ACTH, corticosteroids, and catecholamines—all are stress hormones.

The direct measurement of ACTH in the blood is not yet practical on a wide scale owing to complexities in chromatographic bioassay techniques (a process of filtering and separation for the isolation and evaluation of components of a given solution). As a result, many clinicians and researchers choose to measure a somewhat indirect indicator of ACTH—the corticosteroids.

17-OHCS

Corticosteroid refers to the hormones which are released during the stress response by the adrenal cortex (as discussed in Chapter 2).

Levels of corticosteroid activity can be assessed in the form of a product of their utilization within the body—the 17-hydroxycorticosteroids (17-OHCS). 17-OHCS can be chromatographically measured from both plasma and urine samples. Table IV provides general guidelines for 17-OHCS levels in adult human beings.

In general, 17-OHCS levels have been found extremely useful in the measurement of psychogenically induced stress (Mason, 1972). However, the use of this endocrine measurement is not without its problems. 17-OHCS represents a state-dependent variable which is vulnerable to natural diurnal fluctuation, sympathomimetic substances, and psychogenically induced stress responses. In his review of endrocrine research, Mason (1972) emphasizes the need to sample 17-OHCS levels six to ten times a day over a period of weeks in order to obtain a truly reliable mean baseline for individuals.

Catecholamines

In the preceding section, it was mentioned that 17-OHCS could be used as a measure of the role of the adrenal cortex during the stress response. However, as described in Chapter 2, this does not account for all the activity of endocrine mechanisms during the stress response. The adrenal medulla is another major source of endocrine activity. Catecholamine levels can be used to measure effectively the role of the adrenal medulla during the stress response (see Mason, 1972).

The adrenal medullary catecholamines are adrenalin (epinephrine) and noradrenalin (norepinephrine—the nonmethylated homologue of epinephrine).

Assessments of plasma levels of catecholamines are sometimes

Table IV. Measurement Guidelines for 17–OHCS in Adults

	Plasma levels	Urinary levels
8 A.M. basal levels	10–14 μg/%	5–8 mg/day
Stress response	18–24 μg/%	10–15 mg/day
Extreme stress	>24 μg/%	>15 mg/day

Table V. Measurement Guidelines for Urinary Catecholamines in Adults

	Adrenalin	Noradrenalin
Basal levels	4–5 μg/day	28–30 μg/day
Stress levels	10–15 μg/day	50–70 μg/day
Extreme stress	>15 μg/day	>70 μg/day

too complex to be considered for various research or clinical applications. As a result, most of the research using catecholamine levels as a dependent variable have depended on urinary assessment.

Urinary catecholamine assessment has been historically conducted through the use of chromatographic methodology. The general guidelines for catecholamine levels in adults is provided in Table V.

Catecholamine levels as well as 17-OHCS represent state criteria (state phenomena are acute, transitory phenomena, as opposed to trait phenomena which are more chronic and stable). Historically, plasma levels of catecholamines and 17-OHCS have been used to assess the very short-term stress reactivity because of their greater sensitivity to such fluctuation. Urinary levels of these same chemical indicators have been used for the assessment of somewhat longer short-term effects (day-to-day fluctuation, for example).

ELECTROMYOGRAPHIC MEASUREMENT

Electromyographic (EMG) measurement of the stress response entails assessment of the effects of the stress response on the striate muscle system. Electromyographic measurement may be considered in reality an indirect measurement of striate muscle tension. It is indirect in the sense that the EMG measures the electrochemical activity of the nerves which innervate the given striate musculature, as opposed to measuring the actual pressure caused by the contracting muscles. (Review Chapter 2 for a brief discussion of the psychophysiology of electrochemical neural phenomena.)

The striate musculature has been implicated as an indicator of the stress response since the early work of Edmund Jacobson (1938). Jacobson noted that stress arousal and striate muscle tension are highly correlated in a positive direction.

A report published in 1954 by Shagass and Malmo specifically implicated the frontalis muscle group as a major response component in anxiety and hyperarousal disorders (the frontalis group represents the major muscles of the forehead). The frontalis group was further implicated as an indicator of arousal by Jacobson (1970) who noted that the striate muscles in the facial and laryngeal regions drop significantly during resting states.

In their summary of early biofeedback research, Stoyva and Budzynski (1974) indicated that their selection of the frontalis group for EMG biofeedback was based on the premise that the frontalis muscles act as somewhat of a generalized indicator of striate muscle activity elsewhere in the body. Therefore, by monitoring frontalis activity the clinician should be able to obtain at least a gross idea of the level of stress arousal in various other striate muscle groups.

Although not without some dispute, many investigations have concluded the EMG measurement of frontalis activity does not only generalize to other upper-body striate muscles (Freedman & Papsdorf, 1976; Glaus & Kotses, 1977, 1978), but can serve as a useful indicator of generalized activity of the sympathetic nervous system (Arnarson & Sheffield, 1980; Budzynski, 1979; Malmo, 1966).

A practical advantage in the use of the EMG measurement of the stress response is the ease of access to the muscle groups. Although most clinicians generally use the frontalis muscles, the trapezius (upper), brachioradialis, and sternocleidomastoid muscle groups can be useful in the measurement of the stress response as well.

The major question at hand is to what degree do these muscles actually reflect acute versus chronic stress arousal? The answer to this question is unclear at this point in that striate muscle tension has both state and trait measurement qualities.

CARDIOVASCULAR MEASUREMENT

Cardiovascular measurement of the stress response entails assessment of the effects of the stress response on the heart and vascular systems. Perhaps the two most popular cardiovascular measurement criteria are peripheral blood flow (PBF) and heart rate (HR).

In research settings PBF is usually assessed by plethysmographic techniques. Plethysmography focuses on the volume of blood in the anatomical area under assessment. The most common areas for plethysmographic assessment of the stress response are the fingers, toes, calves, and forearms. During the stress response the vast majority of individuals suffer a reduction of blood volume in these areas. This is generally thought to be a function of direct neural impulses to the blood vessels causing a vasoconstrictive effect, as well as a function of adrenal medullary norepinephrine. A decline in blood flow to these areas will cause a decline in skin temperature at these local sites as well.

In clinical settings PBF is usually assessed on the basis of skin temperature recorded from any of the four anatomical areas mentioned above. Skin temperature is clinically more convenient than having to rely on plethysmography. It is generally more meaningful to the client as well.

HR activity during the stress response is thought to be a function of direct neural innervation and epinephrine from the adrenal medulla. HR is usually assessed on the basis of some optical plethysmographic technique, or on the basis of an electrocardiogram (EKG). The plethysmographic assessment of HR is far more convenient but is subject to greater inaccuracy. The EKG assessment of HR is certainly more accurate, but it suffers from practical limitations.

ELECTRODERMAL MEASUREMENT

Electrodermal measurement of the stress response entails assessment of the effects of the stress on the state-electrical characteristics of the skin.

The most commonly used electrodermal measurement of the stress response has been the phenomenon of skin resistance (sometimes known as GSR). The basic GSR paradigm involves introducing a mild electrical current between two surface electrodes. In this paradigm the skin acts as a resistor. This fact can help us measure the stress response, if we remember that during the stress response most individuals excrete varying amounts of salt-based perspiration through the sweat ducts in the skin. The perspiration acts to alter the resistance of the skin to a measurable degree. GSR measures have been found to be vulnerable to many sources of error (see Hassett, 1978, for a discussion of these). As a result, many professionals have begun seeking alternatives to the measurement of the electrodermal phenomenon.

The measurement of skin potential (SP) is one useful alternative to the GSR in the measurement of electrodermal activity. The SP paradigm consists of the measurement of the skin's natural bioelectric activity, rather than introducing an electric current to the surface of the skin as in GSR. One advantage of SP over GSR is that SP has a shorter time delay between the introduction of a stimulus and the electrodermal response. The average delay with the GSR is two to three seconds. This time is cut in half in most cases when using the SP.

Robert Edelberg (1972) and Stern, Ray, and Davis (1980) present among the most useful discussions of the measurement of electrodermal phenomena.

PSYCHOLOGICAL MEASUREMENT

The psychological measurement of the stress response refers to the measurement of the "psychological" effects of the stress response. There currently exist numerous and diverse methods for the measurement of psychological states and traits. To cover this topic fully would require a volume of its own. Therefore, what we shall do in this section is merely highlight the paper-and-pencil questionnaires that a clinician might find most useful in measuring the psychological effects of the stress response.

Minnesota Multiphasic Personality Inventory (MMPI)

The Minnesota Multiphasic Personality Inventory (Hathaway & McKinley, 1967) is perhaps the most valid and reliable inventory for the assessment of long-term stress on the personality structure of the client. The numerous clinical and content scales of the MMPI yield a wealth of valuable information. These numerous scales sample a wide range of "abnormal" or maladjusted personality traits (a personality trait is a rather chronic and consistent pattern of thinking and behavior).

The MMPI consists of 10 basic clinical scales developed on the basis of actuarial data:

1. Hs: Hypochondriasis
2. D: Depression
3. Hy: Conversion Hysteria

4. Pd: Psychopathic Deviate
5. Mf: Masculinity–Femininity
6. Pa: Paranoia
7. Pt: Psychasthenia (trait anxiety)
8. Sc: Schizophrenia
9. Ma: Hypomania (manifest energy)
10. Si: Social Introversion (preference for being alone)

In addition to the highly researched clinical scales, the MMPI has four validity scales which act to give the clinician a general idea of how valid any given set of test scores is for the client. This unique feature of the MMPI increases its desirability to many clinicians.

Over the years, the MMPI items have given rise to numerous other scales in varying stages of validation (see Dahlstrom, Welsh, & Dahlstrom, 1975).

The MMPI offers a virtual wealth of information to the trained clinician; its only major drawback appears to be its length (550 items), although a shortened version (366 items) is available.

The Sixteen Personality Factor (16 P–F)

The Sixteen Personality Factor (Cattell, 1972) does much the same thing that the MMPI does by assessing a wide range of personality traits. The 16 P–F measures sixteen "functionally independent and psychologically meaningful dimensions isolated and replicated in more than thirty years of factor-analytic research on normal and clinical groups" (Cattell, 1972, p. 5).

The 16 P–F consists of 187 items distributed across the following 16 scales:

Reserved–Outgoing
Less Intelligent–More Intelligent
Affected by Feelings–Emotionally Stable
Humble–Assertive
Sober–Happy-Go-Lucky
Expedient–Conscientious
Shy–Venturesome
Tough-minded–Tender-minded
Trusting–Suspicious
Practical–Imaginative
Forthright–Astute
Self-Assured–Apprehensive
Conservative–Experimenting
Group-Dependent–Self-Sufficient
Undisciplined Self-Conflict–Controlled
Relaxed–Tense

Compared to the MMPI, the 16 P–F has far fewer actuarial data to support it. However, it tends to be less complex to score and interpret than the MMPI.

Taylor Manifest Anxiety Scale (TAS)

The Taylor Manifest Anxiety Scale (Taylor, 1953), unlike the inventories described above, measures only one trait—anxiety. Its 50 items are derived from the MMPI. The TAS measures how generally anxious the client is and has little ability to reflect situational fluctuations in anxiety.

State–Trait Anxiety Inventory (STAI)

The State–Trait Anxiety Inventory (Spielberger, Gorsuch, & Lushene, 1970) is a highly unique inventory in that it is two scales in one. The first 20 items measure state anxiety (a psychological state is an acute, usually situationally dependent condition of psychological functioning). The second 20 items measure trait anxiety. This is the same basic phenomenon as that measured by the TAS. The STAI can be administered in full form (40 items) or can be used to measure only state anxiety or trait anxiety.

Affect Adjective Checklist (AACL)

Another unusual measuring device is the Affect Adjective Checklist (Zuckerman, 1960). Like the STAI, the AACL can be used to measure a psychological state or trait. The AACL achieves this by using the same items (21 adjectives) and merely changing the instructions. The client may use the checklist of adjectives to describe how he or she feels in general, or under a specific set of conditions—"now" for instance. Zuckerman and Lubin (1965) later expanded the AACL by adding specific items to assess hostility and depression. The new scale is called the Multiple Affect Adjective Checklist (MAACL).

Subjective Stress Scale (SSS)

The Subjective Stress Scale (Berkun, 1962) is a scale which is designed to measure situational (state) effects of stress on the individual. The scale consists of 14 descriptors which the client can use to identify his or her subjective reactions during a stressful situation. Each of the 14 descriptors comes with an empirically derived numerical weight, which the clinician then uses to generate a subjective stress score.

Profile of Mood States (POMS)

The Profile of Mood States (McNair, Lorr, & Droppleman, 1971) is a factor-analytically derived self-report inventory "which measures six identifiable mood or affective states" (McNair, Lorr, & Droppleman, 1971, p. 5):

- Tension–Anxiety
- Depression–Dejection
- Anger–Hostility
- Vigor–Activity
- Fatigue–Inertia
- Confusion–Bewilderment

The POMS consists of 65 adjectives. Each adjective is followed by a five-point rating scale which the client uses to indicate the subjective presence of that condition. The instructions ask the client use the 65 adjectives to indicate "How you have been feeling during the past week including today." Other time states have been used, for example: "right now," "today," and for "the past three minutes."

The POMS offers a broader range of state measures for the subjective assessment of stress when compared to the STAI, the AACL–MAACL, and the SSS.

LAW OF INITIAL VALUE

When attempting to measure the stress response, the clinician should take into consideration the role of individual client differences in the manifestation of the stress response. No two clients are exactly alike in their manifestation of the stress response. When measuring the psychophysiological reactivity during a stress response, the clinician must understand that the client's baseline level of psychophysiologic activity affects the subsequent degree of reactivity in that same psychophysiological parameter. This is Wilder's Law of Initial Values (Wilder, 1950). In order to compare individual's stress reactivity (assuming variant baselines), a statistical correction must be made in order to assure that the correlation between baseline activity and stressful reactivity is equal to zero. Such a correction must be made in order to compare groups as well. Benjamin (1963) has written a very useful paper which addresses the necessary statistical corrections that must be made. She concludes that a covariance model must be adopted in order to correct for the Law of Initial Values, though specific calculations will differ when comparing groups or individuals.* It must be remembered that the Law of Initial Values will affect not only the measurement of stress arousal but stress reduction as well.

SUMMARY

In this chapter we have described briefly some of the most commonly used methods of measuring the effects of the stress response. The methods described have included physiological and psychological, criteria. We have also seen that these criteria may be further broken down as state or trait criteria.

The most important question surrounding the measurement of the stress response is "How do you select the most appropriate measurement criterion?" The answer to this question is in no way clear-cut. Generally speaking, to begin with you should consider the state versus trait measurement criterion issue. Basically, state criteria should be used to measure immediate and/or short-lived phenomena. Trait criteria should be used to measure phenomena which take a longer term to manifest themselves and/or have greater stability and duration. The psychological criteria discussed in this chapter are fairly straightforward as to their state or trait nature. The physiological

*One useful formula for correcting for the Law of Initial Value when comparing individuals is the Autonomic Lability Score (ALS) (Lacey & Lacey, 1962). The ALS is form of covariance and therefore consistent with Benjamin's recommendation. The ALS is expressed

$$\text{ALS} = 50 + 10\left[\frac{Y_z - X_z r_{xy}}{(1 - r_{xy}{}^2)^{0.5}}\right]$$

where X_z = client's standardized prestressor autonomic level, Y_z = client's standardized poststressor autonomic level, and r_{xy} = correlation for sample between pre- and poststressor levels.

criteria are somewhat less clear. Some physiological criteria possess both state and trait characteristics. Furthermore, normal values for blood and urinary stress indicators may vary somewhat from lab to lab. Therefore, the clinician should familiarize him- or herself with the lab's standard values. Before using physiologic measurement criteria in the assessment of the stress response, the reader who has no background in physiology would benefit from consulting any useful physiology or psychophysiology text (see, for example, Brown, 1967; Greenfield & Sternbach, 1972; Levi, 1975; Selye, 1976; Stern, Ray, & Davis, 1980). Finally becuase no two clients are alike in their response to stressors, the clinician might consider measuring multiple and diverse response mechanisms (or stress axes) in order to increase the sensitivity of any given assessment procedure designed to measure the stress response.

PART THREE

THE TREATMENT OF THE STRESS RESPONSE

The primary focus of this text is on providing a practical and clinically useful guide to the treatment of excessive psychophysiological stress. The previous two parts may be thought of as a preface for a better understanding of this the third and final part—the treatment of the stress reponse. Our goal is to present a unique and clinically useful discussion of numerous and diverse treatment options between the covers of a single textbook. In order to achieve that goal we have, out of choice as well as necessity, condensed a large amount of information pertaining to each of the therapeutic options discussed. In doing so, we have attempted to address the key generic issues of clinical concern. This strategy, hopefully, yields for the reader a new perspective from which to view many of these interventions while minimizing the inevitable errors of omission. To compensate for the latter we have cited primary sources and more elaborate discussions wherever useful.

Finally, the "how to" presentations of the following treatment options are designed not as prescriptions but simply as models which the clinician may use in order to develop ultimately a useful clinical tool. In the final analysis, it must be the clinician who determines the ultimate suitability of employing any given therapeutic intervention and to what degree on an individual client-to-client basis.

CHAPTER 5

Self-Responsibility as a Therapeutic Force

The purpose of this chapter is to address the issues of self-responsibility in the treatment of the stress response. Health care is seen by many as being in a phase of change. The traditional medical model where the patient/client assumes a totally passive role in his or her treatment appears to be on the decline. In place of such a model we see emerging individual self-responsibility. This model manifests itself in the form of the individual's becoming an active participant with the clinician in the treatment paradigm. Although such a model does have the potential to be taken to a dangerous extreme (as in the case of the individual's diagnosing and treating him- or herself without the direction of a trained clinican), or perhaps perceived as a threat by some clinicians, the role of self-responsibility in health care will probably not recede. Self-responsibility plays a particularly important role in the treatment of the stress response. The purpose of this chapter, therefore, becomes to examine that role.

In Chapter 1 we stated that by far the greater part of stress in a client's life is self-initiated and self-propagated. In this chapter we shall explore this important theme of self-responsibility as it relates to the avoidance of pathogenic stress.

HUMAN DEVELOPMENT AND SELF-RESPONSIBILITY

As infants we had little control over our environment. Furthermore, our physical and intellectual development was so limited that we were not really able to meet our own needs. Consequently, we had to rely on significant others in our environment for the most fundamental things. We did make our comforts and discomforts known (usually heard), but basically others dictated our experiences to us. We were virtually helpless and at the mercy of others, usually our parents.

As we grew older, increased intellectual and motor development resulted in increased behavioral options' becoming available to us. Although these options were usually under numerous restrictions, we were well on our way to expanding our realm of self-responsibility.

As we approached school age, our ability to affect personal decisions expanded. Most of us quickly learned that there was a negative consequence in not exercising those personal choices within the generally accepted rules and regulations of our social systems.

With the further development of intellectual and motor skills and the augmentation of higher-level decision-making skills and moral and value systems, the teenage years became more marked with personal choices and responsibilities. The notion here is that the individual is continuing to make the shift from environmental support systems to self-support and self-responsibility mechanisms. From the teen years on, it is the individual who is willing to take responsibility for his or her own choices, decisions, and behavior who is regarded as "mature" and well-developed, psychologically speaking.

PHILOSOPHICAL PERSPECTIVES ON SELF-RESPONSIBILITY

Man has always been free to make choices or decisions for himself, given an environment that would permit such choices to be made. Even in times of persecution, strife, or war, individuals have had certain choices as to whether they would flee, fight, attempt to affect a compromise, or acquiesce. It was Aristotle who firmly believed that man is the being who makes himself. Further support for the concept of self-responsibility can be found in the writings of Thomas Aquinas, who stated, "Man differs from the irrational creatures in . . . that he is master of his own acts."

The humanistic/existential theorists viewed man as essentially free to accept responsibility for directing his own life and in shaping his own destiny. The individual becomes what he or she "decides" to become, and must accept the responsibility for the course of his or her life; as Jean Paul Sartre has stated, "We are our choices" (see Sartre, 1956). The core theme of humanistic/existential theorists such as Rollo May, Jean Paul Sartre, and Victor Frankl is that "Man creates himself."

SELF-RESPONSIBILITY AND EXCESSIVE STRESS

Before the process of self-responsibility can be utilized in the alleviation of excessive stress, its role must be understood in the creation of excessive stress. The initial sections of this chapter attempted to provide a basic introduction to the concept of self-responsibility. In this section we shall attempt to provide a justification for the statement that most of the stress in a client's life is self-initiated and self-propagated.

Hans Selye has stated, "It is not what happens to you that matters, but how you take it." This statement was in direct reference to the excessive stress that so many people suffer from. This important concept as applied to disease is not new. Albert Ellis (1971, 1973), for example, has developed a theory which states that emotional disturbance results, not from the actual events which take place in an individual's life, but from the irrational beliefs with which individuals meet those events. As a basis for his theory, Ellis quotes the Greco-Roman philosopher Epictetus, who reportedly stated, "Men are disturbed not by things, but by the views which they take of them."

Ellis's A–B–C Theory of Emotional Disturbance may be summarized as follows:

A	→	B	→	C
Activating Experience		Belief (interpretation)		Emotional Consequence

In condition A, something happens to the client (late for an appointment). In condition B, the client generates some "irrational" or otherwise inappropriate belief about self as a result of the original experience (stupidity for being late, worthlessness, incompetence, etc.). Condition C represents the consequence of the irrational belief (guilt, depression, shame, hostility, etc.). These emotional consequences are direct functions of the belief (interpretation) that the client holds concerning the A—activating experience. The emotional consequences *are not* caused by the actual experience itself. As Ellis summarizes, "It is not the event, but rather it is our interpretation of it, that causes our emotional reaction."

This position, that excessive stress and emotional disturbance is a function of the way the individual interprets his or her environment, can indeed be supported through examination of the stress-response process itself. The reader will recall Figure 8 (Chapter 2) which details the stress-response process. From this figure, reproduced here as Figure 10, it becomes obvious that whether or not most stimuli (environmental events or endogenous cognitions) become stressors (causing a stress response) appears to be determined by the integration of cognitive interpretation and affective responses given those stimuli (see Kirtz & Moos, 1974; Lazarus, 1966, 1976; Malmo, 1972). If a stimulus is not interpreted as being a threat or a challenge to the person, the stress response, generally speaking, will not result. Thus most stress responses that clients undergo are indeed self-created and will last as long as the client allows them to.

Of course, there are stimuli whose stressfulness is not dictated by the interpretive processes of the neocortex. These are substances which create a stress response merely by the body's metabolism of them. These substances are known as sympathomimetics, because they stimulate the sympathetic nervous system, resulting in a form of

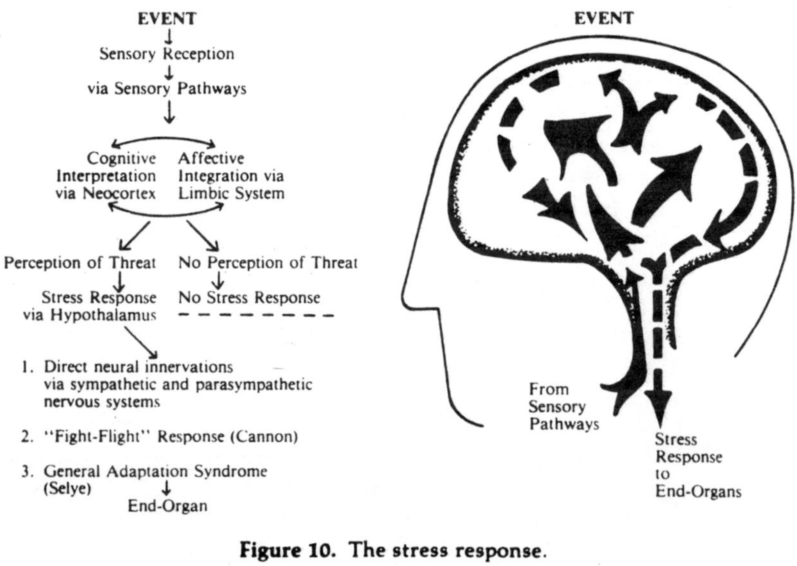

Figure 10. The stress response.

stress response (Levi, 1967). The most common mode of exposure to sympathomimetic stimuli is through diet, although nicotine in cigarette smoke is another source. Chapter 6 more fully addresses the issue of diet in the stress response.

Even in the case of the sympathomimetics, however, we still find that it is the client who chooses to eat, drink, or smoke these stress-causing stimuli. So, once again, the stress response appears to be largely the responsibility of the individual who suffers its effects. As Rollo May has stated, "Man is the being who can be conscious of and therefore responsible for, his existence."

THE ROLE OF THERAPEUTIC CLIENT EDUCATION

The preceding section has attempted to provide a rationale for the statement that excessive stress is self-initiated and self-propagated. If the clinician accepts this premise of client self-responsibility for excessive stress, then it seems logical to seek to harness the self-responsibility mechanism in the treatment and alleviation of excessive stress in that same client's life.

In order to harness the process of self-responsibility in a therapeutic vein, the client must first be given an accurate understanding of the nature of the problem (see Meichenbaum & Novaco, 1978), and then the numerous potential remedies available (see Everly, 1980c; Girdano & Everly, 1979). This is the process of therapeutic client education.

The process of client education, technically speaking, continues in various forms for the duration of the treatment process. In utilizing therapeutic client education, the clinician should attempt to include the following major components:

1. The first major component of client education consists of addressing the most common misconceptions concerning the stress response. There exist many misconceptions about stress and psychosomatic phenomena. Many of these misconceptions can adversely affect the client's motivation to seek and continue treatment. Such misconceptions may adversely affect the client's motivation to adhere to treatment protocols as well. For these reasons, it is generally useful for the clinician to anticipate these misconceptions and confront them early in the course of intervention. Table VI represents a compilation

Table VI. Stress Mythology

Listed below are 7 of the most commonly held misconceptions about stress. How many of these misconceptions you have held?

1. *"Stress related symptoms and psychosomatic diseases are all in my head, therefore they can't really injure me."*

This commonly held belief is false, because stress affects not only the mind but the body as well. A psychosomatic disease which results from stress is a "real" disease that can be very dangerous to your health, such as ulcers and high blood pressure, to mention only two.

2. *"Only weak people suffer from stress."*

The truth of the matter is that it is the hard-driving, overachieving "workaholic" who is most prone to suffer from excessive stress. Yet we are all potential targets.

3. *"I'm not responsible for the stress in my life—stress is unavoidable these days—we're all victims."*

In reality, you are responsible for most of the stress in your life. This is so because stress results not so much from what happens to you as from how you react to the things which happen to you. This stress is often your unconscious choice.

4. *"I always know when I begin to suffer from excessive stress."*

The fact is that the more stress you are under, the less sensitive you become to its symptoms, until the stress reaches a point where the symptoms can no longer be ignored.

5. *"It is easy to identify the causes of excessive stress."*

This statement is only half true. For many individuals, the cause of stress can be easily identified by recognizing the stressful symptoms and analyzing the immediate environment for the cause. With some individuals, the symptoms of stress do not appear until the stressor is gone. In cases like this, the symptoms appear in the form of mental and/or physical exhaustion.

6. *"All people respond to stress in the same way."*

This statement is very false. The fact of the matter is that we are all individuals. We differ dramatically in the things that cause us stress, the symptoms and diseases that we suffer from as a result of excessive stress, and in the treatment that proves effective for our excessive stress.

7. *"When I begin to suffer from excessive stress, all I have to do is sit down and relax."*

Although relaxation is a very useful tool in overcoming stress, few people know how to relax deeply. Techniques such as meditation, Hatha Yoga, and quiet contemplation are generally the most effective ways to relax deeply, as opposed to watching TV or listening to the radio. Remember, vacations and other forms of recreation aren't always relaxing.

---

of some of the most commonly held misconceptions about stress. It is entitled Stress Mythology and is based upon a survey of 405 adults who were asked to generate a list of statements describing the nature of stress and psychosomatic disease (Everly, 1980d). After eliminating the statements which were indeed valid in their description of the characteristics of stress, a Q-Sort methodology was applied to the remaining statements which were, in one way or another, misconceptions. Table VI represents the major misconceptions about stress and psychosomatic disease which emerged. Following each misconception, a brief statement appears which is designed to correct the misconception. Table VI is designed to be reproduced by the clinician and given to each client for discussion.

2. The second major component of therapeutic client education entails having the client learn what the general nature of the stress response really is. This involves having the client learn the basic fundamentals of the psychosomatic concept, that is, how thoughts and emotions can affect the body, and how stress can be a positive force (eustress) as well as a negative force (distress).

3. The third component of client education focuses on the role that excessive stress plays in causing disease. Here the clinician attempts to provide the client with a basic understanding of how excessive stress can lead to certain diseases.

4. The fourth component involves having the client develop self-awareness of how he or she experiences/manifests the stress response, that is, what are his or her idiosyncratic symptoms of excessive stress. Ultimately, the client should be able to distinguish the signs of eustress from those of distress.

5. Fifth, the client should be able to develop a self-assessment capability in order to identify his or her personal stressors. It is important for the client and the clinician alike to remember that stressors are idiosyncratic to each client. If the client can identify his or her sources of stress, then constructive steps can be taken to avoid the stressors, or at least to become better prepared to encounter them.

6. Finally, the sixth component of therapeutic client education should consist of having the clinician nonjudgmentally communicate to the client the active role that he or she has played in the creation of excessive stress and the active role that he or she must play in its alleviation.

These six components of client education may be best disseminated using a combination of strategies such as bibliotherapy, self-awareness exercises, didactic/support groups, and even a more traditional tutorial approach. "Nonclinical" educational approaches such as these have been found useful in reducing stress (Everly, 1980a,b; Girdano, 1977).

To reiterate, the major theme in therapeutic client education is the concept of the client's self-responsibility for the creation and alleviation of excessive stress. However, it is most important that this theme of self-responsibility be *noncritically* emphasized by the clinician throughout the entire educational process (see Shapiro & Shapiro, 1979); nor should an emphasis on self-responsibility discourage a client from seeking professional guidance for health problems (see Halberstam, 1978).

THE ROLE OF COUNSELING AND PSYCHOTHERAPY

Counseling and psychotherapy may be thought of as playing an important role in the treatment of excessive stress. The utility derived from the use of this generic intervention may be viewed from several perspectives.

First of all, consider that by far the most effective (though not always practical) way of alleviating excessive stress is for the client to take responsibility to avoid, minimize, or modify his or her exposure to stressors. In order to do this, the client must first understand what his or her stressors are. Didactic and indirect client education, as well as insight psychotherapy, can play an important role in treating excessive stress by assisting the client in *identifying* what the stressors really are. Once this identification process has been successfully completed, active attempts at avoidance, minimization, or modification of stressor exposure may be undertaken.

The second application that counseling/psychotherapy may have is in the *development* of life-style behavior modifications. Life-style behavior modifications can allow the client consciously to reduce exposure to stressors before they can begin to affect a stress response. Such techniques as dietary modification, time management, assertiveness training, and outright conscious avoidance of stressors that are not amenable to modification may be useful. Such overt avoidance becomes maladaptive only when it leads to the creation of other stress reactions in equal or greater intensity. Of course, the reduction in exposure to stressors might also result from the client's self-initiated avoidance behaviors based on the more direct client-education component, rather than what may be yielded through less direct counseling/psychotherapeutic processes.

Third, and perhaps most important, counseling/psychotherapy can alter personality to a less stress-vulnerable disposition. It will be recalled from earlier sections of this text that most of the stress a client undergoes is a function of the way the client interprets his or her environment—the perceptions, attitudes, and/or values, if you will. The major utility of counseling/psychotherapy in a treatment paradigm for excessive stress may lie in the fact that through these interventions the client can change his or her perceptions, attitudes, and values about the environment. Counseling/psychotherapy may actually restructure the personality of the client to a position which is far less vulnerable to initiation and propagation of excessive psychophysiological stress arousal. Indeed, clients often emerge from counseling/psychotherapy with less hostility, less suspicion, an improved self-concept, and increased problem-solving skills (Bergin & Garfield, 1971; Meltzoff & Kornreich, 1970). Such personality alterations tend to reduce the perceived stressfulness of one's environment. In effect, counseling/psychotherapy may be thought of as attacking the "root" of the problem as it generally or specifically exists in the cognitive/affective domain. Or from a more psychodynamic perspective, such intervention may be thought of as resolving the "internal conflict" that may indeed be responsible for the initiation and propagation of the psychophysiological stress arousal. Such interventions would certainly address any issues of the so-called symptom-substitution phenomenon should that exist.

We must also consider the positive effects of catharsis that often occur during counseling/psychotherapy. Such cathartic relief has been shown to be therapeutic (see Lazarus, 1976) and may act to reduce arousal states (see Lang, 1971).

Finally, it can be argued that behavior change in the direction of independence and self-responsibility is the ultimate goal of counseling/psychotherapy. Therefore, counseling and psychotherapy have added utility in the treatment of excessive stress in that they can foster an active role for the client in the treatment of his or her stress problem.

SUMMARY

In this chapter we have tried to describe the role of client self-responsibility as a therapeutic force in the treatment of excessive stress. In doing so, we have examined therapeutic client education and the role of counseling and psychotherapy. Both these therapeutic interventions involve and are ultimately aimed toward the client's assuming responsibility for the cause, but more important, the alleviation of excessive stress in his or her life.

Having the client assume self-responsibility as described above is not without its difficulties, however. Clearly, many clients derive some secondary gain from excessive stress. This is particularly true of the role of "victim." As mentioned earlier, client responsibility for the creation of the original stress problems should be handled by the clinician in a nonjudgmental, nonpunitive manner. If the clinician is not careful, some clients will interpret self-responsibility as reason for self-guilt. This can usually be avoided by focusing primarily on the alleviation of stress, rather than its cause, and by assuring the clients that if they had the power to create the problem, they must also have the power to alleviate it.

Finally, although we have mentioned self-responsibility as a major component in therapeutic client education and counseling/psychotherapy, it was not our intent to limit it to those interventions exclusively. Without question self-responsibility is a major component in the implementation of all therapeutic interventions. In the final analysis, it is the client who takes responsibility for practicing meditation, exercising, or even taking his or her medication. As Victor Frankl has summarized it: "Life ultimately means taking the responsibility to find the right answer to its problems."

CHAPTER 6

Dietary Recommendations and the Stress Response

It was mentioned in the previous chapter that the stress response can be affected by one's diet. In this chapter we shall address the issue of how diet may relate to excessive stress. We shall directly address this issue in the form of general dietary recommendations for individuals who are vulnerable to chronic, excessive stress. Following each recommendation, we shall provide a discussion of the rationale behind it. It must be mentioned in preface that there is a paucity of research pertaining directly to diet and dietary intervention in relation to the stress response. As a result, some of this discussion will be based on our own clinical observations.

RECOMMENDATION NO. 1: OBTAIN WELL-BALANCED NUTRITION.

Rationale: The individual should take care to consume a well-balanced diet. Well-balanced nutrition is essential for both physical and mental well-being, though its importance may be ignored when the individual feels overwhelmed by stress. Learning to take the time to consider one's diet is an important part of learning to cope with stress.

Basic good nutrition consists of eating a variety of foods from the four food groups—milk and milk products, meat and meat alternates, fruits and vegetables, and breads and cereals. Table VII gives the key nutrients obtained from each group. Table VIII shows the recommended number of servings that should be consumed daily from each group by adults.

Table VII. Key Nutrients Provided by Each Food Group

Milk and milk products	Fruits and vegetables
Calcium	Vitamin A
Vitamin D	Vitamin C
Protein	Fiber
Riboflavin	Bread and cereals
Meat and meat alternates	Thiamin
Protein	Niacin
Iron	Riboflavin
Thiamin	Iron
Niacin	Fiber

Concern over cardiovascular disease and other major diseases in which diet plays a role led the U.S. Senate to make recommendations regarding the eating habits of Americans (Select Committee on Nutrition and Human Needs, 1977). The U.S. Department of Agriculture and the Department of Health, Education, and Welfare made similar recommendations (USDA/HEW, 1980). Because excessive stress has been implicated as a factor contributing to the development of cardiovascular disease (Eliot, 1979; Selye, 1976), we feel that each of the dietary goals enumerated by the U.S. Senate Select Committee on Nutrition has particular relevance for all individuals with vulnerability to excessive stress. These dietary goals are provided in Table IX. Adherence to these guidelines may also have a remedial effect on certain conditions of diffuse anxiety, irritability, and fatigue which are diet-related and/or exacerbated through excessive stress.

RECOMMENDATION NO. 2: EAT BREAKFAST AND SPACE MEALS EVENLY THROUGHOUT THE DAY.

Rationale: Breakfast is a source of important nutrients. Studies

Table VIII. Recommended Servings from Each Food Group for Adults

Milk and milk products	Fruits and vegetables
Two or more servings daily; examples of one serving dishes include: 1 cup milk 2 slices cheese 1 cup cottage cheese 1 cup yogurt	Four or more servings daily including a a citrus fruit or tomato to provide vitamin C. One serving of dark green or yellow or orange vegetable should be eaten every other day for vitamin A.
Meat and meat alternates	Bread and cereals
Two or more 3-ounce servings daily of meat, fish, poultry, or cheese. Eggs, dry beans, peas, nuts, and peanut butter are acceptable meat alternates.	Four or more servings of whole grain or enriched breads and cereals daily.

Table IX. U.S. Dietary Goals[a]

1.	To avoid overweight, consume only as much energy (calories) as is expended; if overweight, decrease energy intake and increase energy expenditure.
2.	Increase the consumption of complex carbohydrates and "naturally occurring" sugars from about 28% of energy intake to about 48%.
3.	Reduce the consumption of refined and processed sugars by about 45% to account for about 10% of total energy intake.
4.	Reduce overall fat consumption from approximately 40% to about 30% of energy intake.
5.	Reduce saturated fat consumption to account for about 10% of total energy intake; and balance that with polyunsaturated and monounsaturated fats, which should account for about 10% of energy intake each.
6.	Reduce cholesterol consumption to about 300 mg a day.
7.	Limit the intake of sodium by reducing the intake of salt to about 5 g/day.

[a] Source: Select Committee on Nutrition and Human Needs, U.S. Senate. *Dietary Goals for the United States* (2nd ed.). U.S. Government Printing Office, 1977.

have shown that those who skip breakfast tend to have shorter attention spans and work less efficiently than those who eat breakfast (Robinson, 1972). Midmorning tiredness or depression is also more frequent among breakfast skippers. A good breakfast is not necessarily a traditional one (in fact, eggs and bacon for some individuals may not be advisable as a routine breakfast, because of their high cholesterol and fat content). Breakfast should, however, contain some source of high-quality protein, such as milk, cottage cheese, yogurt, peanut butter, or leftover meat. Fruit or fruit juice and bread and/or cereal can make a breakfast that will provide energy throughout the morning. Certainly one of the worst habits for the distressed individual to fall into is to consume only a cup of coffee for breakfast. This issue will be addressed more directly in the next recommendation.

There is nothing sacred about "three meals a day." Many people find that they feel better with smaller, more frequent meals spaced throughout the day. Research has demonstrated that more frequent, smaller meals are actually a more desirable way to obtain nutrition (Bray, 1972). Most important, nutrients should be distributed throughout the day to meet the physical and mental needs of the individual. The optimal distribution may even vary from day to day in the same individual depending on each day's schedule. Fewer than three meals per day is generally not recommended as a slump in energy often occurs during the long period between meals. It is also difficult to obtain all needed nutrients in fewer than three meals without eating uncomfortably large meals. Whatever the number of meals or snacks eaten throughout the day, they should each include some foods chosen from the four food groups. "Empty calorie" foods (i.e., foods which offer little more than calories) should be limited, especially in the overweight individual.

RECOMMENDATION NO. 3: AVOID OR MINIMIZE CONSUMPTION OF METHYLATED XANTHINES.

Rationale: Caffeine, theophylline, and theobromine are methylated xanthines. Pharmacological actions attributable to them are: central nervous system and cardiac muscle stimulation, cardiac necrosis, gluconeogenesis, and diuresis (Cutting, 1972; Graham, 1978; Selye, 1976). In effect, these agents actually stimulate a psychophysiological stress response.

It is with their role as CNS stimulants that we are most concerned. In fact, it is this stimulant effect that largely accounts for the widespread use of beverages and foods that contain these sympathomimetic agents. Other than the oft-desired effects of alertness and reduced fatiguability, however, these substances can cause such unpleasant effects as headache, irritability, nervousness, and sleeplessness (Stephenson, 1977). The pharmacological dose for caffeine is considered to be 50–200 mg (Greden, 1974). There is, of course, individual variation in susceptibility to the stimulating effects; but it is advisable that stress-prone individuals avoid, or at least greatly curtail use of, foodstuffs containing methylated xanthines.

Methylated xanthines are found in coffee, tea, chocolate, and cola beverages. Caffeine is the commonest of these compounds, and the most powerful CNS stimulant. Table X presents the amount of caffeine in common dietary sources. In addition to these sources, many prescription and over-the-counter medications contain significant quantities of caffeine. The physician should bear this in mind before prescribing medications or advising patients regarding over-the-counter drugs.

Effects of large doses of caffeine may be indistinguishable from the symptoms of anxiety neurosis which include nervousness, headache, and gastrointestinal irritation (Greden, 1974; Stephenson, 1977). It should be pointed out, however, that even small doses of caffeine, less than 200 mg, are known to bring about undesirable effects. Stress-prone individuals may be particularly susceptible to these effects and are best advised to avoid caffeine and the related methylated xanthines completely.

Table X. Caffeine Content of Common Beverages[a]

Coffee (brewed)	100–110 mgs/6 oz. serving
Coffee (instant)	70–75 mg/6 oz. serving
Coffee (decaffeinated)	3–5 mg/6 oz. serving
Tea (instant)	30–36 mg/6 oz. serving
Tea (brewed)	50–100 mg/6 oz. serving
Cola beverages	36–65 mg/12 oz. serving
Cocoa	6–142 mg/5 oz. serving
Chocolate	20 mg/1 oz. serving

[a] Sources: Johns Hopkins Hospital Dietary Manual (1973); Stephenson (1977); Massachusetts General Hospital Dietary Manual (1976).

RECOMMENDATION NO. 4: TAKE SPECIAL CARE TO CONSUME A DIET THAT PROVIDES ADEQUATE LEVELS OF NUTRIENTS POTENTIALLY VULNERABLE TO EXCESSIVE STRESS.

Rationale: A definitive statement on exactly how excessive stress affects general nutritional status is currently lacking; however, we are beginning to accumulate data on the metabolic effects of excessive stress with regard to certain specific nutrients. Ohlsen (1958) and Scrimshaw (1969) reported data indicating that human beings can experience a negative nitrogen balance as a result of excessive stress. This nitrogen loss is a result of the catabolic metabolism of protein. A useful dietary intervention for nitrogen loss would be a well balanced diet "relatively rich in protein" (Cuthbertson, 1964).

Another nutrient implicated in the stress response is ascorbic acid (vitamin C). Evidence suggests that vitamin C is depleted during the stress response. "One of the most characteristic consequences of exposure to acute stress is the loss of ascorbic acid from the adrenal cortex" (Selye, 1976, p. 572). Hodges (1970), Maas, Gleser, and Gottschalk (1961), and Kuhl, Wilson, and Ralli (1952) have reported data which show that urinary excretion of ascorbic acid increases in human beings during exposures to stressors. It is now thought that ascorbic acid requirements do indeed increase during excessive stress, but to what degree is not known.

Emotional status and psychophysiological arousal may have some effect on calcium levels as well. Everson (1960) reports cases of individuals who underwent negative calcium balance during periods of high stress. Calcium excretions have been shown to increase in chimpanzees who were forced to undergo a stressor episode (Sabbot, McNew, Hoshizaki, Sedgwick, & Adey, 1972).

Finally, there is evidence that the B-complex vitamins may be susceptible to depletion during the stress response. It is known that the B-complex vitamins are constituents of the adrenal cortical hormones which are active during the stress response (Mountcastle, 1974). Pfeiffer (1975) has stated that B-6 and zinc are depleted during the stress response. The implications of these facts are unclear at this time, however.

To what real degree the loss of any of the nutrients mentioned adversely affects biochemical and behavioral outcome is unknown. Similarly, the degree to which vitamin/mineral supplementation affects those variables is unknown. It may be argued, however, that chronic excessive stress does theoretically increase the client's requirement for certain nutrients.

SUMMARY

Much is yet to be learned about the effects of psychophysiological stress on nutritional status. It would appear, based on data available thus far in the literature, that severe stress adversely affects nutritional status, and that diet can initiate or exacerbate levels of stress arousal experienced by the client. The qualitative effects in any one individual, however, are hard or impossible to assess, and must certainly depend on the degree and chronicity of the stress as well as the individual's nutritional status prior to onset. We have chosen to omit a discussion of the potential for allergiclike reactions to some foods which have received popular press coverage, for example, white sugar and milk products. Although we feel that stress reactions can occur in predisposed individuals from ingestion of these foods, such reactions lack sufficient clarification of scope and mechanism to be included in this chapter. The chronically stressed individual should strive to obtain needed nutrients in a balanced diet. Where stress may be increasing nutritional needs, an increase in food intake should cover the needs, if the food is well chosen to provide a wide range of nutrients. Specific vitamin or mineral supplementation is most indicated in conditions where significant nutrient deficits exist. Such deficits may result from nutrient exhaustion, malnutrition, or malabsorption. Radical alterations in diet should never be made, however, unless the individual client is under the supervision of a knowledgeable clinician.

CHAPTER 7

The Pharmacological Treatment of the Stress Response

The purpose of this chapter is to provide a practical introduction to the pharmacological treatment of excessive stress. In presenting this material, we have attempted to provide information which will be useful to both the medically and the nonmedically trained clinician.

Man's search for relief from distress often leads him to a pharmacological solution and the desire for instant relief. The expectation that such relief is possible has produced an upsurge in the development and sales of substances intended to reduce the effects of stress, to alter the state of consciousness and produce relief from the difficulties of everyday life. The fact that the minor tranquilizers remain the top-selling pharmaceuticals would seem to attest to this conclusion. The fact that such a pharmacological panacea does indeed exist in the minds of many people has led to a major abuse problem in this form of treatment of the stress response.

Yet the use of medications can be most beneficial in certain cases, and it is the purpose of this chapter to describe those instances in which pharmacology can be helpful to the practitioner in offering the client an adjunctive therapy in dealing with specific types of difficulties. Also, it will provide a practical guide to the selection and use of the appropriate drugs, as well as offer insight as to their general use for the nonprescribing practitioner.

Strictly speaking, the pharmacological treatment could include the treatment of the most peripheral manifestations of the stress response, such as the use of antacids in the treatment of gastric ulcer, or aspirin or other analgesics for the treatment of tension headache; however, we shall be addressing ourselves in this chapter primarily to the use of those medications whose purpose it is to relieve that subjective state of distress described as tension or anxiety and reduce psychophysiological overactivity.

Many clinicians agree that pharmacological intervention can play a useful role in the treatment of the stress response. Perhaps its greatest utility comes in its ability to relieve the symptoms of excessive stress which are acutely intense and/or which interfere with other forms of therapy. Therefore, the most constructive use of pharmacological interventions is generally felt to be limited to the short term (such as two or three weeks) with the main goal that of decreasing the symptoms enough to permit other, longer-lasting forms of treatment to have effect.

It must be kept in mind that, as in almost every other form of therapy we have discussed, the relationship with the clinician is certainly an important element in the success of the treatment. This is reflected in patient compliance in taking the medication regularly and reporting improvement, side effects, or fears and concerns. We shall not discuss here the element of the placebo effect in the use of medications: however, it must be kept in mind that the faith in the clinician and the expected effect of the medication has been shown by many authors to be as important as the medication itself (see Harlem, 1977; Jones, 1977).

In this chapter we shall describe several categories of medication used in the treatment of the stress response. We shall describe the mechanisms of action and their major indications, contraindications, and side effects. Furthermore, we shall provide examples of specific medications and dosages within each class. Our intention is to be concise and practical as we provide a basic guide for the understanding and/or implementation of such a treatment option.

SEDATIVE-HYPNOTICS—AN INTRODUCTORY HISTORY

"The term sedative-hypnotic is intended to denote the dose-dependency of the effect of these drugs" (Swonger & Constantine,

1976, p. 113). At low doses these drugs produce a sedative effect, at high doses they can induce sleep. This is perhaps the oldest class of medications to be discussed in this chapter. One of its earliest representatives is ethyl alcohol, probably the oldest "tranquilizer" known to man. Another useful pharmacological agent (introduced around 1850) was the bromide salts. These proved to be a fairly good central-nervous-system depressant; however, the possibility of intoxication made their usefulness somewhat limited. The use of chloral hydrate as a sedative was begun around 1869.

The next form of sedative-hypnotic medication which became available was the barbiturates, which are still being used by some practitioners for the treatment of anxiety. But because of the tendency to produce tolerance and their addictive potential, they are not very desirable in the treatment of chronic stress.

Following the barbiturates, the next major drug to be produced for the treatment of the syndrome was meprobamate, a propanediol, which was manufactured beginning in 1957. Its addictive properties also made it less than desirable, although this was not known at first.

Finally, in 1960, the "new age of anti-anxiety medications" began with the development of chlordiazepoxide (Librium) by the Hoffmann-LaRoche company.

What all these substances seem to have in common is their ability to decrease anxiety and, in larger doses, to produce sleep. Though all these agents decrease anxiety and are often lumped together by authors, it may be useful in the context of this chapter to consider separately the barbiturate and the nonbarbiturate sedatives and hypnotics, followed by the anti-anxiety agents, which are more specific in dealing with anxiety and seem to work at a different level in the central nervous system.

THE BARBITURATE SEDATIVE-HYPNOTIC AGENTS

These drugs appear to have their major locus of action in the reticular formation and the cerebral cortex. They all produce depression of the central nervous system, and as the dosage is increased, the response progresses from sedation to respiratory depression and ultimately death. They can be used to reduce restlessness and agitation and must be administered in small doses for this purpose, in order not to interfere with alertness and psychomotor performance. They have been used by practitioners particularly in treating the psychogenic component of organic diseases, gastrointestinal, cardiovascular, or respiratory, reducing the anxiety resulting from the somatic symptoms. Their most common use now is in the treatment of insomnia, although, as mentioned before, some physicians still rely heavily on these medications for the treatment of anxiety.

The barbiturates have been classified as long-, intermediate-, and short-acting. The major disadvantage of the barbiturates is that they tend to induce liver enzymes, which means that they make the liver work faster to metabolize them as well as other substances. This is particularly dangerous when a client is getting other medication along with a barbiturate. A classic example is the client who is taking barbiturates and dicumarin (a medication to decrease blood coagulability) simultaneously. While the patient is taking barbiturates, the amount of dicumarin needed to produce a therapeutic effect is greater than normal because it is being metabolized at a greater rate than normal by the liver enzyme induced by the barbiturate. If the patient were to stop the barbiturate, in one to two weeks the effect of the same amount of dicumarin would be dangerously increased, because the liver would no longer be metabolizing it at the rapid pace caused by the barbiturate induction of its enzymes. Because of this induction of enzymes, a tolerance is ultimately built up to the barbiturates themselves, and more medication has to be used to obtain the same effect as

Table XI. Commonly Prescribed Barbiturates

Generic name	Trade name	Common doses for adults
Phenobarbital (long-acting)	Luminal	As a sedative: 30–120 mg daily in 2–3 divided doses. As a hypnotic: 100–320 mg at bedtime.
Amobarbital (intermediate-acting)	Amytal	As a sedative: 50–300 mg daily in divided doses. As a hypnotic: 65–200 mg at bedtime.
Pentobarbital (short-acting)	Nembutal	As a sedative: 100–200 mg daily in 3 divided doses. As a hypnotic: 100–200 mg at bedtime.
Secobarbital (short-acting)	Seconal	As a sedative: 100–300 mg daily in divided doses. As a hypnotic: 100–200 mg at bedtime.

previously. Perhaps the major disadvantage of these medications is the addictive potential they have; and abrupt withdrawal from them may lead to delirium, convulsions, coma, and death. This type of withdrawal is also the case with alcohol.

Another disadvantage to barbiturates is that they are a relatively nonspecific central-nervous-system depressant, and the only way to use them in treating the stress response is to use very small dosages, that is, dosages that do not produce drowsiness, and for a very brief period of time. However, in reality, as regards the stress response, we feel that there is no advantage to using the barbiturates given other pharmacological options. Table XI presents commonly prescribed barbiturates.

Overdosage of barbiturates will produce a picture similar to drunkenness with ataxia. Eventually profound shock, hypotension, tachycardia, respiratory depression, coma, and death due to depression of medullary centers for respiration will occur.

NONBARBITURATE SEDATIVE HYPNOTICS

These act in the same way as the barbiturates and though they were originally thought to be nonaddictive, we now know that dependence can result. They include such drugs as Placidyl, Doriden, and Quāālude. They are probably somewhat less potent, and also it is felt that they offer no advantage in the treatment of the stress response. Other sedative-hypnotics include chloral hydrate and paraldehyde, which again offer no advantage in the treatment of the stress response, the former being used primarily as a sleep aid and the latter as a treatment in alcohol withdrawal. Bromide salts are no longer in use at all for the treatment of the stress response, but they have in the past been available in over-the-counter preparations. The bromides came into use in the mid-1800s as antianxiety agents, but problems arose because of their relatively long half-lives and tendency to accumulate in the body causing a bromide psychosis. It should not be overlooked, however, that the bromide salts do sometimes find their way into people's bodies, often through the use of bromide-salt-containing substances. Table XII presents the commonly used nonbarbiturate sedative-hypnotics.

Table XII. Commonly Prescribed Nonbarbiturate Sedative Hypnotics

Generic name	Trade name	Common doses for adults
Ethchlorvynol	Placidyl	As a sedative: 200–600 mg in divided doses. As a hypnotic: 500–1000 mg at bedtime.
Glutethimide	Doriden	As a sedative: 250–750 mg in divided doses. As a hypnotic: 250–1000 mg at bedtime.
Methaqualone	Quāālude	As a sedative: 300–450 mg in divided doses. As a hypnotic: 150–400 mg at bedtime.
Chloral hydrate		As a sedative: 300–1500 mg in divided doses. As a hypnotic: 500–1000 mg at bedtime.

THE ANTIANXIETY AGENTS

In this section we shall present numerous types of medications which are commonly prescribed with the primary intention of reducing anxiety and psychophysiological arousal without inducing a hypnotic effect.

The Propanediols

As mentioned earlier in this chapter, when meprobamate (a compound of the propanediol group) was first introduced, it was hoped that it was an agent that would be a major advance from the barbiturates; however, it has been found that, though it is probably better at relieving anxiety than the barbiturates, it may have an almost equal potential for addiction and abuse. Interestingly, there is a member of this class of drugs named tybamate, which has an extremely short half-life, and in which very little addiction potential has been found. Both these drugs, however, are much less effective than the benzodiazepines and are not typically recommended for the treatment of stress. Their major disadvantages, as with the barbiturates, are impairment of motor function, development of drowsiness, and induction of hepatic enzymes. In conclusion, the propanediols, such as meprobamate and tybamate, may be classified in between the sedative-hypnotics and the next drug class to be discussed—the benzodiazepines.

The Benzodiazepines

All the evidence gathered so far would indicate that the benzodiazepines as a class are extremely effective as antianxiety medications. Several generic compounds which belong to the benzodiazepine group, such as chlordiazepoxide (Librium), diazepam (Valium), Flurazepam (Dalmane), and oxazepam (Serax) are considered less toxic and less addicitive than the sedative-hypnotic medications described thus far. The very popularity alluded to at the beginning of this chapter is a testimony to either their effectiveness or the belief in that effectiveness. It is generally felt that the benzodiazepines have their effect on the limbic system, and therefore do not interfere with cortical function in the same way as the other medications described. Several possible mechanisms have been described for the way in which the benzodiazepines may work pharmacologically. Stein, Wise, and Berger (1973), for example, offer the finding that oxazepam (a derivative of benzodiazepine) may somehow be related to serotonin (another neurotransmitter) turnover in terms of its antianxiety action; however, the significance of this finding is still somewhat unclear.

The major advantage in the use of the benzodiazepines for the treatment of the stress response is the fact that in the dosage ranges generally recommended, they do not significantly reduce cortical functioning and therefore impair ability to work or concentrate. They appear to enhance interaction in those people who are overly anxious, inhibited, and isolated, thus allowing them to become more amenable to therapy. The other main advantage is the large difference in the level of medication that it takes to be effective, as compared with the level considered to be lethal. It is virtually impossible to commit suicide with the benzodiazepines without combining them with another drug that also acts as a depressant of the central nervous system.

The major disadvantage lies in the half-lives of the drugs. The half-life for Librium is 30 to 40 hours, for Valium and its active metabolites about 96 hours. Thus, with repeated dosages, blood levels rise over a period of days. This can potentially lead to more depression of the central nervous system than one had anticipated. This can be especially troublesome in older people. Also, there can be a withdrawal syndrome from benzodiazepines; and though this may not be of the magnitude of the withdrawal syndrome from barbiturates, the psychological and physiological addictive properties of the benzodiazepines are becoming much more familiar to the physician, and they are being prescribed with much more caution. Another disadvantage to the benzodiazepines is their ability to compromise respiratory function through centrally mediated mechanisms. This can obviously be a problem with people with lung disease.

Antihistamines

There are several types of antihistamines that have been used in treating anxiety; however, the one that is most frequently used is hydroxyzine. The main reason for using antihistamines in the treatment of anxiety is not for their primary pharmacological property, which is to antagonize the peripheral effects of histamines, but for their side effect, which is sedation, and for this reason can be used to treat anxiety and insomnia. This type of medication seems to be somewhat useful for this purpose, and patients do not seem to build up a tolerance to it. In low doses it does not seem to cause significant impairment of mental alertness or coordination, and it appears not to produce cortical depression. It, like the benzodiazepines, has a wide margin of safety between the therapeutic and the lethal doses. There have been no reported cases of addiction or deaths related to its use. The commercial names for hydroxyzine are Vistaril and Atarax.

Beta Adrenergic Blocking Agents

In those patients whose anxiety and psychophysiological stress arousal are manifested by peripheral autonomic symptoms primarily, it has been found helpful by some physicians to use propranolol. This is a medication which appears to act by blocking synaptic transmission to the beta group of adrenergic receptors. Since this is a peripheral and not a centrally acting phenomenon, it will reduce symptoms associated with anxiety and stress arousal, but does not alter consciousness in any way. This drug is not officially approved for this particular use. It must also be taken with care in patients who would be susceptible to beta adrenergic blockade, such as those with asthma. The trade name for propranolol is Inderal.

Tricyclic Antidepressants

For those patients in whom anxiety and depression are part of the same clinical picture, it has been found that tricyclic antidepressants may be of benefit in relieving both the depressive and the anxiety components. These drugs have their mechanism of action in blocking reuptake of norepinephrine and serotonin at the synapses of the central nervous system. It will be recalled from earlier in this book that norepinephrine and serotonin are neurotransmitters at synapses in the brain. There is a hypothesis that it is the relative decrease in the availability of these substances, or increase in their destruction, that accounts for depression in some people. It is further hypothesized that the tricyclic antidepressant agents act by blocking the reuptake of these neurotransmitters at the presynaptic neurons, and thus produce a relief from depression. One of the side effects of the antidepressants is sedation. This is particularly true with the amitriptyline and doxepin tricyclics. One particularly interesting use of tricyclic antidepressants has been in panic attacks, where it has been found that the use of the tricyclic imipramine can prevent occurrence. This can be done with a dose as small as 10 mg a day, although in some patients it is necessary to increase the dosage to as high as one would normally use in treating depression. Typically, the sedative or antianxiety effect of the tricyclic antidepressants is seen soon after taking the medication, and sometimes the medication is given only at night, in order to take advantage of the rather shorter-acting sedative component of the medication.

The major disadvantage to the use of tricyclic antidepressants is in their side effects, which can be particularly bothersome. These are generally anticholinergic in nature, and present such symptoms as dry mouth, difficulty with accommodation of vision, urinary retention, and a particular danger to patients with narrow-angle glaucoma. There are cardiovascular risks, particularly postural hypotension and cardiac arrhythmia. They have been known to cause psychomotor slowing and difficulties in concentration and planning. The margin of safety in dosage of the tricyclics as compared with the benzodiazepines is much less, and the possibility is present of paradoxical reaction with increased anxiety and depression. Finally, they may also precipitate a psychosis in those individuals who have an underlying psychotic disorder.

Phenothiazines

In those individuals in whom anxiety is part of a more hyperactive, distractible, obsessional, disorganized picture, the use of major tranquilizers is sometimes helpful. Major tranquilizers are purported to have their effect centrally, as do the tricyclic antidepressants. The effect of the major tranquilizers supposedly is in blockade of the neurotransmitter dopamine at its receptor site. Dopamine is another neurotransmitter in the central nervous system, and it has been speculated that it is a disorder of the dopamine system which is manifested by psychosis.

For the purpose of this discussion, the major tranquilizers are useful only in those cases in which the stress response reaches severe proportions, threatening to disorganize thought processes, and where it would be useful to help the individual reduce the psychomotor response to the stress and be able ultimately to integrate his thought processes in a more functional way. It is not a step which should be lightly taken by the practitioner, since it has been found that even small doses of phenothiazine can produce tardive dyskinesia, a syndrome manifested by abnormal movements, particularly of the face and tongue and sometimes of the body as a whole, which appears after a period of use of even small doses of phenothiazines, and for which there is as yet no cure known. However, this medication may be

Table XIII. Medications Used to Treat Anxiety[a]

Generic name	Trade name	Doses
Meprobamate	Miltown	1200–1600 mg/day in divided doses.
Tybamate	Tybatran	750–2000 mg/day in divided doses.
Diazepam	Valium	6–40 mg/day in divided doses.
Chlordiazepoxide	Librium	15–100 mg/day in divided doses.
Flurazepam	Dalmane	15–30 mg/day in divided doses.
Oxazepam	Serax	30–120 mg/day in divided doses.
Hydroxyzine	Atarax	50–400 mg/day in divided doses.
Propranolol	Inderal	30–120 mg/day in divided doses.
Amitriptyline	Elavil	75–300 mg/day in divided doses.
Doxepin	Sinequan	75–300 mg/day in divided doses.
Imipramine	Tofranil	75–300 mg/day in divided doses.
Chlorpromazine	Thorazine	10–100 mg/day in divided doses for stress.
Thioridazine	Mellaril	10–100 mg/day in divided doses for stress.
Haloperidol	Haldol	1–5 mg/day in divided doses.

[a] Dosages are based on experience of authors.

useful in those individuals described above, and therefore should not necessarily be withheld as long as therapeutic benefit has been properly weighed against possible risk factors. It is felt that the phenothiazine compounds chlorpromazine (Thorazine) and thioridazine (Mellaril), the more sedating phenothiazines, can be useful in small doses in the treatment of excessive stress. The side effects of these medications tend to be as mentioned above with regard to the tricyclic antidepressants with common anticholinergic side effects. In those clients in whom anticholinergic side effects would be most difficult, and those in whom cardiovascular factors would mitigate against using phenothiazine type drugs, another alternative is to use a butyrophenone, which is a drug class related to the phenothiazines. The butyrophenone compound haloperidol (Haldol) has somewhat less sedating effects and less anticholinergic side effects, but more extrapyramidal side effects, which would be manifested by a stiffness in gait, a decreased facial expressiveness, a feeling of restlessness, movement disorder, and so forth, all of which are reversible when the drug is withdrawn.

Table XIII lists the commonly used doses of the previously mentioned medications for reducing anxiety and psychophysiological arousal.

SUMMARY AND CONCLUSIONS

As mentioned at the beginning of this chapter, our purpose has been to describe some of the pharmacological interventions which may be useful as an adjunct in the overall treatment of the stress response. Some of the same cautions as mentioned in other chapters must be repeated here. No medication is an answer in itself. It must be given in the context of a total therapeutic relationship, primarily in order to facilitate that relationship at a point at which it is being interfered with by excessive anxiety. It is thus used to further the relationship. It owes its effectiveness to the relationship and should never be used instead of it. Medication, we feel, should be used in as small a dosage as possible for as short a time as possible.

Pharmacotherapy has been said to be both an art and a science. It is important to know not only one's medications, but also one's client, and one must be able to balance therapeutic benefit against potential risk; therefore, appropriate medications can be determined on a client-to-client basis only.

The purpose of the chapter has been to familiarize the reader with some of the possible pharmacotherapeutic modalities available to the clinician treating the stress response and to indicate some of the benefits and difficulties associated with their use.

It is impossible in a review such as this to mention all of the possible drugs that can be used in such a condition, and new ones are being evaluated and tried almost daily. It is hoped that this brief review will serve to indicate some of the possible tools the practitioner has in his therapeutic armamentarium in the overall treatment of the stress response.

Those readers interested in a more in-depth discussion of the pharmacological interventions may see Swonger and Constantine (1973), Bassuck and Schoonover (1977), Shader (1975), or the latest edition of *AMA Drug Evaluations.*

CHAPTER 8

The Clinical Use of Relaxation Techniques

GENERAL CONSIDERATIONS

The purpose of this chapter is to provide a rationale and general introduction for the clinical use of behavioral techniques for relaxation. More specifically, this discussion will focus on techniques which the client may employ for the self-inducement of relaxation. So to provide a common frame of reference, we shall use the term *relaxation* to refer to an awakened state of hypoaroused psychophysiological functioning, experienced organism-wide or within any given bodily system.

Among the most commonly used techniques for autogenic (self-induced) relaxation are neuromuscular relaxation, meditation, controlled breathing, and various forms of biofeedback.

RATIONALE FOR THE CLINICAL USE OF RELAXATION TECHNIQUES

The use of behavioral autogenic techniques for relaxation has long been popular in the cultures of the Eastern world. Yet these techniques have only recently found their way into the research and clinicial settings of the Western world.

Though still relatively new, the clinical utilization of behavioral relaxation techniques have proven highly useful in the treatment of excessive stress and its clinical syndromes. The client's development and consistent implementation of the generic skill of relaxation may be considered therapeutic in the treatment of the stress response for several apparent reasons:

1. The practice of relaxation techniques may yield a temporary "trophotropic state." This state was first cogently described by Hess (1957), and it was popularized in clinical settings by Benson (1975). The trophotropic state is characterized by a generalized state of decreased psychophysiological activity, and may be described as an awakened state of hypometabolic functioning. This state of generalized relaxation appears to be mediated via the parasympathetic nervous system (Hess, 1957). Deep relaxation such as this appears to be conducive to health, in that (a) it is the complete physiological opposite of the sympathetic stress response, and (b) it appears to facilitate psychophysiological restoration within the body (see Benson, 1975; Davidson, 1976; Emmons, 1978; Jacobson, 1978; Shapiro & Giber, 1978; Stoyva, 1979; Stoyva & Budzynski, 1974).

2. The chronic practice (once or twice a day for several months) of these techniques may create a state of lowered limbic and hypothalamic activity (see Gellhorn, 1969; Gellhorn & Kiely, 1972; Glueck & Stroebel, 1978; Stoyva, 1977; Weil, 1974). This may explain the reported development of a less anxious attitude, a sort of prophylactic "anti-stress" disposition in clients who practice relaxation for several months. Therefore, operationally, the clinician would hope to see a reduction in the client's predisposition to undergo excessive psychological and physiological arousal during stressor episodes (see Gevarter, 1978; Jacobson, 1978; Luthe, 1969, Vol. 4; Stoyva, 1976; Stoyva & Budzynski, 1974).

3. There have been reported shifts in the personality constellations of individuals who practice relaxation techniques over a sustained period of time. These shifts have been reported in the direction of "positive mental health" (see Emmons, 1979; Everly, 1980a,b; Girdano, 1977; Kendall, 1967; Shapiro & Giber, 1978; Townsend *et al.*, 1975). Among the most notable of such changes are apparent shifts toward an internal locus of control, as well as improvement in self-esteem. However, the studies on which these conclusions are based must be considered preliminary until more and

better-controlled studies can be undertaken. Nevertheless, such findings have important implications for the process of psychotherapy, as well as for psychological health in general (see Carrington, 1977).

Given such overall findings as these, the clinician can see the emergence of a therapeutic rationale which fits virtually all clinical orientations. Let us now progress to a discussion of important clinical issues which are relevant to the use of relaxation strategies.

INDIVIDUAL CLIENT DIFFERENCES IN RELAXATION

This section addresses the role that individual client differences play in the clinical implementation of relaxation techniques.

"Inadequate recognition of individual differences is a methodological deficiency that has seriously slowed psychological research. Lip service is paid to individual differences, but in reality they are largely ignored" (Tart, 1975, p. 140). Researchers are only now beginning to realize that individual subject differences are important variables in the outcome of all behavioral-sciences research. Few things in the behavioral sciences are readily attributable to "main effects;" rather, "interaction effects" usually explain far more variation in research.

Clinicians must ultimately reach the same conclusion that researchers are beginning to, that is, that the effectiveness of a given treatment paradigm is a function of the interaction of the treatment with various client idiosyncracies. Rather than ask the question whether a treatment works or not, perhaps we should pose the question according to Paul (1967, p. 111): "WHAT treatment, by WHOM, is the most effective for this INDIVIDUAL with THAT specific problem, and under WHICH set of circumstances?"

These issues become of vital importance in the application of relaxation techniques. Peper (1976) argues effectively that there are very subtle qualities in the clinical application of biofeedback, for example, which significantly contribute to success or failure.

Unfortunately, at this time we have progressed only to the point that we realize that individual client differences do exert a major influence on clinical outcome. We have not yet discovered any specific variables which seem to predict the outcome of relaxation techniques. The most promising area of research resides in the personality construct as predictor of success in relaxation; however, no generally accepted results have yet been generated.

In summary, Luthe and Blumberger (1977) point out that not all relaxation techniques are useful for all clients. Therefore, the need to match clients selectively to specific relaxation techniques seems obvious. We have found that this matching process can proceed on the basis of a broad spectrum of knowledge and experience on the part of the clinician, as well as on the basis of input from the client. The clinician may wish to allow the client to express preferences for techniques based on a simple trial-and-error exposure before therapy actually begins. The clinician should be open to the use of a multidimensional treatment model in order to meet the idiosyncratic needs of the client (Girdano & Everly, 1979).

CLINICAL PRECAUTIONS AND UNDESIRABLE SIDE EFFECTS

Until just recently it was assumed by many that the use of relaxation techniques was a totally benign therapeutic intervention. With the increasing popularity and utilization of these techniques, however, several clinical precautions and undesirable side effects have emerged. It is important for the clinican to be aware of these potential problems.

Based on the research and clinical observations of Luthe (1969), Emmons (1978), Stroebel (1979), and Everly (1978b), five major typologies of potential areas for behavioral relaxation training are described below.

Loss of Reality Contact

The loss-of-reality-contact reactions to relaxation training include acute hallucinations (both auditory and visual) and delusions (usually of the paranoid type). Various forms of nonpsychotic dissociative reactions may similarly occur, for example, depersonalization, and unfamiliar somatic sensations. It is, therefore, usually unadvisable to use deep-relaxation techniques with clients who suffer from affective or thought-disturbance psychoses. Care should also be taken with clients who utilize nonpsychotic fantasy excessively. In such conditions, the use of deep relaxation may exacerbate the problem.

Drug Reactions

Clinical evidence has clearly indicated that the induction of a trophotropic state may actually intensify the effects of any medication or other chemical substance that the client may be taking. Of special concern would be clients taking insulin, sedatives/hypnotics, or cardiovascular medications. All such clients should be carefully monitored. Although in many cases chronic relaxation may ultimately result in long-term reductions in required use of medications. When such an outcome occurs, the functional intensification of the medication may be considered highly desirable.

Panic States

Panic-state reactions are characterized by high levels of anxiety concerning the loss of control, insecurity, and, in some cases, seduction. Diffuse, free-floating worry and apprehension have also been observed. With such clients it is generally more desirable to provide a more concrete relaxation paradigm (such as neuromuscular techniques or biofeedback), rather than the abstract relaxation paradigms (such as meditation). Similarly, it is important to assure the client that it is he or she who is really always in control—even in the states of "passive attention" which will be discussed in the following chapter on meditation.

Premature Freeing of Repressed Ideation

It is not uncommon for deeply repressed thoughts and emotions to be released into the client's consciousness in response to a deeply relaxed state. Although in some psychotherapeutic paradigms such reactions are considered desirable, they could be perceived as destructive by the client if such reactions are unexpected and/or too intense to be dealt with constructively at that point in the therapeutic process. Before implementation of relaxation techniques, the clinician may wish to inform the client of the possibility of the arising such ideation. Similarly, the clinician must be prepared to render support to the client should such thoughts emerge (see Adler & Morrissey-Adler, 1979; Glueck & Stroebel, 1978).

Excessive Trophotropic States

In some instances, the use of relaxation techniques that were intended to be therapeutic may induce an excessively lowered state of psychophysiological functioning. If this occurs, several phenomena may result:

1. *Temporary Hypotensive State.* This is an acute state of lowered blood pressure which may cause dizziness, headaches, or momentary fainting, particularly if the client rushes to stand up following the relaxation session. The clinician should know the client's resting blood pressure before employing relaxation techniques. Caution should be used if the client's resting blood pressure is lower than 90 mm/Hg systolic and 50 mm/Hg diastolic. Dizziness and fainting can often be aborted if the client is instructed to open his or her eyes and to stretch and look around the room at the first signs of uncomfortable light-headedness. Similarly, the client should be told to wait one to three minutes before standing up following the relaxation session.

2. *Temporary Hypoglycemic State.* This is a condition of low blood sugar which may follow the inducement of the trophotropic state. This condition is most likely to last until the client consumes some form of foodstuff. Deep relaxation, like exercise, appears to have in some clients an insulinlike action, and may induce such a condition if the client has a tendency for such conditions, or has not eaten properly that day. The acute hypoglycemic state just described may result in symptoms similar to the hypotensive condition.

3. *Fatigue.* Although relaxation techniques are known to create a refreshed feeling of vigor in many clients, a very few have reported feeling tired after relaxation practice. This is a highly unusual result and may be linked to an overstriving to relax on the part of the client. The clinician should inform the client that the best outcome in any attempt at relaxation is achieved when the client *allows* relaxation to occur, rather than making it happen.

Behavioral relaxation techniques are being used in a wide variety of settings, presumably because of their effectiveness and their seeming simplicity. Although undesirable side effects are rare, we now know that relaxation techniques and the trophotropic state are not totally benign. Therefore, they must be used in a responsible manner by the clinican. This means being aware of the precautions and potential undesirable side effects. The work of Luthe (1969) stands as the most important comprehensive treatment of this subject.

SUMMARY

Behavioral techniques which the client may use for the self-inducement of relaxation are powerful therapeutic interventions when used properly. Such techniques have particular utility in the treatment of excessive stress reactions. However, the clinician must be aware of the role that (1) individual client differences and (2) precautions and undesirable side effects play in their utilization. The clinician must assess the ultimate value of teaching clients skills in relaxation on an individual client-to-client basis. Although we remain unconvinced that there are any global contraindications for relaxation, we do feel that the precautions mentioned in this chapter are worthy of consideration. It is also important for the clinician to emphasize that the practice of relaxation techniques represents a *skill*, and that this skill can be obtained only through consistent practice. It is incumbent on the clinician to help the client develop this skill, and yet it cannot be taught, it must be learned.

The most widely used behavioral techniques for relaxation are meditation, neuromuscular relaxation, breath control, and the biofeedback methodologies. Therefore, we shall expand our discussion of these modalities in the following four chapters. However, in the final analysis the clinician must assess the ultimate suitability of every relaxation technique on a client-to-client basis.

Finally, Appendix A contains a relaxation-training report. This general form is designed to be used by clients to summarize their experiences while learning to relax. Its purpose is to provide guidelines that will structure expectations and elicit valuable information from clients with regard to their experiences while relaxing, whether in the office or at home. Most of the methods for teaching relaxation that we shall discuss in subsequent chapters are highly dependent on home practice. In our experience, this relaxation-training report facilitates that home training.

CHAPTER 9

Meditation

The purpose of this chapter is to provide a clinically useful introduction to meditation.

In our Western culture, *meditation* refers to the act of thinking, planning, pondering, or reflecting. Our Western definitions, however, are not representative of the essence of the Eastern world's notion of meditation. In the Eastern tradition, meditation is a process by which one attains "enlightenment." It is a growth producing experience along intellectual, philosophical, and, most importantly, existential dimensions. Within the context of this book, we shall use the term meditation to mean, quite simply, the autogenic practice of a genre of techniques which have the potential for inducing the trophotropic state in the practicer through the utilization of a repetitive focal device. Inherent in a high level of achievement using these procedures is a mental state characterized by a nonegocentered and intuitive mode of thought processing.

HISTORY OF MEDITATION

Some the the earliest of written records on the subject of meditation come from the Hindu traditions of around 1,500 B.C. These records consist of scriptures called the Vedas, which discuss the meditative traditions of ancient India.

The sixth century B.C. saw the rise of various forms of meditation—Taoist in China, Buddhist in India—and even the Greeks delved into meditation.

The earliest known Christian meditators were the desert hermits of Egypt in the fourth century A.D. Their generic meditative practices strongly resembled those of the Hindu and Buddhist traditions.

In the eleventh and twelfth centuries A.D. the Zen form of meditation, called "zazen," gained popularity in Japan.

Finally, in the 1960s a wave of meditative practice was begun in the United States in a form representing a "Westernized" style in the Hindu tradition. It was brought to this country by Maharishi Mahesh Yogi and is called "Transcendental Meditation" (TM).

TYPES OF MEDITATION

The practice of meditation represents the practice of a given technique or procedure which has the potential of inducing the awakened trophotropic state, as mentioned earlier. Although there exist many kinds of meditation, one element common to all forms of meditative technique is a stimulus, or thing, which the meditator will focus his or her awareness on. According to Naranjo and Ornstein (1971), it is something to "dwell upon," in effect, a focal device.

Meditative techniques may then be categorized by the nature of their focal devices. Using this criterion, there are four forms of meditative technique.

1. *Mental Repetition.* This form of focal device involves dwelling on some mental event. The classic example of a mentally repetitive focal device is the "mantra." A mantra is a word or phrase which is repeated over and over, usually silently to oneself. We would include chanting under this category as well. TM uses a mantra format. The TM mantra is chosen from several Sanskrit words. Herbert Benson (1975) employs the word "one" as a mantra for the hypertensive patients he treats. A Tibetan Buddhist mantra in verse form is "Om mani padme hum." The Christian prayer "Lord Jesus Christ, have mercy on me" is said to be a form of mantra as well.

2. *Physical Repetition.* This focal device involves the focusing of one's awareness on some physical act. An ancient Yogic (Hindu) style of repetitive meditation focuses on the physically repetitive act of breathing. Various forms of breath control and breath counting (called "pranayama") serve as the basis for one form of Hatha Yoga. The aspect of Hatha Yoga best known to the public involves the practice of postures (called "asanas"). The Moslem Sufis are known for their

practice of continuous circular dancing, or whirling. The name "whirling dervishes" was given to the ancient practitioners of this style. Finally, the popularity of jogging in the United States has given rise to the study of the effects of such activity. One effect reported by some joggers is a meditativelike experience. This could be caused by the repetitive breathing or the repetitive sounds of the feet pounding the ground.

3. *Problem Contemplation.* This focal device involves attempting to solve a problem with paradoxical components. The Zen "koan" is the classic example. In this case, a seemingly paradoxical problem is presented for contemplation. "What is the sound of one hand clapping?" is one of the most commonly known koan.

4. *Visual Concentration.* This focal device involves visually focusing on an image. It could be a picture, a candle flame, a leaf, a relaxing scene, or anything else. The "mandala" is a geometric design which features a square within a circle, representing the union of man with universe. This is often used in Eastern cultures for visual concentration.

MECHANISMS OF ACTION

Exactly how the meditative technique works, no one knows for sure. However, significant insight is yielded into this problem by examining the common link between all forms of meditation—the focal device. This stimulus to "dwell upon" appears to be the critical ingredient in the meditative procedure (Benson, 1975; Glueck & Stroebel, 1975, 1978; Naranjo & Ornstein, 1971; Ornstein, 1972; White, 1974).

The role of the focal device appears to be to allow the intuitive, nonegocentered mode of thought processing (thought to be activity of the brain's right neocortical hemisphere) to dominate consciousness in place of the normally dominant analytic, egocentered mode of thought processing (thought to be left-hemisphere activity). The focal device appears to set the stage for this shift to occur by sufficiently engaging the left hemisphere's neural circuitry to allow the right hemisphere to become dominant (see Davidson, 1976; Naranjo & Ornstein, 1971; Ornstein, 1972). The focal device may occupy the left hemisphere by engaging it in some monotonous task, such as attending to a mantra, focused breathing, or a set of postures. Or, the focal device may overload and frustrate the left hemisphere. This would be the case when the meditator dwells on seemingly paradoxical problems, as in Zen, or when the meditator engages in intense physical activity, as practiced by the Sufis (whirling dervishes), the Tantrics, or perhaps even the American jogging enthusiast.

When the focal device is successfully employed, the brain's order of processing appears to be altered. "When the rational (analytic) mind is silenced, the intuitive mode produces an extraordinary awareness" (Capra, 1975, p. 26). This awareness is the goal of all meditative techniques when practiced by the devoted practitioner.

This state of "extraordinary awareness" has been called many things. In the East, it is called "nirvana" or "satori." A liberal translation of these words yields the word "enlightenment." Similar translations for this state include "truth consciousness" or "Being-cognition." In the early Western world, those few individuals who understood it called it the "supraconsciousness" or the "cosmic consciousness."

More modern research investigations have attempted to qualify the neurophysiology of this supraconscious state. To date, research investigations in the neurophysiological domain have been inconclusive. Results of early studies point in the direction of lowered frequency of brain-wave production with increased amplitude during the supraconscious state. More recent investigations in the neurophysiology of meditation point toward a shift from left-hemisphere dominance to right-hemisphere, as mentioned earlier (Pagano & Frumkin, 1977; see also Davidson, 1976, and Orme-Johnson & Farrow, 1978, for reviews). In the final analysis, we may find this state to result from some combination of lowered neocortical activity occuring in a dominant right hemisphere.

It is crucial at this point to emphasize that meditation and the achievement of the supraconscious state are not always the same! It should be made clear to the client that meditation is the *process*, or series of techniques, which the meditator employs to achieve the desired *goal* of the supraconscious state.

THERAPEUTIC HALLMARKS TO THE SUPRACONSCIOUS STATE

As just mentioned, the "extraordinary awareness" of the supraconscious state is the desired goal of the devoted practitioners of all meditative styles. However, it is important for the clinician *and* client alike to understand that achievement of this state is never assured, and that this state may not be achieved every time by even the very experienced meditator. Given this fact, the question must then arise, "Is the time spent in the meditative session wasted if the meditator is unable to achieve the supraconscious state?" The answer to this question is clearly No! Positive therapeutic growth can be achieved without reaching the ultimate supraconscious state. The rationale for this statement lies in the fact that there exist several "therapeutic hallmarks" which are inherent in the process of meditation as one approaches the supraconscious state. Whereas Shapiro (1978) discusses five steps in meditation: (1) Difficulty in Breathing, (2) Wandering Mind, (3) Relaxation, (4) Detached Observation, and (5) Higher State of Consciousness, we should like to expand upon these hallmarks which we see in the meditative process.

The first and most fundamental of these hallmarks resides in *practice itself*. Even the ancient Hindu and Zen scriptures on meditation point out that it is far more important to *attempt* to achieve the supraconscious state than it is to actually reach that state. It should be clear to the twentieth-century clinician that, simply by taking time out to meditate, the client is making a conscious effort to improve health. This effect, by definition, is the antithesis of the behavior pattern that leads to excessive stress. Similarly, by emphasizing to the client the importance of simply meditating, rather than achieving the supraconscious state, the clinician will remove much of the competitive, or success-versus-failure, component in this process.

The second hallmark toward the supraconscious is a noticeable increase in *relaxation*. At this point, the client begins autogenically to induce a state of trophotropic relaxation. This is the awakened state of hypometabolic functioning referred to in the literature (see Benson, 1975). This state is therapeutic in that: (1) the body is placed into a mode which is equal or superior to sleep with regard to the restorative functions performed (Orme-Johnson & Farrow, 1978); and (2) ergotropically stimulating afferent proprioceptive impulses are reduced (Davidson, 1976).

The third hallmark toward the supraconscious is that of *detached observation* (see Shapiro, 1978). In the Indian scriptures this hallmark is described as a state in which the meditator remains "a spectator, resting in himself" as he observes his environment. This state is an egoless, passive state of observation in which the meditator simply "coexists" with the environment, rather than confronting or attempting to master it. It is a nonanalytic, intuitive state. One similar experience that many individuals have had is that of "highway hypnosis." This state is often experienced by individuals driving on monotonous expressways. At one point they notice they are at Exit #6, a mere moment later they may notice they are at Exit #16, yet have no immediate memory of the 10 exits in between. Many call this a "daydreaming state." It is important to note that the driver of the car was fully capable of driving; this is not a sleep state. If an emergency had arisen, the driver would have been able to react appropriately. Therefore, the clinician should explain that this state is not one of lethargy or total passivity (a major concern for many clients).

The final step in the meditative experience is the "supraconscious state." This state appears to be a summation of all the previous states except in greater intensity. Davidson (1976) has characterized its nature as:

1. A positive mood (tranquillity, peace of mind)
2. An experience of unity, or oneness, with the environment; what the ancients called the joining of microcosm (man) with macrocosm (universe)
3. A sense of ineffability
4. An alteration in time/space relationships
5. An enhanced sense of reality and meaning
6. Paradoxicality, that is, acceptance of things which seem paradoxical in ordinary consciousness

Because the clinician will be bombarded with questions concerning the nature of the clients' meditative experiences, let us place common experiences on a continuum for better understanding (See Figure 11).

This continuum of meditative experiences is not totally progressive from one discrete state to another. A meditator may jump from any one state to another and back again. On the other hand,

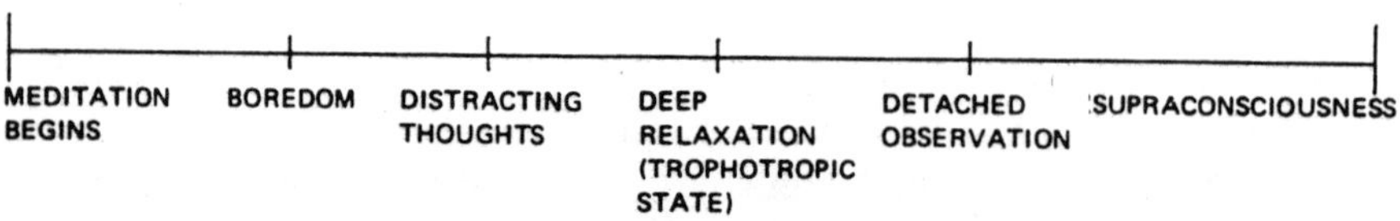

Figure 11. A meditative continuum.

varying degrees of depth within each state can be experienced. Note that boredom and distracting thoughts often precede more positive effects. The clinician should explain to the client that this is natural, and that he or she should be tolerant of such occurrences and simply return concentration to the focal device.

The meditator should be discouraged from *evaluating* the meditative sessions, for this sets up a success–failure paradigm. Simple descriptive reports to the clinician are useful, so as to monitor the course of the activity for a period of two to three weeks. A daily log might be kept by the client, as long as it is *descriptive* and *not evaluative*.

RESEARCH ON THE CLINICAL APPLICATIONS AND EFFECTS OF MEDITATION

Well-controlled research studies on the clinical effectiveness of meditation are in the minority at this time (see Shapiro & Giber, 1978, for a discussion and review). Nevertheless, those studies which do exist and which are relatively well-controlled point to a potentially wide range of stress-related therapeutic applications for meditation. Specifically, meditative techniques of the mantra type have been found useful:

1. In the treatment of generalized autonomic arousal and excessive ergotropic tone (Benson, Beary, & Carol, 1974)
2. In the treatment of anxiety and anxiety neurosis (Benson, Beary, & Carol, 1974; Emmons, 1978; Girodo, 1974; Vahia, 1972)
3. In the treatment of phobias (Boudreau, 1972)
4. For increasing "self-actualization" and "positive mental health" (Emmons, 1978; Nidich, 1973)
5. As an adjunct in the treatment of drug and alcohol abuse (Benson, 1969; Lazar, 1975)
6. As an adjunct in the treatment of essential hypertension (Benson *et al.*, 1974; Datey, 1969)

In order to assess objectively the therapeutic efficacy of meditation, one must not allow the poor quality of many of the early research and clinical reports, as well as the somewhat commercial reputation that meditation may have, to bias one's perspective. Although it is clear that the clinical use of meditation needs further validation, we feel that applications cited above have substantial potential, as well as preliminary validation (see Carrington, 1977, for further review).

Having provided a rationale for the clinical use of meditation, let us now examine its implementation.

HOW TO IMPLEMENT MEDITATION

The following discussion is provided as a guide to the clinical use of meditation.

Preparation for Implementation

In addition to the general precautions for relaxation mentioned in an earlier chapter,

1. Determine whether the client has any contraindications specifically for the use of meditation. For example, affective or thought-disturbance psychoses may possibly be exacerbated by meditation. Similarly, the clinician should use care with clients who demonstrate a tendency to employ nonpsychotic fantasy, as in the schizoid personality. It should also be noted here that some compulsive Type-A individuals appear to have greater difficulty in learning to meditate effectively than do less compulsive individuals. Boredom and distracting thoughts appear to compete with the meditation.

2. Inquire into the client's previous knowledge or experience in meditation. Pay particular attention to any mention of cultic or religious aspects. These are the most common misconceptions which clients find troublesome. Some will feel that if they meditate they will be performing a sacrilegious act.

3. Provide the client with a basic explanation of meditation.

4. Describe to the client the proper environment for the practice of meditation. This is described in the next section below.

Components within Meditation

In his book *The Relaxation Response*, Benson describes four basic components in successful meditation:

1. A quiet environment
2. A mental device

3. A passive attitude
4. A comfortable position

Based on our research and clinical experience, we would generally agree, but would wish to expand Benson's paradigm to some extent.

The first condition we would recommend is a *quiet environment*. The quiet enviroment is absent of external stimuli that would compete with the meditative process. Many clients will state that it is impossible to find such a place. If this is so, then some creativity may be needed. The client may wish to use some music or environmental recordings to "mask" distractions. In our laboratory experiments, we have found the steady hum of a fan or an air conditioner to be effective as a masking noise. Sounds of steady, low to moderate amplitude can actually be relaxing. In situations where this is not possible, the client may elect to wear a blindfold and/or ear plugs to reduce external stimulation.

The second condition (for physically passive meditation) is a *comfortable position*. Muscle tension can be disruptive to the meditative process. When first learning, the client should have most of his or her weight supported. The notable exceptions would be the head and neck. By keeping the spine straight and the head and neck unsupported, there will be enough muscle tension to keep the client from falling asleep. If the client continually falls asleep during meditation, then some posture which requires greater muscle tension should be used.

The third condition is a *focal device*. This is the link between all forms of meditation, even the physically active forms, as discussed earlier. The focal device appears to act by allowing the brain to alter its normal mode of processing.

The fourth condition is a *passive attitude*. This attitude has been called "passive volition" or "passive attention" by some. Benson (1975) states that this "passive attitude is perhaps the most important element" (p. 113). With this attitude, the client "allows" the meditative act to occur, rather than striving to control the meditative process. As Greenspan (1979) has noted, "The patient can only begin to win by surrendering resistance and allowing the . . . process to proceed" (p. 18).

If the client is unable to adopt this attitude, he or she will ask questions such as:

"Am I doing this correctly?"—usually indicative of concern of performance.

"How long does this take?"—usually indicative of concern for time.

"What is a *good* level of proficiency?"—usually indicative of concern for performance outcome, rather than process.

"Should I try to remember everything I feel?"—usually indicative of overanalysis. The more the client dwells on such thoughts as these, the less successful he or she will be. Distracting thoughts are completely normal during the meditative process, and are to be expected. However, adoption of a passive attitude allows the client to recognize distracting thoughts and simply return concentration to the focal device. A fascinating discussion of the passive attitude may be found in a paper written by Erik Peper (1976).

The fifth and final condition that we would recognize is a *receptive psychophysiological environment*. By this we mean a set of internal psychophysiological conditions which will allow the client to meditate. We have noted, for example, that clients who are psychophysiologically aroused when they attempt to meditate have a very low success rate. Therefore, we have found it necessary to teach the clients to put themselves in a more "receptive condition" for meditating (this would apply to biofeedback, hypnosis, and guided imagery as well). To achieve this receptive condition, the client may wish to use a few neuromuscular-relaxation techniques before the meditation, in order to reduce excessive muscle tension. We have recommended that the client take a hot bath before meditating. In some instances, clients have reported high levels of success if they meditated while sitting in a hot tub. We have found this seldom-mentioned concept of psychophysiological receptivity to be a critical variable in our own clinical experiences. Therefore, we would expand the meditative continuum (Figure 11) to include this variable (see Figure 12).

Example Protocol

Provided below is an example of a protocol* for a physically passive mantra-like form of meditation. Examine it and make notes in the margins provided as to what changes you might make in order to make the protocol more effective for your specific needs.

*This protocol is written as if being spoken directly to a client. It is adapted from D. Girdano & G. Everly, *Controlling Occupational Stress: A Self-Management Program.* An audio cassette program published by Robert J. Brady Co., Bowie, Maryland, 1980.

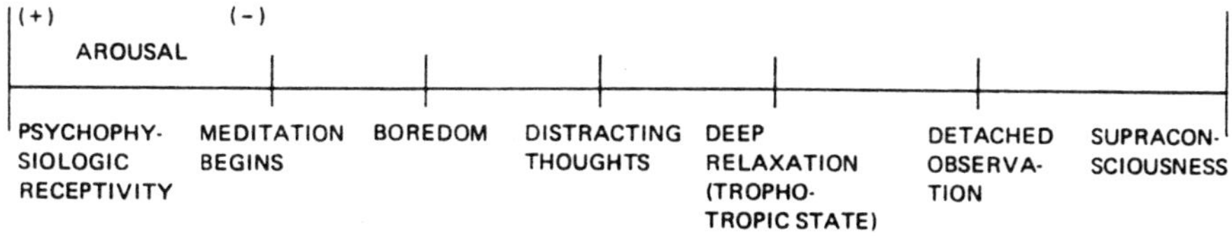

Figure 12. Arousal and the meditative continuum.

BACKGROUND INFORMATION

The purpose of these instructions is to familiarize you with the use of meditation as a way of reducing the stress in your life. These instructions consist of background information and specific directions for the use of four techniques that you may choose from in order to meditate. Follow all the instructions closely. Later you may wish to modify a part of the technique to fit a personal preference or situation, but in the initial learning phase you should do all the exercises exactly as instructed. Once you have chosen one of the meditative techniques, employ that technique as instructed for 15 to 20 minutes of uninterrupted meditation once or twice a day.

Some people, not familiar with the nature and origins of meditation, confuse its pure form with its possible uses. There are important differences. The techniques of meditation presented here represent techniques derived from the ancient Eastern philosophies which have then been blended with modern relaxation and stress-reduction techniques. Although some of the techniques were used in the practice of specific religions, to say that meditation is a religious practice is like saying wine is a religious instrument simply because many religions use wine in their ceremonies. Meditation is a technique of quieting the mind, which, of course, is a necessary prerequisite for reducing anxiety and tension.

As taught here, a quiet mind is an end in itself. What you do with this valuable skill is, of course, up to you.

The fundamentals of meditation are often misunderstood, as meditation itself is difficult to define. Meditation is not a physiological state. Nor is it any specific psychological feeling. It is not a religion. Rather, as used here, meditation is a technique. Meditation is so basic that it has transcended time, cultures, races, religions, and ideologies. The physiological, psychological, and philosophical goals of meditation cannot be achieved without training, and mastery of technique cannot be achieved except through continued practice.

Although there are many types of meditation, the most popular meditative techniques in Western society are derived from specific practices of ancient Yoga and Zen. Each type of meditation represents a variation of purpose and technique. Those which are presented here are thought to be the best suited for stress reduction. The technique is the easiest to learn and the one most devoid of cultic, religious, and spiritual overtones. It is complete and can be all the meditation one will ever need; or, it may serve as an introduction to more specific types.

There are several essential steps you should follow when learning to meditate.

A first essential step is to find a quiet environment, which means both external and internal. A quiet room away from others who are not meditating is essential, especially while learning. Take the phone off the hook, or at least go into a room without one. Generally, do whatever can be done to reduce external noise. If you cannot completely eliminate the noise, which is often the case in busy households or in college dorms, etc., use ear plugs. Play a record or tape of some soft instrumental sounds, or use any of the numerous environmental sound recordings which are commercially available. Even the steady hum of a fan or an air conditioner can serve effectively to block out, or mask, external noise. You will also wish to turn down, or completely off, any lights in the room. Now that you have quieted your external environment, the next essential step is to work on quieting your internal environment. One way is to reduce muscle tension. Muscle tension represents one of the biggest obstacles to successful meditation. Spend some time relaxing your muscles. One way to reduce muscle tension is to sit comfortably. You may not feel like a real meditator unless you are sitting in the Eastern cross-legged lotus position, but that takes a great deal of flexibility and training. For now, sit comfortably on the floor, or, better yet, sit in a straight-backed, comfortable chair, feet on the floor, legs not crossed, hands resting on the thighs, fingers slightly opened, not interlocked. You should sit still, but remember, meditation is not a trance. If you are uncomfortable or feel too much pressure on any one spot, move. If you have an itch, scratch. Do not assume a tight inflexible position or attitude. Relax. It is best not to lie or support your head or you will tend to fall asleep. Keep the head, neck, and spine in a straight vertical line. A small but significant amount of muscle tension is needed to maintain this posture, and this effort helps prevent sleep from occurring, while at the same time it creates an optimal position for learning to meditate.

There are many types of meditation. Some focus on inner forces, inner power, or self-identity. Others on external things, like words, lights, or sounds. Meditation is a simple natural process. And though techniques may differ, the core experience is essentially the same. The basic meditative experience involves passively concentrating on some stimulus, whether it be a word, an image, your breath, or nothing at all. The stimulus acts as a vehicle to keep distracting thoughts out of your mind. And yet, the harder you concentrate on the stimulus, the harder it is to meditate. Although this sounds confusing, it is true, simply because meditation is a "passive" activity. You must allow the stimulus, whatever it is, to interact passively with you. You must learn to concentrate passively on your stimulus. The skill of passive concentration takes time to develop—so don't be discouraged if it seems difficult for the first few weeks. Just continue to practice.

ACTUAL INSTRUCTION

You are now ready to begin the actual instruction. To begin with, close your eyes. Notice the quietness. Much of our sensory input comes in through our eyes. Just by closing yours eyes, you can do muchto quiet the mind.

THE USE OF BREATH CONCENTRATION

What we are going to do now is clear our minds. Not of all thoughts, but of ongoing thoughts, which use the imagination to increase stress arousal. Focus on your breathing. Shift your awareness from the hectic external world to the quiet and relaxing internal world.

As you breath in, think in. Let the air out. Think out. In and out. Concentrate on your breathing. Think in. Think out. Breath in through your nose and let the air out through the mouth very effortlessly. Just open your mouth and let the air flow out. Do not force it. Become involved with the breathing process. Concentrate on your breathing. In and out. Now, each time you breathe in, I want you to feel how cold the air is, and each time you breathe out, feel how warm and moist the air is. Do that now. (*Pause 60 seconds.*)

THE USE OF ONE

Now we would like to replace the concentration on breathing with the use of a mantra. A mantra is a vehicle which is often a word or phrase. It is merely a vehicle to help control your mind from wandering back to those daydreams. An example of a mantra, suggested by Herbert Benson in his book *The Relaxation Response*, is simply the word "one" (o-n-e). This is a soft, noncultic word which has little meaning as a number. Every time you breath out, say the word "one" to yourself. Say one. One. Say it softly. One. Say the word one without moving your lips. Say it more softly yet until it becomes just a mental thought. (*Pause 75 seconds here.*)

THE USE OF OM

The word "one" is an example of a mantra. A vehicle to help clear your mind. By concentrating on a word without emotion or significance, your mind's order of processing begins to change. The mind begins to wander, with a quieter, more subtle state of consciousness. Many people like to use words from the ancient Sanskrit language, feeling that they represent soft sounds which have spiritual significances which can also be used as a focus for contemplation. The universal mantra is the word "om"; spelled o-m, it also means one. Each time you breath out say the word om. Om. Om. Breathe softly and normally, but now do not concentrate on your breathing. Repeat the mantra in your mind. Just think of saying it. Do not actually move your lips. Just think of it. Do not concentrate on your breathing. Let the mantra repeat itself in your mind. Do not force it. Just let it flow. Gradually the mantra will fade. The mind will be quiet. Occasionally, the quiet will be broken by sporadic thoughts. Let them come. Experience them, then let them leave your mind as quickly as they entered, by simply going stronger to your mantra. Let us now use "om" as a mantra. Say the word om, om. (*Pause here 75 seconds.*) Remember, the mantra is a vehicle to help clear the mind when you cannot do so without it. Also remember, keep your movements to a minimum, but if you are uncomfortable, move. If you are worried about time, look at a clock. Discomfort or anxiety will prevent full attainment of the relaxed state.

THE USE OF COUNTING

A final mantra which you may select from, if you find your mind wandering too much, is a mantra that requires a little more concentration than the three previous meditation techniques.

As you breathe out, begin to count backward from 10 to 1. Say a single number to yourself each time you exhale. As you say the number, try to picture that number in your "mind's eye." When you reach 1, go back to 10 and start over. Let us do that now. (*Pause here 3 minutes.*)

REAWAKEN

Now I want to bring attention back to yourself and the world around you. I will count from 1 to 10. With each count you will feel your mind become more and more awake, and your body become more and more refreshed. When I reach 10, open your eyes, and you will feel the best you've felt all day—you will feel alert, refreshed, full of energy, and eager to resume your activities. Let us begin: 1–2 you are beginning to feel more alert, 3–4–5 you are more and more awake, 6–7 now begin to stretch your hands and feet, 8–now begin to stretch your arms and legs, 9–10 open your eyes *now*! You feel alert, awake, your mind is clear and your body refreshed.

Having read the preceding example, one should note the following points:

1. In the example, the client was given four different mantras to choose from. Such "freedom of choice" may increase clinical effectiveness (refer to Chapters 8 and 15). It is important to ask the client which mantra was the best for him or her, and why. Such questions foster client introspection and self-understanding.

2. The meditation example contains a *reawaken* step, as does the neuromuscular-relaxation example.

3. The clinician should indicate, at some point, when the client should meditate. We have found once or twice a day to be sufficient, 15 to 20 minutes in duration for each session. As with neuromuscular

relaxation, before lunch or before dinner are generally the best times to meditate, although practice in the morning may provide a relaxing start for the entire day.

SUMMARY

In this chapter we have discussed the use of meditation in the treatment of chronic stress. We have included a sample protocol, not as a prescription, but simply to demonstrate how such a protocol may be created.

On the basis of our clinical and research observations, in addition to other reports in the literature, we must conclude that the generic process of meditation can be a very effective therapeutic strategy for excessive stress.

A critical problem arises, however, in finding which specific forms of meditation are best suited for which individuals. This explains our desire to offer at least four different varieties of mantra. By offering several forms of meditative technique to the client, we have noted an increase in our own degree of effectiveness compared to when we taught only one form of meditation.

Overall, our best results have been obtained when clients choose to employ several neuromuscular techniques prior to meditation. This has led us to become sensitive to the concept of *psychophysiological receptivity* for meditation.

Perhaps the greatest task the clinician will face in using meditation as a therapeutic tool is in reducing the mystical, cultic, and religious auras which surround this otherwise extremely valuable therapeutic tool. In the final analysis, however, it is the clinician who must assess the clinical suitability of meditation on a client-to-client basis.

CHAPTER 10

Neuromuscular Relaxation

The purpose of this chapter is to provide a clinically useful introduction to a genre of interventions termed *neuromuscular relaxation* (NMR).

As used in this chapter, the term neuromuscular relaxation refers to a process by which an individual client can perform a series of exercises which will reduce the neural activity (*neuro*) and contractile tension in striate skeletal muscles (*muscular*). This process usually consists of isotonic and/or isometric muscular contractions, which are performed by the client with initial instruction from the clinician.

HISTORY OF NEUROMUSCULAR RELAXATION

The neuromuscular-relaxation procedure presented in this chapter comes from four primary sources: (1) the "Progressive Relaxation" procedures developed by Edmund Jacobson, (2) research protocols developed by the present authors, (3) the research of Bernstein and Borkovec (1973), and (4) the clinical work of Vinod Bhalla applying neuromuscular interventions to the fields of physical medicine and stress.

Research by Jacobson (1938) led to the conclusion that striate muscle tension represented a contraction of muscle fibers. He further concluded that this striate muscle tension played a large role in anxiety states. By teaching individuals to reduce striate muscle tension, Jacobson reported success in reducing subjective reports of anxiety.

After the 1940s C. Atlas developed a program of muscular "dynamic tension" for general health, but the model developed by Jacobson gained greater popularity.

Jacobson calls his system "Progressive Relaxation." This system consists of a series of exercises by which the subject tenses (contracts) and then relaxes selected muscles and muscle groups so as to achieve the desired state of deep relaxation. Jacobson considers his procedure "progressive" for the following reasons:

1. The subject learns progressively to relax the neuromuscular activity (tension) in the selected muscle. This process may require several minutes to achieve maximal neuromuscular relaxation in any selected muscle.

2. The subject tenses and then relaxes selected muscles in the body in such a manner as to progress through the principle muscle groups until the entire body, or selected body area, is relaxed.

3. With continued daiiy practice, the subject tends progressively to develop a "habit of repose" (p. 161)—a less stressful, less excitable attitude, in our experience.

Progressive Relaxation gained considerable popularity when Joseph Wolpe (1958) utilized the same basic relaxation system in his treatment for phobias called "systematic desensitization." This treatment paradigm has become a classic behavioral therapeutic intervention which consists of relaxing the subject before and during exposure to a hierarchy of anxiety-evoking stimuli. Wolpe has successfully employed the principle that an individual cannot be relaxed and anxious at the same time, that is, relaxation acts to inhibit a stress response.

MECHANISMS OF ACTION

Jacobson (1978) argues that the main therapeutic actions of the neuromuscular-relaxation system reside in having the client *learn* the difference between tension and relaxation. This learning is based on having the client enhance his or her awareness of proprioceptive neuromuscular impulses which originate at the peripheral muscular levels and increase with striate muscle tension. These afferent proprioceptive impulses are major determiners of chronic diffuse anxiety and overall stressful sympathetic arousal according to Jacobson. This conclusion is supported by the research of Gellhorn (1967), who demonstrated the critical role that afferent proprioceptive impulses from the muscle spindles play in the determination of generalized ergotropic tone.

Once the client learns adequate neuromuscular awareness, he or she may then effectively learn to reduce excessive muscle tension by consciously and progressively "letting go" or reducing the degree of contraction in the selected muscles. It has been argued that it is difficult for "unpracticed" clients to achieve a similar degree of conscious relaxation because they are not learned in the sensations of tension versus conscious deep relaxation—as a result, measurable "residual tension" will remain during conscious efforts to relax.

More recent studies on progressive relaxation have suggested that there are two principle therapeutic components at work. Although it is generally accepted that the traditional Jacobsonian concept of *learned awareness* of the differences between the tension of contraction compared to the relaxation experienced on the release of contraction is an important therapeutic force, there may be more. It has been suggested that the actual procedure of *contracting* a muscle before attempting to relax it may yield some additional impetus to the total amount of relaxation achieved in that muscle, over and above the process of learned awareness (Borkovec, Grayson, & Cooper, 1978).

RESEARCH ON CLINICAL APPLICATIONS AND EFFECTS OF NEUROMUSCULAR RELAXATION

A review of research and clinical literature on the genre of techniques which would fall under the heading of neuromuscular relaxation (including Jacobson's procedures) reveals a wide range of stress-related therapeutic applications. Specifically, neuromuscular relaxation has been concluded to be effective in the treatment of:

1. Insomnia (Jacobson, 1938; Nicassio & Bootzin, 1974; Steinmark & Borkovec, 1973).
2. Essential hypertension (Deabler, 1973; Shoemaker & Tasto, 1975).

3. Tension headaches (Cox, Freundlick, & Meyer, 1975).
4. Subjective reports of anxiety (Jacobson, 1978; Paul, 1969a).
5. General autonomic arousal and excessive ergotropic tone (Jacobson, 1978; Paul, 1969a,b).
6. Development of a calmer attitude which may act as a prophylactic against excessive stress arousal (see Stoyva, 1977).

On the basis of these research findings and our own clinical observations, we have concluded neuromuscular-relaxation strategies to be an effective component of most treatment programs for chronic stress. Let us now examine a structure for clinical implementation.

HOW TO IMPLEMENT A PHYSICALLY ACTIVE FORM OF NEUROMUSCULAR RELAXATION: PREPARATION

To review, neuromuscular relaxation represents a series of exercises during which the subject tenses (contracts) and then releases (relaxes) selected muscles in a predetermined and orderly manner. Some preliminary activities that the clinician should undertake before implementing the procedures are as follows:

1. In addition to the general precautions for relaxation mentioned in an earlier chapter, determine whether the client has any muscular or neuromuscular contraindications: for example, nerve problems, weak or damaged muscles, or skeletal problems which would be made worse through the neuromuscular exercises. When in doubt, avoid that specific muscle group until a qualified opinion can be obtained.

2. Inquire into the client's previous knowledge or experience of neuromuscular techniques. The clinician must determine whether such knowledge or experience will be detrimental or facilitative in the present situation. It is often helpful to discuss in detail any previous exposure that the client may have had to neuromuscular techniques.

3. Provide the client with background and rationale for use of neuromuscular techniques.

4. Describe to the client the proper environment for the practice of neuromuscular techniques: (a) quiet, comfortable surroundings, darkened, if possible, in order to allow full concentration on bodily sensations; (b) loosen tight clothing; remove contact lens, glasses, and shoes if desired; (c) body should be supported as much as possible (with exception of neck and head if client falls asleep unintentionally).

5. Instruct the client in the differences between the desired muscle "tension" and undesirable muscle "strain." Tension is indicated by a tightened, somewhat uncomfortable, sensation in the muscles being tensed. Strain is indicated by any pain in the muscle, joints, or tendons, as well as any uncontrolled trembling in the muscles. Strain is in actuality excessive muscle tension.

6. Instruct the client in proper breathing. Do not hold the breath while tensing muscles. Rather, breathe normally, or inhale on tensing and exhale on relaxing the muscles.

7. Before beginning the actual protocol with the client, informally demonstrate all the exercises that you will be employing. Take this opportunity to answer any questions that the client may have.

8. Finally, explain to the client exactly "how" you will give the instructions. For example: "In the case of each muscle group that we will focus upon, I will always carefully describe the relaxation exercise to you first, before you are actually to do the exercise. Therefore, don't begin the exercise described until I say, 'Ready? Begin.'"

The exact order of these steps may vary. In order to facilitate client awareness of some of these preliminary points, the clinician may place them on a type of handout.

HOW TO IMPLEMENT NEUROMUSCULAR RELAXATION: PROCEDURE

Whenever possible, begin the total protocol with the lowest areas of the body to be relaxed and end with the face. This is done because once a muscle has been tensed and then relaxed, we attempt to insure that it is not inadvertently retensed. The quasi-voluntary muscles of the face are the most susceptible to retensing, therefore we relax them last to eliminate the opportunity.

The Sequential Steps to Follow for Each Muscle Being Relaxed

Once the clinician is ready to initiate the actual protocol, he or she should be sure to follow a fundamental sequence of steps for *each* muscle group.

Step 1. Describe to the client the specific muscle(s) to be tensed and how it/they will be contracted. "We are now going to tense the muscles in the calf. To begin I'd like you to leave your toes flat on the floor and raise both of your heels as high as you can."

Step 2. Have the client initiate the response with some predetermined cue: "Ready? Begin."

Step 3. Have the client hold the contraction for three to five seconds. During this time you may wish to encourage the client to exert an even greater effort: "Raise your toes higher, higher, even higher."

Step 4. Signal to the client to relax the contraction: "And now relax."

Step 5. Facilitate the client's awareness of the muscles just relaxed by having him or her search for feelings of relaxation: "Now sense how the backs of your legs feel. Are they warm, tingling, do they feel heavy? Search for the feelings."

Step 6. The clinician may wish to encourage further relaxation: "Now let the muscles relax even more. They are heavier and heavier and heavier."

Step 7. Pause at least five to ten seconds after each exercise to allow the client to experience relaxation. Pause 15 to 20 seconds after each major muscle group.

Step 8. When possible, go directly to the opposing set of muscles. In this case, it would involve leaving the heels flat on the floor and raising the toes as high as possible.

Example Protocol

Provided below is a brief protocol* in which the previously discussed components have been included. See whether you can identify the major preliminary activities (only a few can be included in this example). See whether you can identify the sequenced steps (some example muscle groups will have only six or seven of the steps to avoid monotony).

As you read the example, make notes in the margins provided as to what changes you might make in order to make the protocol more effective for your needs in teaching a general NMR protocol.

*This protocol is written as if being spoken to the client. It is adapted from D. Girdano & G. Everly, *Controlling Occupational Stress: A Self-Management Program.* An audio cassette program published by Robert J. Brady Co., Bowie, Maryland, 1980.

BACKGROUND INFORMATION

As early as 1908, research conducted at Harvard University discovered that stress and anxiety are related to muscle tension. Muscle tension is created by a shortening or contraction of muscle fibers. The relationship between stress and anxiety on one hand, and muscle tension on the other, is such that if you are able to reduce muscle tension, stress and anxiety will be reduced as well.

Progressive neuromuscular relaxation is a tool that you can use to reduce muscle tension and, therefore, stress and anxiety. Progressive neuromuscular relaxation is a progressive system by which you can systematically tense and then relax major muscle groups in your body, in an orderly manner, so as to achieve a state of total relaxation. This total relaxation is made possible by two important processes.

First, by tensing a muscle and then relaxing it you will actually receive a sort of running start, in order to achieve a greater degree of muscular relaxation than would normally be obtainable. And, second, by tensing a muscle and then relaxing it, you are able to compare and contrast muscular tension and muscular relaxation. Therefore, we see that the basic premises underlying your muscular relaxation are as follows:

1. Stress and anxiety are related to muscular tension.
2. When you reduce muscular tension, a significant reduction in stress and anxiety will be achieved as well.
3. Neuromuscular relaxation provides you with the unique opportunity to compare and contrast tension with relaxation.

Neuromuscular relaxation has been proven to be a powerful tool which can be used to achieve relaxation and peace of mind. However, relaxation is an active skill and like any skill it must be practiced. The mistake that most individuals make is to rush through this relaxation procedure. Neuromuscular relaxation works, but it takes practice and patience to succeed. But, after all, isn't your health well-being worth at least 15 minutes a day?

PRELIMINARY INSTRUCTIONS

Before beginning the progressive neuromuscular relaxation procedure, let us review some basic considerations.

First, you should find a quiet place without interruptions or glaring lights. You should find a comfortable chair to relax in, though you will find progressive relaxation useful performed lying down in bed in order to help you fall asleep at night as well. You should loosen tight articles of clothing. Ties, sport coats, glasses, and contact lenses should be removed.

Second, the progressive neuromuscular relaxation system requires you to tense each set of muscles for two periods, lasting about five seconds each. However, it is possible to tense each set of muscles up to seven times if you continue to feel residual tension. Muscular tension is not equal to muscular strain. They are not the same. You will know that you have strained a muscle if you feel pain in the muscle or any of the joints around it, or if it begins to shiver or to tremble uncontrollably. In either case, these should be signs to you to employ a lesser degree of tension, or simply avoid that exercise. The entire neuromuscular relaxation procedure lasts about 20 minutes, should you wish to relax your entire body. The time will be less if you choose to relax only a few muscles groups.

Last, don't hold your breath during contractions. Breathe normally, or inhale as you tense and exhale as you release the tension.

ACTUAL INSTRUCTIONS

Your are now ready to relax progressively the major muscle groups in your body, in order to achieve a state of total relaxation. I would like you to settle back and get very, very comfortable. You may loosen or remove any tight articles of clothing, such as shoes or coats, ties or glasses. You should also remove contact lenses. You should try to get very, very comfortable. I would like you to close your eyes. Just sit back and close your eyes. And I would like to begin by directing your attention to your breathing. The breath is the body's metronome. So let us become aware of the metronome. Become aware of how the air comes in through your nostrils and down into your lungs, and as you inhale how your stomach and chest expand, as you exhale how they recede. Concentrate on your breathing. (*Provide 30 second pause here.*)

In the case of each muscle group that we shall focus on, I shall always carefully describe the relaxation exercise to you first, before you are actually to do the exercise. Therefore, do not begin the exercise described until I say, "Ready? Begin."

CHEST

Let us begin with the chest. I would like you, at my request, and not before, to take a very, very deep breath. I would like you to breathe in all the air around you. Let's do that now. Ready? Begin. Take a very deep breath. A very deep breath; deeper, deeper, deeper, hold it . . . and relax. Just exhale all the air from your lungs and resume your normal breathing. Did you notice tension in your chest as you inhaled? Did you notice relaxation as you exhaled? If you had to, could you describe the difference between tension and relaxation? Let us keep that in mind as we repeat this exercise. Ready? Begin. Inhale very deeply, very deeply. Deeper than that. Deeper than that. Deepest of all. Hold it, and relax. Just exhale and resume your normal breathing. Could you feel the tension that time? Could you feel the relaxation? Try to concentrate on that difference in all the muscle groups that we shall be attending to.

(*Always pause 5–10 seconds between exercises.*)

LOWER LEGS

Let us go now to the lower legs and the muscles in the calf. Before we begin, I should like you to place both your feet flat on the floor. Now, to engage in this exercise, I should like you simply to leave your toes flat on the floor, and raise

Figure 13

both your heels at the same time as high as they will go. Ready? Begin. Raise your heels. Raise them both very high, very high, very high (see Figure 13). Hold it, and relax. Just let them fall gently back to the floor. You should have felt some contraction in the back of your calves. Let us repeat this exercise. Ready? Begin. Raise the heels very high, very high, higher this time. Higher. Hold it, and relax. As you relax, you may feel some tingling, some warmth. Perhaps some heaviness as the muscle becomes loose and relaxed. To work the opposite set of muscles, I should like you to leave both your heels flat on the floor, point both sets of your toes very, very high. Point them as high as you can toward the ceiling. This is the same motion that you would make if you lifted your foot off the accelerator pedal in your car (see Figure 14). Except that we shall do both feet at the same time. Let us do that now. Ready? Begin. Raise the toes very high. Raise the toes higher, higher. Much higher. Hold it, and relax. Now let us repeat this exercise. Ready? Begin. Raise the toes high. Higher this time. Highest of all. Hold it, and relax. You should feel some tingling or heaviness in your lower legs. That feeling is there. You must simply search for it. So take a moment and try to feel that tingling, warmth, or perhaps that heaviness that tells you that your muscles are now relaxed. Let those muscles become looser and heavier and even heavier. (*Pause for 20 seconds.*)

THIGHS AND STOMACH

The next set of muscles that we shall concentrate on is those of the thigh. This exercise is a simple one. At my request, I should like you simply to extend both your legs out in front of you as straight as you can (see Figure 15). (*If*

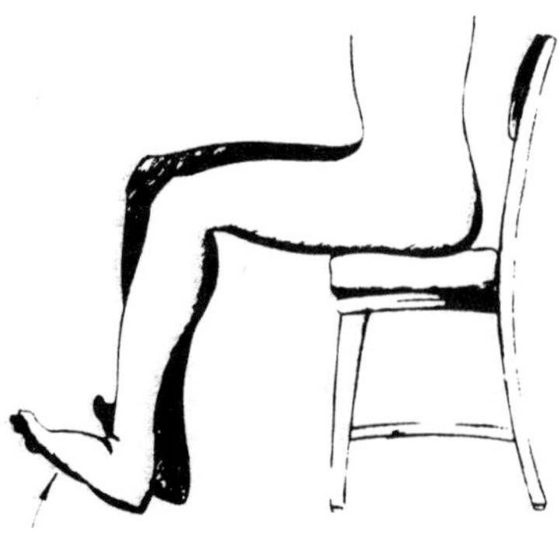

Figure 14

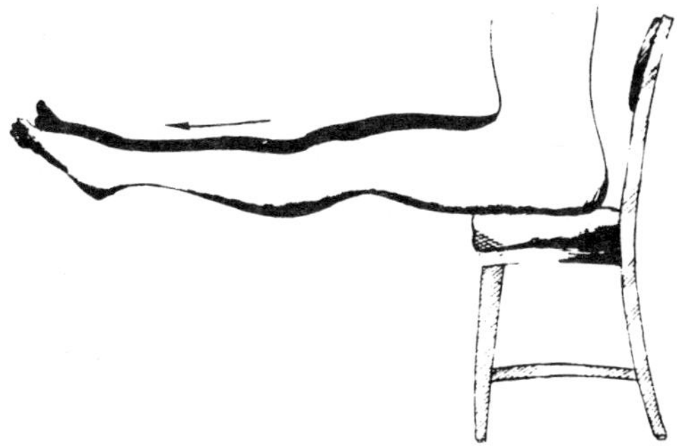

Figure 15

this is uncomfortable for the client, let him or her exercise one leg at a time.) Remember to leave your calves loose. Do not tense them. Let us do that now. Ready? Begin. Straighten both your legs out in front of you. Very straight. Very straight. Straighter than that. Much straighter. Hold it, and relax. Just let the feet fall gently to the floor. Did you feel tension in the top of your thighs? Let us repeat this exercise. Ready? Begin. Straighten both your legs out. Very straight. Straighter this time. Straightest of all. Hold it, and relax. To work the opposite set of muscles, I should like you to imagine that you are at the beach and are digging your heels down into the sand (see Figure 16). Ready? Begin. Dig your feet down into the floor. Very hard. Very hard, Harder than that. Harder. And relax. Now let us repeat this exercise. Ready? Begin. Dig your heels down into the floor. Very hard. Very hard. Harder. Harder than that, and relax. Now, the tops of your legs should feel relaxed. Let them become more and more relaxed—more and more relaxed. Concentrate on that feeling now. (*Pause here 20 seconds.*)

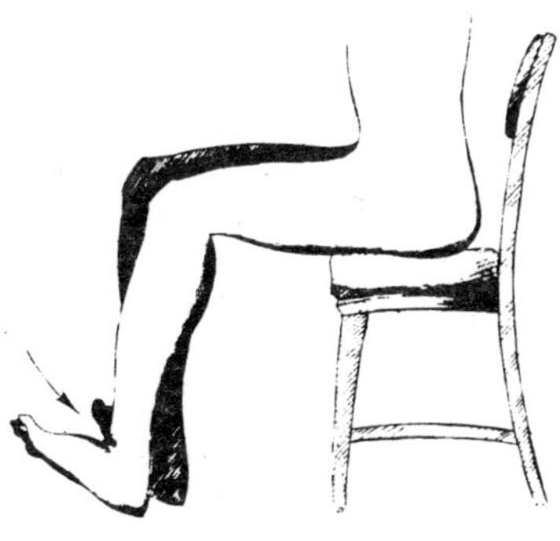

Figure 16

Figure 17

HANDS

Let us move now to the hands. The first thing that I should like you to do, with both your hands at the same time, is make very tight fists (See Figure 17). Clench your fists together as tightly as you can. Ready? Begin. Clench your fists very tightly. Very tightly. Tighter. Tighter than that. Hold it, and relax. This exercise is excellent if you type or do a lot of writing during the day. Now let us repeat. Ready? Begin. Clench both your fists very tightly. Very tightly. Tightest of all. Hold it, and relax. To work the opposing muscles, simply spread your fingers as wide as you can (see Figure 18). Ready? Begin. Spread your fingers very wide. Wider. Wider than that. Hold it, and relax. Now let us repeat this exercise. Ready? Begin. Spread the fingers wide. Wider.

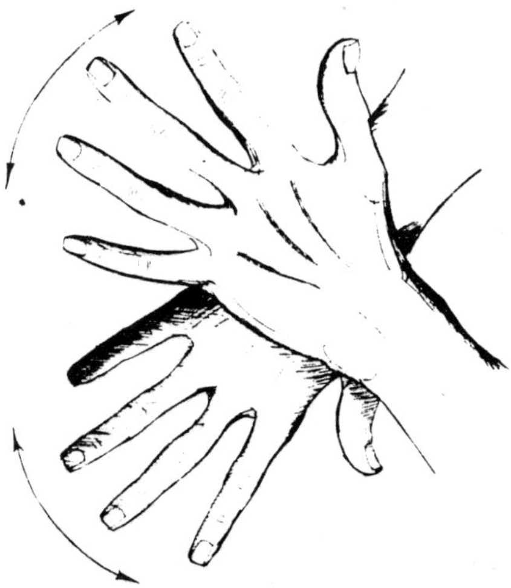

Figure 18

Wider. Widest of all. Hold it, and relax. Concentrate on the warmth or tingling in your hands and forearms. (*Pause here 20 seconds.*)

SHOULDERS

Now let us work on the shoulders. We tend to store a lot of our tension and stress in our shoulders. This exercise simply consists of shrugging your shoulders vertically up toward your ears. Imagine trying to touch your ear lobes with the tops of your shoulders (see Figure 19). Let us do that now. Ready? Begin. Shrug your shoulders up high. Very high. Higher than that. Much higher than that. Hold it, and relax. Now let us repeat. Ready? Begin. Shrug the shoulders high. Higher. Higher. Much higher. Highest of all. Hold it, and relax. Let us repeat this exercise one more time. Ready? Begin. Shrug the shoulders as high as you can. Higher. Higher than that. Hold it, and relax. Very good. Now just concentrate on the heaviness in your shoulders. Let your shoulders go, let them completely relax—heavier and heavier. (*Pause here 20 seconds.*)

FACE

Let us move now into the facial region. We shall start with the mouth. The first thing I should like you to do is smile as widely as you possibly can (see Figure 20). An ear-to-ear grin. Ready? Begin. Very wide smile. Very wide. Very wide. Wider. Wider than that. Hold it, and relax. Now let us

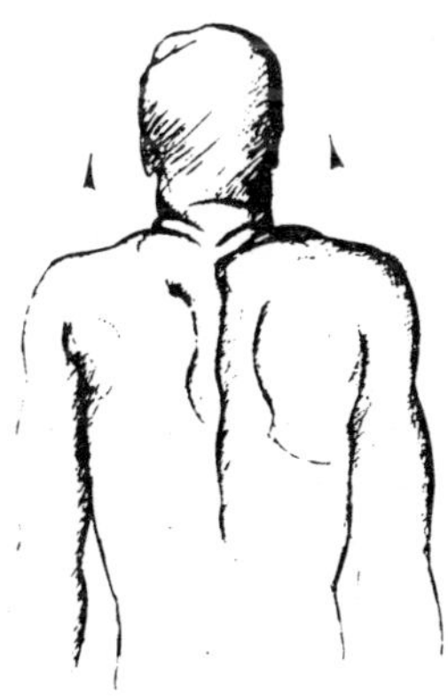

Figure 19

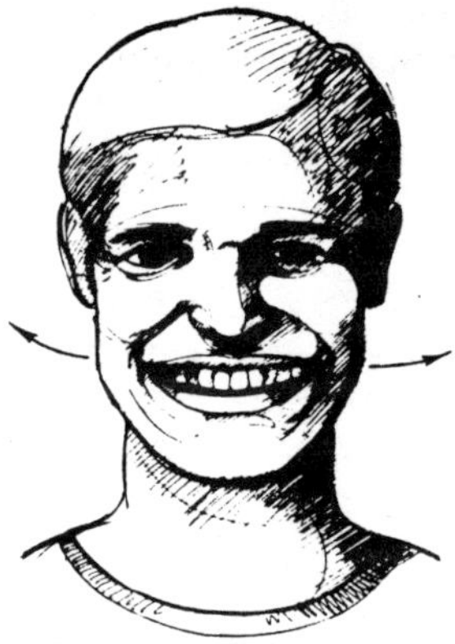

Figure 20

repeat this exercise. Ready? Begin. Grin very wide. Wide smile. Much wider. Much wider. Hold it, and relax. The opposite set of muscles will be activated when you pucker or purse your lips together, as if you were trying to give someone a kiss (see Figure 21). Ready? Begin. Pucker the lips together. Purse them together very tightly. Tighter than that. Tighter than that. Hold it, and relax. Now let us repeat that exercise. Ready? Begin. Purse the lips together. Tighter. Tighter than that. Tightest of all. Hold it, and relax. Let your mouth relax. Let the muscles go—let them relax, more and more; even more.

Now let us move up to the eyes. I should like you to keep your eyes closed, but to clench them even tighter. Imagine that you are trying to keep shampoo suds out of your eyes (see Figure 22). Ready? Begin. Clench the eyes very tightly. Very tight. Very tight. Tighter than that. Tighter, and relax.

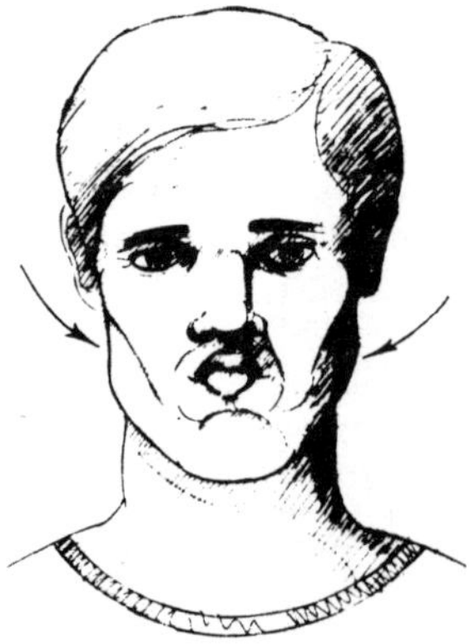

Figure 21

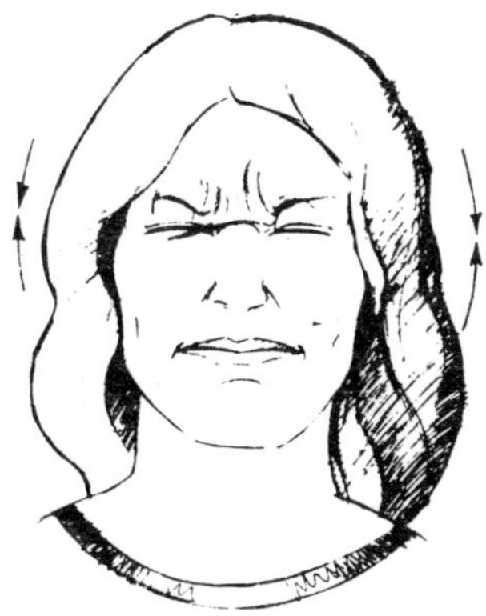

Figure 22

Let us repeat this exercise. Ready? Begin. Clench the eyes, tighter. Tighter. Tighter. Hold it, and relax.

The last exercise consists simply of raising your eyebrows as high as you can. Now, remember to keep your eyes closed, but raise your eyebrows as high as you can (see Figure 23). Ready? Begin. Raise the eyebrows high. Higher than that. Much higher. Much higher. Hold it, and relax. Now let us repeat this exercise. Ready? Begin. Raise the eyebrows higher. Higher than that. Highest of all. Hold it, and relax. Let us pause for a few moments to allow you to feel the relaxation in your face. (*Pause 15 seconds.*)

CLOSURE

You have now relaxed most of the major muscles in your body. To make sure that they are all relaxed, I shall go

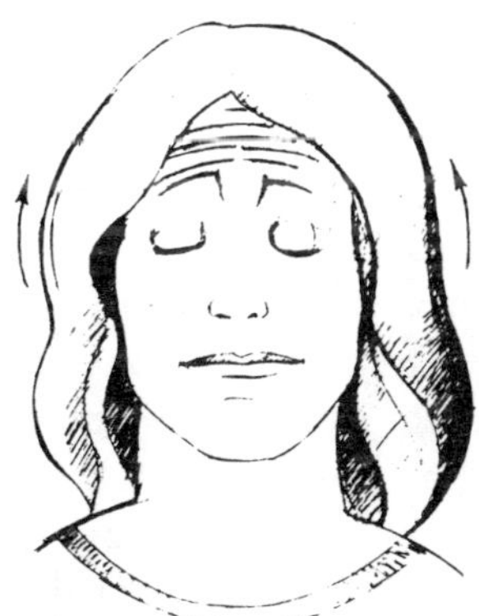

Figure 23

back and name the muscles that we have just activated and just relaxed. And, as I name them, let them go even further into relaxation. You will feel a sense of relaxation descend over your entire body in a warm wave. You will feel the muscular relaxation now in your forehead, and as it goes down into your eyes, down into your cheeks, you can feel the heaviness of relaxation descend into your jaws, into your neck, down through your shoulders, to the chest, and arms, to the stomach, into your hands. Relaxation is descending into your legs, into the thighs and calves, and down to the feet. Your body now feels very heavy. Very relaxed. This is a good feeling. So take a moment and enjoy this feeling of relaxation. (*Pause here 2 minutes.*)

REAWAKEN

Now I want you to bring your attention back to yourself and the world around you. I shall count from 1 to 10. With each count you will feel your mind become more and more awake, and your body more and more refreshed and responsive. When I reach 10, open your eyes, and you will feel the *best* you've felt all day—you will feel alert, refreshed, full of energy, and eager to resume your activities. Let us begin: 1–2 you are beginning to feel more alert, 3–4–5 you are more and more awake, 6–7 now begin to stretch your hands and feet, 8– now begin to stretch your arms and legs, 9–10 open your eyes *now*! You feel alert, awake, your mind is clear and your body refreshed.

Having read the example protocol, one should note the following points:

1. Having completed the desired groups of muscles, the clinician should go back and provide the client with a final opportunity to achieve further relaxation, or "closure." Here the clinician simply goes back and names the major muscles relaxed, and he instructs the client to release any residual tension. This is demonstrated in the example protocol under the heading "Closure."

2. In cases where the entire body is relaxed, we have observed in many clients a deeply relaxed state that carries over, or lingers, for several minutes to an hour or so. This can be highly desirable, if the goal of the relaxation is to hasten sleep, or simply to act as a tranquillizing agent. However, for clients who must go back to work or study, etc., within a brief time after relaxation, it becomes desirable

to show them how to "reawaken" or energize themselves. One such technique is provided in the example protocol under the heading "Reawaken."

3. Inform the client when to practice at home or at work. Inform the client that it is best to practice the technique twice a day—though once a day has been found to be effective for many. We have found the best times typically to be before lunch and before dinner, since digestive processes seem to interfere with effective concentration. In the treatment of insomnia, these techniques should be done while lying in bed at the end of the evening as the client attempts to go to sleep.

4. Emphasize to the client that a big advantage in the use of neuromuscular relaxation resides in its flexibility. That is, clients can elect to employ the entire system, relaxing the entire body, or select one or two muscle groups which seem to be the most tense. This obviously cuts down on the time needed to complete the exercises, and creates a symptom-specific intervention role for NMR which can be highly useful.

5. Finally, reemphasize that the technique of neuromuscular relaxation is a *skill*, that will be developed *only* through consistent practice.

SUMMARY

The series of exercises presented in the example represents a *brief* protocol, not as a prescription for use with clients so much as an example of how such a protocol may be created. Usually greater specificity is included for muscle groups, and even individual muscles, depending on the requirements of the client. It is important to mention that Jacobson clearly emphasizes the utility of relaxing the facial muscles, particularly the throat, mouth, and eyes, to obtain maximal relaxation. Therefore, far more specialization directed toward those muscle groups may be considered in developing a protocol.

The clinician may encourage the client to develop his or her own personalized protocol. The clinician may further encourage or provide the client with a home practice tape.

Jacobson's text *You Must Relax*, represents an excellent resource for

Table XIV. Summary Checklist of Neuromuscular Relaxation Components

Preparation for implementation:

_____ 1. Identify contraindications.

_____ 2. Inquire as to previous knowledge/experience in techniques.

_____ 3. Provide client with background/rationale for use of technique.

_____ 4. Describe proper environment for practice of technique.

_____ 5. Instruct client in the difference between muscle "tension" and muscle "strain."

_____ 6. Instruct client in proper breathing.

_____ 7. Informally demonstrate all specific muscular contractions to be used.

_____ 8. Describe "how" you will provide instruction and cues.

Implementation of sequential steps for *each* muscle being relaxed:

_____ 1. Describe the specific muscle and "how" it will be contracted.

_____ 2. Signal the client to begin contraction.

_____ 3. Hold contraction and encourage greater contraction.

_____ 4. Signal the client to release tension, that is, relax.

_____ 5. Facilitate the client's awareness of muscles just relaxed through verbal and intonational cues.

_____ 6. Encourage further relaxation.

_____ 7. Pause and allow client to become aware of sensations.

_____ 8. Proceed with opposing muscle group, if applicable.

additional and far more specific exercises. However, in the final analysis, it is up to the clinician to assess the clinical suitability of any form of neuromuscular relaxation on an individual basis.

Table XIV may be used as a checklist of important procedural points that should be covered when teaching clients neuromuscular relaxation. As each step is completed, simply check (√) it off. This same table may be used to evaluate clinical student's mastery of these procedures. It is designed to be reprinted from this text and used clinically or in educational settings.

Finally, Appendix B contains a different version of neuromuscular relaxation. It consists of a physically passive form which utilizes focused sensory awarenss and directed concentration for the reduction of striate muscle tension. The clinician may consider this as a potential clinical alternative to the form of neuromuscular relaxation just described.

CHAPTER 11

Voluntary Control of Respiration Patterns in the Reduction of Excessive Stress

The purpose of this chapter is to discuss using voluntary control of respiration patterns in the reduction of excessive stress. As used in this text, voluntary controlled respiration refers to the process by which the client exerts voluntary control over his or her breathing pattern—in effect, breath control. There exist hundreds of diverse patterns of controlled respiration; we shall examine only several which we feel have particular introductory utility for the clinician concerned with the treatment of the stress response. The exercises presented here are by no means to be considered the only exercises that may be used. We have simply chosen several patterns which we have found to be extremely simple to learn, as well as effective. Simply stated, the goal of voluntary controlled respiration in the treatment of excessive stress is to have the client voluntarily alter his or her rhythmic pattern of breathing so as to create a more relaxed state. The following discussion is most relevant to that stated goal.

HISTORY

Voluntary control of respiration patterns (breath control) is perhaps the oldest stress-reduction technique known. It has been used for thousands of years to reduce anxiety and to promote a generalized state of relaxation. The history of voluntary breath control dates back centuries before Christ. References to voluntary breath control for obtaining a relaxed state can be found in the Hindu tradition of Hatha Yoga. In fact, Hatha Yoga (the yoga of postures) is essentially built on various patterns of breathing. These patterns are called *pranayama*. The term *pranayama* means breath control, or breath restraint. According to Hewitt (1977), however, *pranayama* may be more loosely translated to mean relaxing breath control. As Hatha Yoga flourishes today, so does the practice of voluntary control of respiration.

While in ancient India breath control was developing in the Hindu tradition, the Chinese were practicing it as well. The development of the movement arts of T'ai Chi and Kung Fu saw the inclusion of controlled breathing as a basic component in both art forms. These "martial arts" have enjoyed a rebirth of popularity in the United States. Breath control remains an important component of both.

Perhaps the most widely used form of breath control today is in the form of the procedure for "natural" childbirth. In this form of childbirth various types of controlled breathing are used to reduce pain for the mother during delivery and to facilitate the descent of the child through the birth canal.

In this chapter we shall concern ourselves only with voluntary controlled breathing patterns that seem most useful as general aids to relaxation, without any specific goal other than common stress reduction.

BASIC PATTERNS OF BREATHING

In this section, we shall describe briefly the fundamentals involved in the breathing process, by examining the four phases of the respiratory cycle and describing three basic types of breathing.

According to Hewitt (1977), there are four distinct phases of the breathing cycle which are of relevance in learning voluntary control of respiration patterns (the clinician will find this phasic division useful in teaching any form of deep-breathing technique):

1. Inhalation (inspiration). Inhalation occurs as air is taken into the nose or mouth, descends via the trachea, the bronchi, and bronchioles, and finally inflates the alveoli, which are the air sacs constituting the majority of the lobes of the lungs.

2. The pause which follows inhalation. During this pause, the lungs are retaining their inflated characteristic.

3. Exhalation (expiration). This occurs as the lungs are deflated, emptying the waste gases from the alveoli into the same system used for inhalation.

4. The pause which follows the exhalation phase. During this phase, the lungs are at rest in a deflated state.

According to Ballentine (1976), there are three basic types of breathing. These are named and differ primarily according to the nature of the inhalation initiating the breathing cycle: clavicular, thoracic, and diaphragmatic.

The clavicular breath is the shortest and shallowest of the three. It can be observed as a slight vertical elevation of the clavicles, combined with a slight expansion of the thoracic cage upon inhalation.

The thoracic breath represents (in varying degrees) a deeper breath—deeper in the sense that a greater amount of air is inhaled, more alveoli are inflated, and the lobes of the lungs are expanded to a greater degree. It is initiated by activation of the intercostal muscles which expand the thoracic cage up and outward. The thoracic breath can be observed as a greater expansion of the thoracic cage, followed by an elevation of the clavicles on inhalation. Thoracic breathing is the most common breathing pattern.

Finally, the diaphragmatic breath represents the deepest of all the breaths. In this breath the most air is inhaled and the greatest number of alveoli are inflated. In addition, for the first time the lowest levels of the lungs are inflated. The lower third of the lungs contains the greater part of the blood when the individual stands vertically, therefore the diaphragmatic breath oxygenates a greater quantity of blood per breathing cycle than the other types. During the diaphragmatic breath, the diaphragm (a thin, musclelike structure which separates the thoracic and the abdominal cavities) flattens downward on inhalation. This forces air to descend into the lungs, and at the same time it forces the organs in the abdominal cavity to be pushed down and forward. The movement of the diaphragm becomes the major cause of the deep inhalation. The full diaphragmatic breath may be observed as the abdominal cavity expands outward, followed by expansion of the thoracic cage, and finally elevation of the clavicles.

Variations of the diaphragmatic breath are considered by many to be the simplest and most effective form of controlled respiration in the reduction of excessive stress. Therefore, we shall limit ourselves to discussing the role of diaphragmatic patterns in reducing excessive stress. It would, however, be helpful to the clinician to learn to identify all three basic patterns of breathing in clients.

MECHANISMS OF ACTION

Although the specific mechanisms involved in stress reduction via breath control may differ from technique to technique, a general therapeutic force is thought to be the ability of the diaphragmatic breath to induce a temporary trophotropic state.

Hymes (1980) notes that the tone of the sympathetic and of the parasympathetic nervous systems is greatly affected by the process of respiration. Harvey (1978) concludes that "diaphragmatic breathing stimulates both the solar plexus and the right vagus nerve in a manner that enervates the parasympathetic nervous system thus facilitating full relaxation" (p. 14). Finally, Pratap, Berrettini, and Smith (1978) have proposed a neural mechanism through which diaphragmatic breathing may reduce neocortical activity (as is useful in anxiety reduction):

> It is clear from the description of this practice that it evokes a strong Hering–Breuer reflex. The afferent limb of the Hering–Breuer reflex consists of stretch receptors in the lung which are excited as inspiration proceeds. The resultant impulses ascend via the vagus nerve to the Pontine Apneustic Center. . . . The excessive stimuli (physiologically speaking) evoked by this practice may functionally alter some areas of the ascending reticular activating system, thereby suppressing sensory input to the cortex bringing about a steadying of the mind. (p. 174)

Ballentine (1976) notes that expiration increases parasympathetic tone. It is interesting to note that during most types of diaphragmatic breathing expiration is protracted, therefore a protracted period of parasympathetic relaxation is apparently created. In summary, Hymes (1980) states, "Autonomic functioning may be voluntarily shifted back to calm by exercising conscious breath control (with an associated reduction of anxiety and pain)" (p. 10).

Unfortunately, there is no substantial body of research literature directed specifically toward one type of therapeutic breath pattern, although research efforts, at the Eleanor N. Dana Laboratory of the Himalayan International Institute, for example, have been directed toward improving this condition. Until such research is undertaken, voluntary breath control may suffer from the stigma of an ancient forgotten remedy.

Finally, independent of any predominantly physiological mechanisms, voluntary breath control may prove therapeutic from a predominantly cognitive perspective as well. The rationale for this statement comes from the fact that concentration on respiration patterns acts to compete with obsessive cognitive thought patterns, and perhaps even compulsive behaviors. This point must be assessed on a client-to-client basis.

HOW TO IMPLEMENT

Voluntary breath control appears to be the most flexible of the interventions for the reduction of excessive stress. It can be utilized under a wide variety of environmental and behavioral conditions.

Despite its versatility, voluntary breath control should not be used without precaution. When breathing is used as a meditative device, the precautions discussed in the chapter on meditation would seem to apply. Apparently, the major precaution which is unique to voluntary breath control is one against hyperventilation. Hyperventilation may be simply defined as a condition where the client "overbreathes." Overbreathing can quickly create a state of hypocapnia (diminished CO_2 levels in the blood) followed by an excess in the bicarbonate ion and an insufficiency in the hydrogen ion (Lum, 1975). The resultant symptoms can include: palpitations, tachycardia, Raynaud's phenomenon, tunnel vision, dizziness, grand mal seizures, shortness of breath, chest pain, tingling in the lips, fingers, and/or toes, epigastric pain, tetany, anxiety, weakness, and loss of consciousness—to mention only a few. Many of these symptoms could appear after several minutes of prolonged hyperventilation. Dizziness and tingling appear to be among the earliest of warning signs that the client is beginning to hyperventilate. Hewitt (1977) adds to the list of precautions for breath control:

> No more than momentary pauses between inhalation and exhalation are safe for persons with lung, heart, eye, or ear troubles, or for persons with high blood pressure. . . . Persons with low blood pressure may pause

> briefly after breathing in, but should make no deliberate pause after breathing out. The breath should not be deliberately held during pregnancy. (pp. 79–80)

Unfortunately, Hewitt offers no clinical or physiological rationale for these statements. Therefore, the clinician reading this text must reach his or her own conclusions regarding this matter. It is interesting to note, however, that Lum (1975) states that one form of diagnosis of hyperventilation "rests on reproducing the patient's symptoms by voluntary hyperventilation in a form which the patient recognizes and on taking reasonable steps to exclude significant pathology" (p. 378).

Listed below are three diaphragmatic breathing exercises that are reported to be useful in promoting a more relaxed state. In teaching any form of diaphragmatic breathing, the clinician must monitor the activities of the client to assure proper techniques. Hewitt (1977) offers the following guidelines, which we feel are appropriate for all forms of diaphragmatic breathing:

> You fill the lungs to a point of fullness without strain or discomfort. (p. 90)
> If after retention [of the inhalation] the air bursts out noisely, the suspension has been overprolonged; the air should be released in a steady smooth stream. . . . Similarly, following the empty pause, the air should unhurriedly and quietly begin its ascent of the nostrils [as the new inhalation begins]. (p. 73)

We have found these general guidelines useful in having clients avoid overbreathing, as well as other inappropriate breathing practices. These guidelines should be followed when instructing a client in each of the following three breathing exercises.

BREATHING EXERCISE NO. 1. This breathing technique may be thought of as a "complete breath." In fact, variations of this breath appear in the Yogic literature with similar names. The technique is extremely simple to complete. In order to assist the clinician in teaching the exercise to clients, we shall describe it according to the four phases of breath described by Hewitt (1977).

Inhalation. The inhalation should begin through the nose if possible. The nose is preferred to the mouth because of its ability to filter and warm the incoming air. On inhalation, the abdomen should begin to move outward, followed by expansion of the chest. The length of the inhalation should be two to three seconds (or to some point less than that where the lungs and chest expand without discomfort).

Pause after inhalation. There should be no pause. Inhalation should transfer smoothly into the beginning of exhalation.

Exhalation. Here the air is expired (through the mouth or the nose, whichever is more comfortable). The length of this exhalation should be two to three seconds.

Pause after exhalation. This pause should last only one second, then inhalation should begin again in a smooth manner. We have found that this exercise can be repeated by many clients for several minutes without the initiation of hyperventilation. However, the client should usually be instructed to stop when light-headedness occurs.

BREATHING EXERCISE NO. 2. This breathing exercise may be thought of as a form of "counting breath," of which variations appear in the Yogic literature. The term counting is applied to this exercise because the client is asked literally to count to him or herself the number of seconds each of the four phases of the exercise will last. In order to assist the clinician in teaching this exercise, we shall describe it according to the four phases of breathing described by Hewitt (1977).

Inhalation. The inhalation should begin through the nose if possible. The abdomen should begin to move outward, followed by expansion of the chest. The length of the inhalation should be two seconds (or to some point less than that where the lungs and chest expand without discomfort). The length of the inhalation should be counted silently, as, One thousand, Two thousand.

Pause after inhalation. There should be a pause here, following the two-second inhalation. The counted pause here should be one second in duration.

Exhalation. Here the air is expelled. The counted exhalation should be three seconds in duration.

Pause after exhalation. This counted pause should last one second. The next inhalation should follow smoothly. We have found that this exercise can be repeated by many clients for several minutes without the occurrence of hyperventilation. However, the client should usually be instructed to stop when light-headedness occurs.

BREATHING EXERCISE NO. 3. This technique, developed by G. S. Everly, is designed to rapidly induce (within 30 to 60 seconds) a state of relaxation. Research has shown it to be effective in reducing muscle tension and subjective reports of anxiety as well as some potential for reducing heart rate (see Everly, 1979a,b; Vanderhoof, 1980). The following description is presented as if instructing a client.

During the course of an average day, many of us find ourselves in anxiety-producing situations. Our heart rates increase, our stomachs may become upset, and our thoughts may race uncontrollably through our minds. It is during such episodes as these that we require fast-acting relief from our stressful reactions. The brief exercise described below on this page has been found effective in reducing most of the stress reaction that we suffer from during acute exposures to stressors—in effect, a quick way to "calm down" in the face of a stressful situation.

The basic mechanism for stress reduction in this exercise involves deep breathing. The procedure is as follows:

Step 1. Assume a comfortable position. Rest your left hand (palm down) on top of your abdomen. More specifically, place your left hand over your navel. Now place your right hand so that it rests comfortably on your left. Your eyes can remain open. However, it is usually easier to complete Step 2 with your eyes closed (see Figure 24).

Step 2. Imagine a hollow bottle, or pouch, lying internally beneath the point at which your hands are resting. Begin to inhale. As you inhale imagine that the air is entering through your nose and descending to fill that internal pouch. Your hands will rise as you fill the pouch with air. As you continue to inhale, imagine the pouch being filled to the top. Your rib cage and upper chest will continue the wavelike rise that was begun at your navel. The total length of your inhalation should be two seconds for the first week or two, then possibly lengthening to two and a half or three seconds as you progress in skill development (see Figure 25).

Step 3. Hold your breath. Keep the air inside the pouch. Repeat to yourself the phrase, "My body is calm." This step should last no more than two seconds.

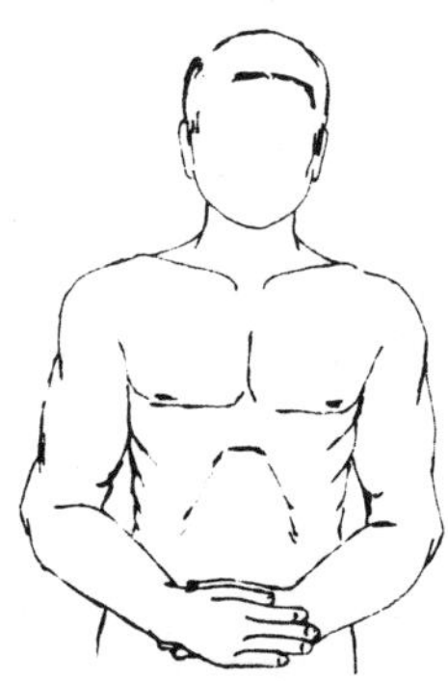

Figure 24

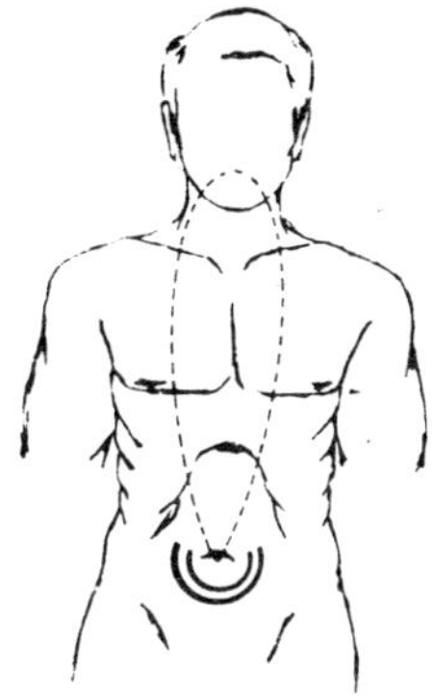

Figure 25

Step 4. Slowly begin to exhale—to empty the pouch. As you do, repeat to yourself the phrase, "My body is quiet." As you exhale, you will feel your raised abdomen and chest recede. This step should last as long as the two preceding steps, or may last one second longer, after a week or two of practice. (*Note*: Step 1 need only be used during the first week or so, as you learn to breathe deeply. Once you master that skill, you may omit that step.) Only repeat this four-step exercise three to five times in succession. Should you begin to fell light-headed, stop at that point. If light-headedness recurs with continued practice, simply shorten the length of the inhalation and/or decrease the number of times you repeat this four-step exercise in succession.

Practice this exercise 10 to 20 times a day. Make it a ritual in the morning, afternoon, and evening, as well as during stressful situations. Because this form of relaxation is a skill, it is important to practice at least 10–20 times a day. At first you may not notice any on-the-spot relaxation. However, after a week or two of regular practice, you will increase your capabilities to temporarily relax "on-the-spot." Remember, you must *practice regularly* if you are to master this skill. Regular, consistent practice of these daily exercises will ultimately lead to the development of a more calm and relaxed attitude—a sort of antistress attitude—and when you do have stressful moments, they will be far less severe. (Adapted from *The Stress Mess Solution*. Brady/ Prentice-Hall, 1980.)

SUMMARY

In this chapter we have presented a discussion of voluntary controlled patterns of respiration as they may be used to reduce excessive stress. As mentioned earlier, the goal of voluntary controlled respiration in the treatment of excessive stress is to have the client voluntarily alter his or her rhythmic pattern of breathing so as to create a more relaxed state.

We have discussed the three basic types of breathing patterns—clavicular, thoracic, and diaphragmatic. The first two are associated with (and may stimulate) a sympathetic response. The latter is associated with (and may stimulate) a parasympathetic response (see Ballentine, 1976). It has been found useful, in our experience, for the clinician to learn to recognize these patterns in clients. It is also useful to teach clients how to recognize such patterns in themselves.

Although the literature (especially the Yogic) presents numerous and diverse respiratory techniques for relaxation, we have focused upon the diaphragmatic breath. This emphasis is based on the conclusion that variations of diaphragmatic breathing are the simplest to teach, and among the most effective for achieving a relaxed psychophysiological state in the client. For these reasons, the clinician may find the variations of the diaphragmatic pattern most clinically useful.

In the final analysis, the clinician must assess the suitability of using voluntary controlled respiration with each client individually. The clinician may attempt teaching the client several breathing exercises, in order to assess which may be of most utility to that individual. We have presented three simplistic variations of the diaphragmatic breath, not as prescription but as example variations of a basic type of breath control (diaphragmatic breathing) which has been found useful in reducing excessive stress. Many other useful variations exist (see Hewitt, 1977; Jencks, 1977). The clinician must assess their utility on a case-by-case basis.

The major drawback that we have mentioned to the use of breath control in stress reduction is the hyperventilation reaction. We have found this to be virtually no problem when the client uses breathing exercises, such as those described in this chapter for short periods of time, and ceases when light-headedness ensues. The Yogic literature includes references that no more than 15 minutes of any hour should be spent in pranayama practice. Once again, however, this issue must be assessed on a case-to-case basis.

In conclusion, Hymes (1980) states that "control of the breath may be a major practical key to the smooth and balanced functioning of the autonomic nervous system and contribute to a healthier body and a more tranquil mind" (p. 10). We concur with this analysis, and would add that, if nothing else, teaching the client simply to pause and breathe more slowly may indeed be therapeutic in a life-style which encompasses potentially pathogenic time urgency.

CHAPTER 12

Biofeedback in the Treatment of the Stress Response

The purpose of this chapter is to provide a basic introduction to biofeedback in general, and as it relates to the treatment of the stress response.

Biofeedback may be conceptualized as a procedure in which data regarding an individual's biological activity are collected, processed, and conveyed back to him, so that ultimately he can modify that activity. It is the construction of a "feedback loop" which may be envisioned as in Figure 26.

Feedback loops exist in almost all functions of the human body, from the rate-modifying feedback loops concerned with the most elementary biochemical reactions to the most complex human endeavors. Information regarding the result of any event is necessary at some level, if it is to be modified in any but random fashion.

Thus, the concept underlying biofeedback is an elementary one in all biology, yet one which has not yet been widely put to use in the therapeutic sciences. In the traditional medical model, the patient presents a physiological disturbance, and data regarding his physiological functioning are collected by the clinician, who draws conclusions and institutes appropriate therapy, the patient playing a passive role. This interaction as visualized below represents an

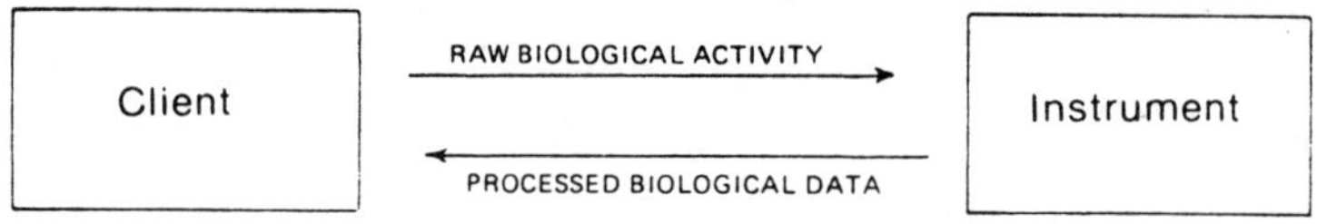

Figure 26

indirect closed loop of information, starting and ending with the patient, and including information-gathering devices, the clinician and therapeutic devices.

As can be seen from a comparison of Figures 26 and 27, the principle on which biofeedback is based involves the active participation of the patient in the modification of his condition.

Consider the case of a function like breathing, in which, when one turns one's attention to it, one is aware of it, but which continues without conscious awareness. The question of awareness, of course, does not even enter into the picture in terms of visceral autonomic responses generally. It is as if there are priorities for the human brain, with many functions carried out at subcortical levels—especially those that must be maintained in an ongoing fashion, such as heartbeat and biochemical reactions. Although this may be the most efficient way for an organism to function, it keeps it from being able to monitor many of its autonomic functions consciously, and thus consciously change them. This is what biofeedback provides for the individual—the potential to exert some control over autonomic biological activity.

Given the appropriate information, as in biofeedback, it is being increasingly found that man can learn to change bodily functions

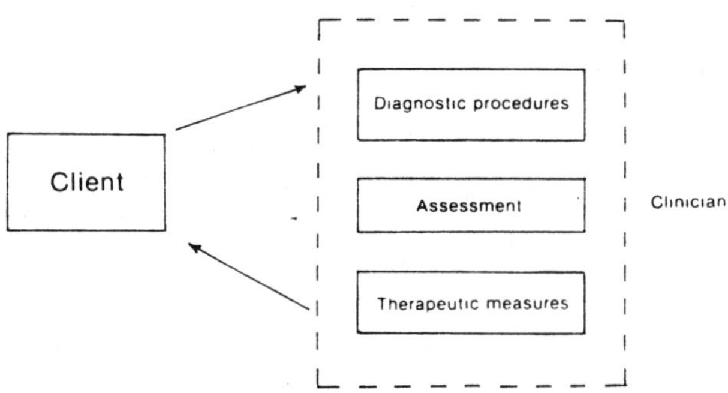

Figure 27

which were heretofore thought to be inaccessible to him. This includes greater finite control over the activities of both the voluntary and the autonomic nervous systems.

The purpose of this chapter is to amplify and elaborate on the principles on which biofeedback is based, and outline how it may be of benefit in the treatment of the stress response. We shall also describe some of the historical trends which have led to the present state of the art of biofeedback. We shall then discuss some of the biofeedback modalities in current use, and, finally, examine the role of the therapist in the biofeedback paradigm.

HISTORY

The term "biofeedback" is relatively new, reportedly having been coined at the first annual meeting of the Biofeedback Research Society in 1969 as a shortened version of "biological feedback." Although the term itself is new, the foundations are less so.

The historical development of biofeedback can be traced back to the early 1900s and the work of Pavlov and Watson on one hand and Thorndike on the other. Pavlov and Watson's research in the classical conditioning of the autonomic nervous system was thought to be discretely separate from the work of Thorndike in the operant conditioning of the musculoskeletal system. Early researchers were convinced that conditioning that affected the autonomic nervous system had to be accomplished through a classical conditioning paradigm (an S $\longrightarrow$ R model involving conditioning on the basis of association rather than as a function of behavioral consequence as in an operant model). This idea persisted for many years. At the same time, according to a review by Gatchel and Price (1979), case reports were emerging of individuals who reportedly could voluntarily alter autonomic functioning (see Lindsley & Sassaman, 1938; Luria, 1958; McClure, 1959; Ogden & Shock, 1939). However, the mechanisms by which these changes were effected were unknown.

In the early 1960s, research reported the ability of subjects to alter heart rate (Frazier, 1966; Shearn, 1962; see Engel, 1972, for an early review).

At the same time, Basmajian (1963) was reporting the ability of patients to control single motor-unit activity. With the development of an electromyographic biofeedback system, Budzynski and Stoyva began delving into the applications of biofeedback in the facilitation of general relaxation and in the treatment of tension headaches (see Stoyva & Budzynski, 1974, for a review).

During this period, the Menninger group led by the Greens was delving into the application of thermal biofeedback to clinical conditions (see Green & Green, 1979).

Finally, the early work of Kamiya (1969) and Brown (1977) in electroencephalographic biofeedback gained widespread attention for applications in relaxation and alteration of consciousness, although it was Sterman's (1972, 1973) work in the clinical applications in the treatment of epilepsy that appeared to have the most clinical utility.

In recent years, biofeedback has shown even more potential applicability to a host of clinical problems including vasoconstrictive syndromes (Taub & Stroebel, 1978), gastrointestinal disorders (Whitehead, 1978), muscle-contraction syndromes (Budzynski, 1978), and physical rehabilitation (Fernando & Basmajian, 1978), to mention only a few.

Despite these advances, the question remains, "What is biofeedback?" Is it a type of operant paradigm or something else? What is the role, if any, of striate muscle activity on autonomic activity? These questions have yet to be answered.

In conclusion, it should be stated that biofeedback in its present form is a new endeavor, the technology for which has become available only since the end of the Second World War. New methods are being made available almost daily for acquiring, storing, processing, and displaying data, and it is an area in which one can expect a great deal of new research and development in the coming years.

BIOFEEDBACK MODALITIES

In this section we shall briefly overview several types of biofeedback, describing their nature and potential utility.

Electromyographic (EMG) Biofeedback

Description. The term EMG as applied to biofeedback stands for electromyograph. The EMG instrument that is used is one in which electrical impulses are picked up through special metal sensors (electrodes), which are applied to the skin, with electrode jelly used as a conducting medium. The impulse is amplified and processed by the machine in such a way as to produce a display of lights, a deflection of a meter, a sound that correlates with the magnitude of the signal, or any combination of these. They are noted by the client, and he is thus given the information that he needs in order to modify the function—in this case, muscle tension.

The words "stress" and "tension" are often used interchangeably, and the muscle tension itself is a very obvious component of the fight–flight response. When a threat is perceived, any muscle throughout the body may tense; however, some do so in a characteristic way. For example, the muscles in the back of the neck will characteristically become tense as if in an effort to keep the head erect to aid in vigilance. Back, shoulder, and jaw muscles tense when the individual perceives himself as being threatened, or when he is under stress.

Since we are describing striated muscle, it would seem that control would be voluntary, and therefore easily subject to learning. The difficulty arises when the contraction increases so slowly and imperceptibly that the individual is not aware of increased muscle tension until the muscles are already in spasm. The EMG apparatus allows the individual to become aware of small increments of change in muscle tension, thus allowing him to learn to relax the muscles involved.

One can place the EMG electrodes virtually over any striated muscle available to either skin or needle electrodes. Frontalis muscle biofeedback is frequently used for "cultivated low-arousal training" (Stoyva, 1977). Other placements for more generalized relaxation may include wrist to wrist for upper body and ankle to ankle for lower body.

Indications. For the purposes of this chapter, EMG biofeedback is used to treat the stress response primarily in two ways. First, by allowing the client to learn to relax a particular muscle or set of muscles (e.g., the masseter muscles in bruxism). Second, EMG biofeedback may be used to produce a more generalized state of relaxation and decreased arousal (e.g., frontalis muscle EMG biofeedback), thus affecting the stress response more centrally (see Stoyva, 1977; Stoyva & Budzynski, 1974).

Perhaps the two most commonly encountered specific muscle-contraction problems are muscle-tension headaches and bruxism. Budzynski's (1978) review concludes that EMG biofeedback can be highly useful in alleviating or eliminating muscle-contraction headache syndromes. Cannistraci (1975) argues that EMG biofeedback is useful in reducing the clenching and toothgrinding syndromes of bruxism.

Yet, objectively speaking, the effectiveness of EMG biofeedback, or any other form of biofeedback, for that matter, has not been rigorously proven; perhaps because it is usually combined with other forms of therapy, and typically does not appear in a pure form. Like other forms of biofeedback therapy, however, it certainly appears to be a very useful adjunct in the treatment of numerous diseases and the stress response.

Temperature Biofeedback

Description. The use of temperature biofeedback is based on the fact that peripheral skin temperature is a function of vasodilatation and constriction. Thus, when the peripheral blood vessels are dilated, more blood is flowing through them, and the skin is warmer. By measuring the temperature in the extremities, one can get an indication of the amount of the constriction of the blood vessels, and since the constriction–dilation is controlled by the sympathetic portion of the autonomic nervous system, one can get a second, indirect measurement of the amount of sympathetic activity.

The equipment used in thermal biofeedback has the same basic function as the EMG-biofeedback equipment described above—that is, there is a sensor, a processor, and a display. The sensor in this case is a thermistor, a small thermal sensing device which is usually taped to the subject's finger. This is connected to a machine which transforms the electrical signal that the thermistor produces into a signal which is amplified and processed in such a way that once again either lights are displayed, sounds are produced, or a change on a meter is produced to indicate raising or lowering of temperature in very small amounts. Typically, the width of the meter on the biofeedback instrument is plus or minus one degree Fahrenheit.

It seems obvious that skin temperature can be raised only to a theoretical high of core body temperature 98.6° Fahrenheit, although Fuller (1972) reports producing higher than core body temperature. If a patient has a baseline skin temperature of 70°, there is greater change possible in terms of warming than if a patient has a baseline temperature of 94°. The increase in temperature will not be as dramatic.

Indications. Temperature feedback has been useful in those instances in which one needs to be concerned with circulatory functions, such as in Raynaud's disease and peripheral vascular disease (Taub & Stroebel, 1978). It has been utilized in the treatment of migraine headaches and hypertension, in those instances in which one is seeking to control sympathetic activity such as in asthma, and in psychotherapy. In the latter case, it has been found to be useful in the determining of areas in which sympathetic discharges are prominent, and thus may relate to resistance on the patient's part in psychotherapy. One minor difficulty with the technology involved is that there is a short but significant delay of several seconds between the time of sympathetic discharge, vasoconstriction, and lowering of temperature in the extremity. This measurable lowering of temperature may be displayed several seconds after the passing of the event which caused the sympathetic discharge to occur.

Temperature biofeedback has a definite role in the treatment of the stress response in that it is a good indicator of sympathetic-nervous-system arousal. For this reason it is a useful tool in teaching general relaxation, the subject being instructed to try to raise skin temperature. This mode of therapy is often used alone, alternatively with EMG, or in combination with it. The reader should refer to Green and Green (1979) for a useful review of thermal biofeedback .

Electroencephalographic (EEG) Biofeedback

Description. The brain is known to discharge electrical activity continually. The electrical activity that arises in the brain appears to be the result of discharges at synapses. In 1924, Hans Berger developed a method for graphically recording that electrical brain-wave activity. What appears to be recorded by the EEG are those synapses closest to the surface of the brain. There are many ascending pathways to the cortex; however, it is felt that the area that is the most highly represented on the outermost surface of the cortex is the reticular activating system. This is a very difficult set of data to analyze, since a single neuron can have as many as a thousand branchings in the cortex. Therefore, although what is picked up on the EEG is very nonspecific, it is generally agreed that various wave forms do correlate with certain states of consciousness and do reflect activity, particularly in the reticular activating system.

Brain waves have been divided into four categories, depending on their predominant frequency and amplitude. The term "frequency" refers to the number of cycles produced per second or per minute and reflects the number of firings of neurons per unit of time. The amplitude refers to the amount of electricity generated and is a reflection of the number of neurons firing synchronously.

The brain waves may be described as follows. Beta waves have 13 or more cycles per second frequency and low amplitude. They are characteristic of the awake, attentive state. This is the state that one is in when one is focusing one's concentration, or when aroused. Alpha waves are characterized by a frequency of 8 to 13 cycles per second and an amplitude of 20 to 100+ microvolts. This state is supposedly related to the relaxed state characterized by serenity, passive attention, and calm. Theta waves are 4 to 8 cycles per second in frequency and usual amplitude 20 microvolts or less. They are often characterized as being a part of the daydreaming state. Lastly, delta waves are from .5 to 4 cycles per second in frequency and are associated with deep sleep.

There are standard electrode-placement sites; however, exact placement is not too critical from session to session, since what is being measured is a very averaged measurement over a wide cortical area. One of the major problems in this kind of measurement is movement artifact and muscle artifact, as well as artifacts being introduced from electrical systems around the machinery. Typically, the subject is instructed to close his eyes to decrease the amount of arousal from visual stimuli. The instruments are generally equipped so that an upper and lower frequency can be set. Usually the upper frequency is set at a point at which the person gets a feedback sound 50% of the time, with the lower-frequency threshold set at 4 cycles per second below baseline, thus producing a "window" for feedback. The amplitude levels are set so that the lower level is just below that average produced by the person, often about 20 microvolts, and the upper limit well above the highest brain-wave amplitude, that is, about 60 microvolts. This allows an amplitude "window" which excludes noise and most muscle artifact. This is the method described by Fuller in his book *Biofeedback: Methods and Procedures in Clinical Practice.*

Feedback is provided to the subject when both amplitude and frequency are within the desired windows. The type of feedback best for learning will be a function of the preferences of the client. If multiple options are available, it is usually wise to allow the client to select.

Of all the biofeedback modalities, EEG has probably found the fewest proven uses. To summarize a review by Barbara Brown (1977), attempts have been made to increase alpha in order to produce general relaxation. This is purportedly useful in people who exhibit obsessive compulsive patterns, as well as generally high stress/anxiety levels. It has also been used in facilitating sleep and in improving concentration and attention, the latter being particularly through the suppression of alpha in order to concentrate more easily. There has been some speculation as to increasing theta in order to increase creativity; however, reports seem to indicate that there is an ambiguous relationship between increased creativity and increased theta.

Another proposed use of EEG has been in reduction of chronic pain. The idea is to help the patient develop an ability to unfocus his awareness of the pain so that the cycle of pain, tensing up from the pain and thus producing more pain, is broken by focusing one's attention away from it. Some positive results have been reported for this particular use of EEG biofeedback. Biofeedback has also been mentioned in the treatment of epilepsy.

As regards its use in the treatment of the stress response, its main function seems to be in training to increase alpha, decrease arousal, and generally to increase the individual's ability to attend passively; however, as we have mentioned earlier in this chapter, this particular area may have gotten more publicity and greater enthusiasm than it should have. At present, it seems to have found fewer uses than the other biofeedback modalities and is being studied in greater depth in the laboratory.

Electrodermal (EDR) Biofeedback

Description. Electrodermal is a generic term that refers to the electrical characteristics of the skin. There are numerous measurement options available when considering this type of biofeedback. The oldest and most commonly used is the galvanic skin response (GSR). Generally speaking, variation of the skin's electrical characteristics appears to be a function of sympathetic neural activity, therefore when using

EDR biofeedback the client appears to be training to affect sympathetic neural arousal.

Indications. The major uses for EDR are to demonstrate to a subject how mind and body are interrelated. Additionally, an attempt is being made to use the patterns of response in order to see if they can be paired with personality structure; however, this research is considered quite preliminary at present. One of the major uses in psychotherapy is for systematic desensitization, the theory being that one cannot be both relaxed and aroused at the same time, and that phobias and anxiety are therefore amenable to treatment with this modality. In some cases, EDR can be used in order to try to decrease sympathetic arousal in general—perhaps this is its major application in the treatment of the stress response. Finally, it has been used as a tool for exploration in psychotherapy. In this case, the machine is used to demonstrate graphically to both therapist and patient areas of arousal which can be useful as another type of "body language" for interpretation (see Fair, 1979).

PRECAUTIONS

There is really very little in the way of adverse reactions which can occur as a result of biofeedback; however, the practitioner should be aware of certain adverse conditions which may be produced or potentially exacerbated by its use.

First is the case of the patient who is taking medication for any purpose. Biofeedback may be considered a replacement for medication by some patients, and they prematurely or mistakenly stop taking medication prescribed for some other purpose. It is necessary to question clients closely regarding their medication history and to deal appropriately with this matter. Most dramatic are diabetic patients who are taking insulin. In these cases, the inducing of relaxation may reduce the need for insulin and the normal amount that the patient had been taking may now become a dose which could precipitate a hypoglycemic coma. Changes in blood pressure are also an area of potential difficulty in patients who are taking medication for hypertension or hypotension. Additionally, it has been found that for those patients with epilepsy who are in training with biofeedback, especially for slow-wave EEG (6 to 9 Hz), seizure may be more likely to occur. Higher-frequency EEG training, however, may indeed hold more promise in the treatment of epilepsy (see Brown, 1977).

Other problems may arise related to improper training of the patient by the therapist. An example might be treatment of bruxism with unilateral placement of EMG sensors, producing dislocation of the jaw through imbalance of the muscles. Improper muscle biofeedback in the treatment of torticollis may also result in a greater imbalance than before the biofeedback.

The elderly offer another situation in which biofeedback may not be too helpful, as there is the possibility of lowering blood pressure and cortical blood flow. Also, in psychotic individuals, typically biofeedback is not integrated because of their difficulty with cognitive functioning, and it may even be incorporated into a delusional system.

Treatment of cardiac arrhythmia is something that should probably be undertaken by those who are well versed in cardiac physiology and have access to life-support equipment and personnel. Such training often takes place in cardiac-care units.

ROLE OF THE THERAPIST

From what has been said thus far in this chapter, it would seem that the major element in biofeedback is the machinery. This really is not the case. An equally important element in this form of therapy, as in any form of therapy, is the clinician–client dyad. This, more than many kinds of therapies, requires motivation on the client's part to want to get better and to practice between sessions what he has learned. Because of this, his relationship with his clinician is quite important.

One determinant of success in biofeedback appears to be the extent to which cognitive restructuring takes place in the patient so that he can begin to see the ways in which mind and body interact. This again is dependent on his relationship with his clinician, who is able to help him with this process. In this framework, biofeedback can be seen as an adjunct to a more total therapeutic relationship. It is not unlike hypnosis, relaxation therapy, etc., in that it is a tool that can be brought to bear on a symptom or symptom complex, but only within the context of the total therapeutic relationship. In this sense, a clinician is like a theatrical director—he sets the stage for change to

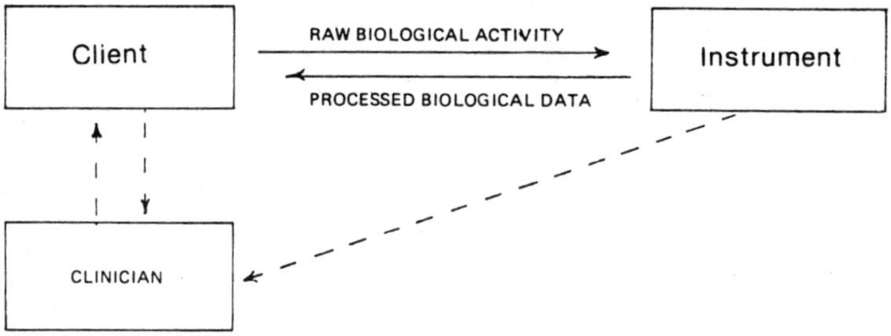

Figure 28

take place, but does not participate in the play himself. He gives useful hints, pointers, feedback, and reinforcement, but he does not change the client himself; he merely facilitates that change. He makes it easier for the client to change through the relationship that he has with him. Our original diagram of the biofeedback situation (Figure 26) may now be modified as indicated in Figure 28.

Thus, the clinician receives information from both the instrument and the client regarding the client's functioning, and feeds information to the client, allowing him to use better the data that he acquires from the instrument alone (clarification, reinforcement, interpretation). In this context, then, the clinician is seen as an important part of the biofeedback loop, even though the responsibility for change and the change itself are carried out by the client. It is possible that some divergent results of biofeedback efficacy by different authors may reflect such "nonspecific factors" as the effect of the clinician. The reader should see Gaarder and Montgomery (1977) for a discussion of this topic.

SUMMARY

In this chapter, we have traced some of the origins of biofeedback and discussed some of the principles on which this form of treatment is based. We have described a few of the biofeedback modalities available to the practicing clinician, and indicated how they are used and in what conditions they have been generally found to be of benefit. We have tried to include to whatever extent possible only clinically useful material which can hopefully aid the clinician in deciding to what extent this therapeutic approach is useful in the treatment of the stress response. We have alluded to the fact that it is only a part of total treatment, that it depends as much on the operator of the machine as on the machine itself, and that it can be a most useful adjunct in treatment.

This is an exciting area of study, and one in which new applications are being discovered almost daily. Biofeedback stands at the frontier between the understanding of the functioning of the mind and the body and of the way in which the brain orchestrates the various functions of the mind–body system. As technology and medical and psychological knowledge increase, this should continue to be a field of great scientific and therapeutic interest. Useful texts which address the clinical applications of biofeedback include Gaarder and Montgomery (1977), Fuller (1972), Gatchel and Price (1979), Blanchard and Epstein (1978), and Basmajian (1979).

CHAPTER 13

Healthful Expression of the Stress Response through Physical Exercise

Having read the initial chapters of this text, which described the nature of the stress response, there appears to be justification for the conclusion that the stress response represents a psychophysiological process which prepares the organism for physical exertion. The increase in blood supply to the heart and the striate muscles, the increase in striate-muscle tension, and the increase in circulating glucose coupled with the decrease in the blood supply to the gastrointestinal system and to the skin are just a few of the signs indicative of a mobilization of the body's resources in preparation for physical activity (see Benson, 1975; Cannon, 1953; Chavat *et al.*, 1964). Based on the discussions sponsored by the World Health Organization, Chavat *et al.* (1964) concluded that when the stress response does not lead to such physically active somatomotor expression, the organism undergoes increased strain, or psychophysiological load:

> What is obvious is that often repeated incidents of . . . [suppressed somatomotor expressions] must imply an increased load on heart and blood-vessels and also considerable, possibly fairly prolonged, changes in blood composition and in chemical environment of the cardiovascular effector cells. (p. 131)

Such potential conditions of psychophysiological overload have been implicated by numerous researchers as a major cause of the development of stress-related psychosomatic disorders (see Kraus & Raab, 1961), as was mentioned in Chapter 3. If, indeed, we have accurately interpreted the "wisdom of the body" as intending for high levels of stress to end in some form of expression, or somatomotor utilization, then a therapeutic rationale for teaching clients how to express the stress response in appropriate and healthful ways quickly emerges. In this chapter, we shall discuss the therapeutic use of physical exercise as a method for the healthful expression/utilization of the stress response.

HISTORY OF THERAPEUTIC EXERCISE

Thousands of years ago, the highly active life-style that was lead by primitive man afforded him sufficient opportunity for physical and psychological expression of dangers, frustrations, and other potential stressors that faced him on a daily basis. However, as mankind progressed from a "physical being" to a "thinking being," he afforded himself fewer and fewer opportunities to release the effects of the stress response. According to Chavat *et al.* (1964), "When in civilized man . . . [stress] reactions are produced, the . . . [physically active] component is usually more or less suppressed" (p. 130). At that point in human development, the once ubiquitous physical activity gained its potential for therapeutic use.

Perhaps the earliest use of exercise in a therapeutic capacity, according to Ryan (1974), was in the fifth century B.C. It was during this time that the Greek physician Herodicus prescribed gymnastics for various diseases. In the second century B.C., Asclepiades prescribed walking and running in conjunction with diet and massage for disease as well as for the ills of an "opulent" society.

In sixteenth-century Europe, Joseph Duchesne is thought to be the first to use swimming as a therapeutic tool. He is said to have used such physical activity to strengthen the heart and lungs. From this time on in Europe exercise gained great popularity in therapeutic and preventive applications.

Following World War I, therapeutic exercise and the study of exercise physiology gained momentum in the United States. Physical fitness came into vogue in the 1960s for the lay public. As more and more people began exercising, new data were being generated on its nature and effects. Today, exercise is enjoying its greatest popularity in the United States. It is being practiced by millions of people and has been "rediscovered" by health-care professionals.

The present discussion looks at exercise as a modern therapeutic tool for the treatment of excessive stress.

MECHANISMS OF ACTION

Although exercise itself represents an intense form of stress reaction, it differs greatly from the stress response implicated in the onset of chronic disease. This point is often one of confusion for the client, who cannot understand why the stress that he or she undergoes during exercise is healthful, when the stress that he or she undergoes in a traffic jam, for example, can be pathologic. Let us examine the mechanisms which may answer this question.

There exist three therapeutic mechanisms of action which explain the clinical effectiveness of exercise in the treatment of excessive stress. They entail (1) those mechanisms which are active during exercise, (2) those mechanisms which are active in the short term following exercise, and (3) those mechanisms which are active in the long term.

The therapeutic mechanisms at work during the acute process of exercising are manifest in the tendency for such physical activity healthfully to utilize the potentially harmful constituents of the stress response. During the stress response, the stress-responsive hormones (primarily cortisol) begin to break down adipose tissue for energy. In this process a form of fat, called triglyceride, is released into the blood stream. High serum levels of such fat have been implicated in the development of atherosclerosis and coronary heart disease (Haskell & Fox, 1974). Through the use of physical activity, however, serum triglycerides actually decline. Similarly, during the stress response a significant demand is placed on the cardiovascular system. Cardiac output (heart rate times stroke volume), blood pressure, and resistance to peripheral blood flow all increase. By the use of *moderate* physical activity, however, these factors are manifest in a more healthful form. Although cardiac output must increase, the rhythmic use of the striate muscles actually assists the return of blood to the heart (increase in venous return). Blood pressure must increase during exercise as well, but usually not so drastically at times when we remain inactive (as in a traffic jam, for example). Finally, we see that during the stress response the resistance to blood flow to the skin and other peripheral aspects increases. During the stress of exercise resistance to blood flow in the skin actually decreases—this has implications for cooling of the body and decline in blood pressure (see Bar-Or & Buskirk, 1974, for a discussion of these cardiovascular dynamics). The examples just described are indicative of the drastically different ways the body responds to the stress of exercise, as versus the stress response that we undergo if we remain static, or inactive. Other examples in pulmonary functions and hemodynamics are similarly available. Clearly, the acute strain on the body is quite different if one undergoes a stress response while one is active, compared to remaining inactive. Although physical activity has the capability of using the constituents of the stress response in a constructive manner, the following passages discuss the therapeutic reactions which last beyond the acute exercise period itself.

The short-term therapeutic mechanisms associated with exercise entail the initiation of a state of relaxation following the physical activity. Clearly, exercise itself represents a powerful ergotropic response mediated by the sympathetic nervous system; however, according to Balog (1978), on completion of exercise the organism may undergo psychophysiological recovery by the initiation of a trophotropic response mediated by the parasympathetic nervous system. This recovery phase is a short-term phenomenon, lasting up to two hours. According to DeVries (1966), gamma motor neural discharge may be inhibited during recovery from physical activity. The gamma motor system is a complementary connection from the cerebral cortex to the striate musculature. The result of such inhibition is said to be a striate-muscle relaxation.

The muscle-relaxant qualities of exercise have important implications for short-term declines in diffuse anxiety and ergotropic tone in autonomic as well as striate muscles. It has been demonstrated that striate-muscle tension contributes to diffuse anxiety and arousal in striate and autonomic musculature through a complex feedback system (Gellhorn, 1967; Jacobson, 1978). This system involves afferent (incoming) proprioceptive stimulation from striate muscles to the hypothalamus and cerebral cortex. Therefore, reduction in striate tension should lead to a generalized decrease in ergotropic tone throughout the body, as well as a decrease in diffuse anxiety levels.

The long-term therapeutic mechanisms of action inherent in exercise are set in motion when exercise is used consistently over a sustained period of time (at least three to four but usually seven to eight weeks). The nature of these mechanisms involves the development of a greater tolerance for high levels of stress.

Inherent in a sustained exercise program are certain highly desirable physical alterations which will so occur as to create a higher level of fitness in the systems of the body which usually undergo the most strain from the stress response. This higher level of fitness aids the body in withstanding high levels of stress, being, in effect, a sort of "hedge" against the pathological characteristics of excessive stress. Wilmore (1977) summarizes these alterations. The most notable are:

1. Increased efficiency of the heart
2. Improved pulmonary function
3. Improved utilization of blood glucose
4. Reduced body fat
5. Reduced resting blood pressure*

To reiterate, these alterations are important to the current discussion of stress because they all contribute to the client's ability to tolerate high levels of stress, thereby working against the pathogenic characteristics of excessive stress when it does occur.

RESEARCH ON THE CLINICAL APPLICATIONS AND EFFECTS OF EXERCISE

A review of relevant literature on the clinical use of exercise in the treatment of stress and stress-related problems reveals its therapeutic potential:

1. Five minutes of stepping (30 steps per min) on a 20-inch bench was found to cause 32% decline in leg-muscle tension one hour after exercise (DeVries, 1963).

2. Fifteen minutes of walking (as to maintain a heart rate of 100 beats per min) was found to be a more powerful muscle relaxant than was 400 mg meprobamate (DeVries & Adams, 1972).

*This finding is the most controversial of the alterations identified. Empirical evidence has yet to prove clearly the validity of this claim. At this time, empirical findings are inconclusive.

3. Exercise programs of jogging, calisthenics, and aquatics have been found useful in reducing muscle tension in men aged 52 to 88 (DeVries, 1970).

4. The psychological effects of exercise have been reviewed by Layman (1974), and she concludes that exercise can be useful for:

a. Treating anxiety
b. Decreasing aggression/combativeness
c. Increasing self-confidence and self-esteem
d. Relieving frustration

(see also Dodson & Mullens, 1969, and Kraus & Raab, 1961).

It is apparent that greater research needs to be conducted on the direct clinical applications of exercise to stress and stress-related disorders. To this point, however, we can conclude that exercise can be effectively used as a muscle relaxant in muscle-tension syndromes. Similarly, we see exercise as a unique psychoactive agent which at least appears to assist the client in moving toward a more positive state of mental functioning. More specifically, we see that the psychodynamics which either predispose the client to excessive stress (poor self-esteem, low tolerance for frustration, poor body image) or to propagate the stress response (depression, anxiety, hostility) can apparently be reduced through certain types of exercise.

We may finally mention the creation of the so-called runner's high—the calm and tranquility reported to occur during or after intense exercise. Reports thus far are totally subjective in nature (see Higdon, 1978). Increased levels of norepinephrine, endorphin, and/or cerebral blood flow have been mentioned as theoretical causes of the effect but its therapeutic practicality is currently unclear.

THE EXERCISE PROGRAM

Types of Exercise

It is generally accepted that the best therapeutic exercises for the purposes germane to our discussion are those which meet three criteria. First, and most important from a physical perspective, exercise should be aerobic. Aerobic exercise is any exercise which involves a sustained increase in oxygen demand (compared to basal metabolic levels), and is usually thought of as an endurance type of exercise. Second, exercise should contain movements which are rhythmical and coordinated, rather than random and uncoordinated. Any exercise which meets both these two criteria may be thought of as useful from a purely physical aspect. The third criterion is critically important but lies in the cognitive and affective domains—physical exercise should be "egoless." Egoless exercise is perhaps best defined in contrast to ego-involved exercise. Exercise is ego-involved if the quality of performance reflects directly on the client's evaluation of self. Egoless exercise, then, is any physical exercise which is void of that self-evaluative component. During egoless exercise, the client is exercising for the intrinsic rewards of the exercise itself. There is no consideration of winning or losing. In fact, competition with others or with one's self should be avoided if it leads to excessive arousal and/or to the potential for self-devaluation. Jogging, for example, is not healthful if the jogger becomes angry because he has lost a race, or simply run slower than usual. Golf is not healthful if the golfer leaves her clubs on the course wrapped around a tree out of disgust for not making the final putt. Whenever exercise and self-esteem become intertwined, the healthful characteristics of that exercise are questionable. Therefore, the role of the clinician becomes that of helping the client to learn to exercise in an egoless manner, where the mere process of exercise itself becomes the major reinforcing aspect. When this stage is reached, chronic adherence to the exercise program will be virtually insured. For an interesting discussion of egoless exercise suitable for the client or the clinician, see Gallwey (1976).

In her review of therapeutic exercise, Layman (1974) identified several forms of physical activity which have been found useful in evoking a positive change in psychological functioning. They were jogging, swimming, weight lifting, dancing, training on a striking bag.

AMOUNT OF EXERCISE NEEDED

The question often arises, "How much exercise is enough to affect a therapeutic outcome?" In order to answer this question, we must define amount in terms of (1) intensity, (2) duration, and (3) frequency.

Perhaps the best index to measure intensity is heart rate. It is generally accepted that to achieve a significant long-term training effect of the cardiovascular and pulmonary systems, the client needs to

Table XV. Maximum Heart Rates Listed by Age[a]

Age	Maximum	85% maximum	80% maximum	70% maximum
25	200	170	160	140
30	194	165	155	136
35	188	160	150	132
40	182	155	145	128
45	176	150	141	124
50	171	145	136	119
55	165	140	132	115
60	159	135	127	111
65	153	130	122	107

[a] Values are listed in beats per minute (bpm).

exercise at an intensity which will force the heart rate to a level between 70% and 85% of maximum. Table XV provides these figures.

However, it is clear that intensities as low as 100 bpm can be useful in many people as cited earlier for muscle relaxation.

In addition to peak intensity, heart-rate recovery can be used to measure intensity of physical exercise. It is generally accepted that, after walking for five minutes post exercise, heart rate should range below 120–110 bpm. It is critical that after exercise a 5 to 10-minute "cool-down" period of walking, stretching, etc. be adhered to. Simply to stop abruptly would cause strain on the heart. If the heart rate remains greater than 120 bpm after a five-minute cool-down, the exercise was probably too intense (of course, consider how vigorously the person cools down in this determination).

As for the variables of duration and frequency, these figures vary from author to author. Eliot (1979) recommends that exercise be done from 15 to 30 minutes, three to five times per week. Pollock (1973) found the optimal schedule to be 20 to 40 minutes, three to four times a week.

WARNINGS IN THE USE OF PHYSICAL EXERCISE

So far we have discussed the benefits of physical exercise with regard to usefulness in treating excessive stress. However, it is important to realize that care must be taken when employing any form of physical activity, especially clinically.

The most critical point to be made in this section is that physical exercise represents a powerful stressor. Intense exercise not only stresses the cardiopulmonary system, but can greatly affect the musculoskeletal system as well.

Physical exercise has the potential to evoke a greater stress response than any psychosocial stressor we can imagine. Although the employment of physical exertion does appear to express most of the potential pathogenic qualities in psychophysiological stress arousal, the sheer quantity of the arousal during physical exercise can be overwhelming to the cardiopulmonary system. Cases are clearly on record of individuals who died from cardiac failure while exercising for their health.

The musculoskeletal system is vulnerable to the strain of physical exercise as well. Numerous joint and connective-tissue problems are related to excessive physical exercise. It is highly recommended that the person use only the proper equipment for exercise, in order to circumvent many of these potential problems.

Exercise is clearly individualistic; what is right for some may not be for others. It is always a good idea to have the family physician assess an individual's physiological readiness to participate in an exercise program and then to suggest reasonable guidelines.

The success of an exercise program depends on its consistent utilization. Therefore, the question of motivation arises. It is important to find an exercise program that is not aversive for the client. The mistake that most clients make is to "overdo" an exercise program. The results are usually soreness, injuries, or the realization that it simply takes too much time. Therefore, have the client engage in a program which will be continued. Emphasize the need for patience and the need to integrate the exercise program into the life-style. It helps to find an exercise partner, one whom the client can exercise with—not compete with.

The cardiovascular, pulmonary, and weight-reducing aspects of the exercise program will manifest themselves within several weeks. The therapeutic psychological effects may take longer to realize, however, so once again the need for patience is required.

Finally, care must be taken in finding the best amount of exercise for the client. Dodson and Mullens (1969) found that "light exercise" actually made psychiatric patients more anxious, whereas longer and more intense exercise, in this case jogging, reduced their anxiety.

SUMMARY

Throughout this text it has been argued that the stress response is a psychophysiological process that prepares the organism for physical activity. When such activity does not result, the stress response may take on pathogenic characteristics. From these facts emerges the therapeutic rationale for the clinical use of exercise in the treatment of excessive stress.

More specifically, exercise is therapeutic from three perspectives: (1) it constructively utilizes the constituents of the stress response during the exercise, (2) it seems to induce some form of parasympathetic activity after termination of the exercise, and (3) it develops a long-term resistance to excessive stress through its effects on the cardiovascular and pulmonary systems; similarly, positive alterations in psychological traits occur as well. Therefore, we see that the therapeutic utility of exercise lies in the fact that it is a healthful way to express actively the stress response.

CHAPTER 14

The Use of Hypnosis in the Treatment of the Stress Response

The purpose of this chapter is to discuss the use of hypnosis in the prevention and treatment of excessive psychophysiological stress arousal. Since this is seen as an introductory chapter and the topic of hypnosis is complex, only some brief background into the nature of hypnosis with the intent of clarifying its role in the treatment of stress will be presented.

As noted earlier in this text, the concept of health care is changing. Although the therapeutic alliance between the clinician and the patient is still as important as ever, the patient's need to participate in his own treatment is becoming more and more prominent. Without such participation, many therapeutic interventions fail or never get initiated. One of the treatment techniques which can be used to facilitate self-regulatory behavior, which can be used either independently or adjunctively to combat stress, and, finally, which fits in very well with the emerging philosophy of the 1980s, is that of hypnosis.

Curiously, in the not so distant past, if a hospital clinical staff were considering a therapeutic disposition and given the choice of hypnotic intervention, they might have rejected it. It has been only during the last three decades that hypnosis itself has been more accepted in medical practice. This occurred only after the American Medical Association in 1958 recognized hypnosis as a bona fide therapeutic tool. The British Medical Association had recognized its legitimacy in 1955. Some of the previous mysticism and magic attributed to hypnosis has been abandoned and replaced by an increasing awareness of the effectiveness and versatility of hypnosis. New therapeutic applications have also been advanced. It is now frequently recognized that hypnotic phenomenon occur naturally. In fact, most hypnosis is autohypnosis. The clinician does not project hypnosis onto the patient. The patient himself decides when hypnosis is used. The capacity, talent, or as Wain (1979) states, "gift," lies with the patient, not the clinician. It is the clinician, however, who sets the stage and the appropriate environment for hypnosis to be effective. The clinician simply creates and delivers the strategy based on his own insight into the patient. Many other misconceptions, concerning hypnosis have also been abandoned. For example, hypnosis is not sleep. The electroencephalogram tracings are more similar to an awakelike state than they are to a sleeplike state. Hypnosis is not for women only; men are as responsive toward hypnotic intervention as are women. Hypnosis is not more readily used with the weak-minded or the severely psychiatrically disturbed. It is the more disciplined mind and the healthier person that tends to be more successful with the use of hypnosis. The secure, mentally healthy patient with a medical problem is typically the most positive responder to hypnotic intervention. Hypnosis is also no longer thought to be successful merely as a placebo or a purely psychological phenomenon, though both factors may contribute to its effectiveness. There appears to be direct physiological effects as well from hypnosis.

In general, hypnotic intervention has come a long way, and more places for its use in medicine are being found. It is no longer thought of as being simply a unilateral treatment but is used adjunctively, in combination with other medical practices, in pain management, oncology, nephrology, surgery, medicine, psychiatry, dentistry, etc. Wain (1979) reports a wide range of successful psychiatric, medical, and surgical applications at Walter Reed Army Medical Center. Specifically, hypnotic intervention has facilitated decreasing medication needs, successful tolerance of risky surgery, and long-term psychotherapy for many, when effectively utilized. An important contributing factor in any use of hypnosis is its facilitative role in the alleviation of stress and perhaps even its prevention.

Now that we have defined what hypnosis is not, what could it be? It has been defined as a psychophysiological state of aroused, attentive, receptive, focal concentration (Spiegel & Spiegel, 1978). Under this state, the individual decreases his peripheral awareness. It occurs either spontaneously, in reponse to another person's signal (heterohypnosis), or through a self-induced signal (autohypnosis). There are other numerous and varied definitions of hypnosis available in any of the basic hypnosis textbooks (Crasilneck & Hall, 1975; Kroger, 1977).

HISTORY

Although it has been suggested that a hypnoticlike phenomenon is reported in the Bible, the history of contemporary medical hypnosis begins with Anton Franz Mesmer, an eighteenth-century Viennese physician. Mesmer felt the hypnotist through his own animal magnetism effected the cures. Following him, the English physician James Braid was the first to maintain that the skill essential to the eventual hypnotic result is that of the patient. He coined the term "hypnotism" and made the procedure more acceptable in medical circles. Following Braid came, Jean Martin Charcot and Pierre Janet. Charcot applied his background in neurology to hypnosis. Janet, his student, emphasized the association of hypnosis and hysteria but placed greatest emphasis on an underlying psychological mechanism—*dissociation.* Along with Charcot and Janet two other Frenchmen, Bernheim and Liebeault, were very influential in the development of hypnosis. Working together in Nancy, they proclaimed that hypnosis was not a pathological condition found in hysterics but a valuable tool that could be used in normal nonhysterics to gain information about the structure of one's personality as well as give facilitative suggestion. Freud trained with Charcot and was familiar with the use of hypnosis. However, he abandoned it for what might have been his own shortcomings. More recently, Milton Erickson is singularly credited by many with bringing the American Medical Association to accept hypnosis as a bona-fide tool. Other influentials are Herbert Spiegel, Martin Orne, T. X. Barber, Ernest Hilgard, Clark Hull, and Ivan Pevoli, all having helped to establish a scientific basis for hypnosis.

MECHANISMS OF ACTION

Exactly what mechanism accounts for the effects of hypnosis remains to be elucidated. Currently there exist widely divergent theories to explain hypnotic phenomena.

The general concept of hypnotic dissociation of awareness can be traced back to the early work of Janet. Hilgard's (1973) "neodissociation" model suggests that hypnotic procedures may be used to alter the natural cognitive hierarchy of attending. The result is a "dissociation" from the normal conscious realities. The patient then selectively attends to a hypnotically restructured hierarchy. The dissociation model suggests that hypnosis acts through a process of redirected awareness.

From a more behavioral orientation, Sarbin and Coe (1972) refer to hypnosis as a form of role enactment in which the patient is engaged. The degree to which the patient is able to assume his or her "role" dictates the level of the hypnotic phenomenon observed. The factors that affect the patient's ability to enact his or her role are motivation, role-related skills, and reinforcement. Barber (1969) argues that hypnosis is a nontrance phenomenon that can be simply explained by antecedent and consequent variables.

Finally, hypnosis can be viewed from a psychophysiological perspective. Mesmer and Charcot were the first to offer a physiological explanation. Spiegel and Spiegel (1978) review studies that implicate the right neocortical hemisphere as being important in hypnosuggestibility. Greenberg (1977), as cited in Spiegel and Spiegel (1978), suggests that the "biological basis of trance capacity" may very well rest in the ability of the reticular activating system to focus attention and integrate the activity of the dominant and nondominant neocortical hemispheres.

Indeed, none of the aforementioned theories has clearly been shown to explain the active mechanisms of the hypnotic phenomenon. It has been suggested that hypnosis is a "polymorphous" phenomenon (Kroger & Fezler, 1976), and that, as such, it may ultimately be found to represent an integration of numerous theoretical postures.

RESEARCH ON THE CLINICAL APPLICATIONS

Hypnosis has had a long history of successful clinical application. Its effectiveness has been documented in enough reports that most clinicians would probably agree that hypnosis can exert a therapeutic effect on numerous clinical problems. Many of the early reports on hypnosis were in the form of case reports. However, in the 1960s hypnosis was subjected to more rigorous investigation. After such inquiry, it appears that hypnosis can still claim therapeutic effectiveness in numerous and diverse disorders, including anxiety and increased sympathetic tone, asthma, neurodermatitis, migraine headache, muscle tension headache, pain syndromes, gastrointestinal disorders, and some cases of essential hypertension. The above are just some of the areas that reflect the appropriateness of hypnotic intervention. It is incumbent upon the reader to realize that it is not the syndrome that responds to hypnotic intervention but the patient. Because the literature is simply too voluminous to cite all primary resources, we shall simply refer the reader to useful reviews by Wain (1980), Kroger and Fezler (1976), Bowers (1976), Fromm and Shor (1972), and Barber (1969).

HYPNOTIC SCREENING

Some clinicians find it facilitative to obtain a measure of the patient's hypnotic capacity, since it is the patient who is going to use this tool. Therefore, the hypnotic strategy to be developed may very well depend on the amount of the hypnotic gift that the patient has, as well as the talent of the clinician to establish the appropriate strategy. Therefore, screening procedures have been developed. Some of the better known screening procedures are those developed by Hilgard and Weitzenhoffer at Stanford, called the Stanford Suggestibility Scale. The Barber scale is a group technique; and the Hypnotic Induction Profile (HIP) developed by Spiegel is a five-minute screening procedure based on eye roll and arm levitation. The HIP allows one to be screened rapidly, and at the same time the patient experiences the hypnotic induction while going through the screening. This sets the stage for the patient to be able to use autohypnosis rapidly, and it allows for rapid induction (see Kroger, 1977, for a comprehensive list of such scales). It is important to make the point that it is the clinician who creates the hypnotic strategy by paying close attention to his patient. The patient contributes not only by his capacity to use the hypnotic intervention but also by his ability to communicate to the clinician. Thus, it is incumbent on the clinician to understand and listen attentively to his patient so that an effective strategy can be developed.

A WORD ABOUT HYPNOTIC INDUCTION

Many methods exist for the induction of hypnosis. Some of the induction procedures include eye fixation, having a patient concentrate on one specific focal point; neuromuscular relaxation; hand levitation; and combinations of the above. The type of induction used depends primarily on the skill and comfort of the clinician in his capacity to implement appropriate induction procedures for the patient but has to take into account the needs of the patient who is the important ingredient in the overall effectiveness of the induction and treatment outcome. (See Kroger, 1977, for a useful review of induction and deepening techniques; see also Erickson, Rossi, & Rossi, 1976.)

THE USE OF HYPNOSIS FOR STRESS REDUCTION

Now that some of the preliminaries with regard to hypnosis have been briefly addressed, let us examine the role of hypnosis in reducing excessive stress. Hypnosis has both preventive and treatment potentials with regard to excessive stress.

From a preventive perspective, hypnosis has three primary applications. We know that hypnosis can be used to induce a deep state of relaxation. The health-promoting benefits of deep relaxation have been underscored throughout this text. Autohypnotic relaxation, when practiced on a frequent and chronic basis, may serve as do minivacations from a hectic environment. One may even see the development of a more relaxed disposition in the individual. Second, autohypnotic techniques can be used by the client to avoid stressors. We will recall that most stressors are a function of the cognitive appraisal of an otherwise neutral stimulus. Autohypnosis may be used to allow the patient to view his or her world a little differently. This application may be extended to the point of allowing the patient cognitively to remove him- or herself from a potential stressor situation. The patient may choose to reengage the stressor when he or she is better prepared to find a solution. Finally, in a related use, hetero- and autohypnosis may be used to facilitate the development of self-confidence in patients. Increased self-confidence may have the effect of moderating stress arousal, thus preventing it from becoming excessive.

Hypnotic techniques may also be used during the elicitation of a stress response. Autohypnosis may be used by the client to interrupt a stressor episode. This can be done by dissociating from the stressor or stress response. This is often the technique used in dentistry or surgery. The patient may choose to perceive him- or herself in a more comfortable/supportive environment, or perceive the situation from a more supportive rather than challenging perspective. This technique can be used in public-speaking anxiety, text anxiety, and any other condition which spawns performance anxiety. Besides changing the on-the-spot perception of the stressor episode, the patient may also use autohypnosis to reduce directly the psychophysiological stress arousal.

SUMMARY

In conclusion, hypnosis, when used in treating excessive stress, can be an easily learned and effective technique allowing the patient to relax deeply and, therefore, obtain all the advantages discussed earlier that accrue from deep relaxation. Furthermore, patients can learn to "neutralize" many stressors, either by distancing themselves from the actual stressor, or distancing themselves from the psychophysiological stress arousal. It must be remembered, however, that the gift of hypnosis lies in the patient, and the clinician must learn to best meet the unique needs of each individual patient to assure therapeutic effectiveness. Of all the techniques addressed in this text, hypnosis may well be the most complex. Therefore, we have not addressed the "how to" issues, as with many of the other techniques. Our purpose has been merely to overview hypnosis and point out its potential uses in treating excessive stress. Therefore, we must refer the reader to the texts previously cited for a more in-depth understanding of the hypnotic phenomenon.

CHAPTER 15

Putting It All Together

HOLISM AND HOLISTIC TREATMENT OF THE STRESS RESPONSE

Up to this point we have attempted to discuss numerous issues which we feel are imperative to the effective clinical treatment of the stress response. We have discussed the nature of the response, detailing the potential mechanisms that may represent its constituents, and also the physiological foundations for the potential end-organ effects of excessive stress. We have discussed various types of stimuli which are common sources of the stress response, and the tools researchers and clinicians may use in order to measure the response. Finally, we have presented numerous options that the clinician may choose from in order to treat excessive stress in his or her client populations.

At this point, we feel that it is appropriate to describe an overall treatment schema, or model, that may be used in the treatment of excessive stress. In effect, this model represents a structure that the clinician may use to organize the therapeutic options already presented in this text. Or, the clinician may simply use this model as a conceptual basis from which to work.

The model that we shall present is one that has gained substantial support from numerous diversely trained clinicians. This treatment model is commonly referred to as a *holistic* treatment model. The term *holism* has come to mean many things to many people. Therefore, we shall operationalize the concept into a pragmatic clinical entity. We shall, further, discuss the clinical assumptions on which holistic therapy is based. Our goal is twofold: to demystify holism to a point of clinical utility, and to attempt to point out that, if extremely popular, holistic therapy is clearly not a panacea.

THE NATURE OF HOLISM

A major theme in Eastern philosophy for over 2,000 years has been the *monistic*, or *holistic* as it is now called, view of mind and body. That is to say, there exists an intrinsic unity between mind and body, and this unity is inseparable. So integrated are these components that it has been said that there can be no mental activity without corresponding somatic (bodily) activity. Although this view of humankind has been in Eastern philosophy for thousands of years, it is only now gaining popularity in Western scientific circles.

Holism is not uniquely an Eastern concept, however. The ancient Greek cultures viewed mind and body as inseparable entities as well. However, the holistic perspective of the ancients was discarded with the advent of "modern" science in the seventeenth century. During this time, the scientific communities adopted a highly mechanistic world view. This world view attempted to explain all human behavior and even the realm of metaphysics via the application of mathematical logic and closed-system perspectives.

The two men most responsible for the adoption of the mechanistic world view by the scientific communities were Isaac Newton and René Descartes. Newtonian physics is noted for its closed-system, mechanistic perspective on the nature of the universe. Yet it was Descartes who shaped the course of modern health-care delivery with the publication of his physiology text *De Homine* in 1662. In *De Homine*, Descartes developed the concept of *dualism*. Descartes's dualism separated the mind from the body, the latter being considered a machine. This separateness was to be generally accepted, not only in medical circles but in philosophical circles as well.

As modern medicine developed over the course of the next several centuries, the dualistic perspective of Newton and Descartes was to provide much of the rationale for the highly specialized and compartmentalized practice that we see today (see Capra, 1975).

Today the Western world is beginning to rediscover holism. The foundations for this renaissance were supplied by the work of Albert Einstein. The work of Einstein led scientists and philosophers alike to begin to view first the universe and later human behavior in the context of open, dynamic systems. From this point of view evolved the hypothesis that *the whole is actually more fundamental than its parts.* This was said to be due to the fact that in reality there are no discrete parts to the whole, but rather, the whole represents a synergistically functioning suprasystem consisting of highly interrelated subsystems. An understanding of the subsystem cannot be achieved until its place in the suprasystem is understood (Capra, 1975; see also d'Espagnat, 1979).

From this brief side-trip into the realm of physics, certain implications for the delivery of health-care services, particularly the treatment of stress, emerge. If indeed there are no discrete parts in human behavior, but rather a complex suprasystem of highly interrelated subsystems, then one may question the appropriateness of treating a client in a highly compartmentalized and fragmented manner, as is often done today. Theoretically, at least, the more highly specialized the treatment plan, the more suspect it is from a holistic perspective.

It will be recalled from Chapter 2 that the entire process that we have called the stress response represents the epitome of holism and holistic human functioning. By this we mean that if viewed in its entirety, from perception of stressor to end-organ effect, the stress response represents a complex system of interrelating subsystems. If, indeed, the stress response is holistic in nature, then it seems reasonable that the treatment paradigm for excessive stress should be designed along holistic principles as well.

Before utilizing a holistic treatment approach for excessive stress, the clinician must understand how holism may apply to clinical intervention; however, no operational guidelines currently exist. Therefore, we have provided a preliminary set of holistic principles for the clinical intervention in the problem of excessive stress.

1. Mind and body are inseparably interrelated.

2. Stress should be viewed from a holistic perspective, that is, stress should be viewed as a function of *interrelating subsystems*, for example, cognitive processes, affective processes, environmental factors, psychophysiological processes, behavioral processes, etc.

3. Diagnostic procedures should follow holistic principles if possible. This means that the diagnostic assessment of excessive stress

should focus not only on singular subsystems, but also on the synergistic role that any subsystem plays in the functioning of the suprasystem.

4. Given the interrelating subsystems that define human stress, holistic treatment should *simultaneously* attend to more than one of the subsystems. Therefore, treatment is initiated from more than one perspective, or dimension, at a time. This is sometimes called a *multidimensional treatment approach*. Once again, if possible, efforts are made to understand the interrelationships between the subsystems as they naturally occur *and* in light of the treatment intervention process (which may disturb original relationships).

5. Holistic treatment recognizes and addresses the role that *individual client differences* play as a moderating variable in treatment outcome. If indeed holistic treatment proves to be superior to traditional compartmentalized treatment models, it will most likely be owing to this fact. The treatment of excessive stress via a holistic model attempts to answer the question, "*What therapy* interventions are most effective for *this individual client* at *this particular time?*" Therefore, holistic treatment attempts to take into consideration client idiosyncracies, whether they be genetic, psychological, physiological, environmental, or temporal/situational. The clinician should realize that there is no such thing as *the best* treatment for excessive stress. Rather, successful outcome is dependent on the moderating role that individual client differences play in the overall treatment process (Paul, 1967; Tart, 1975). Therefore, for treatment to be holistic it must be dynamic (subject to change) as well as multidimensional (affecting more than one subsystem at once).

6. As described in an earlier chapter, the noncritical emphasis on *client self-responsibility* is a major thrust in the holistic treatment of the stress response. A heavy emphasis is placed on the client's accepting responsibility for the creation as well as the alleviation/control of stress in his or her life. This is done with the initial support and general facilitation of the clinician.

7. Finally, the ultimate goal of the holistic treatment model (and the specific goal of the previous assumption) is to foster appropriate *client independence* in the management of excessive stress. Because by far the greater proportion of the stress that one suffers from is self-initiated and self-propagated, successful treatment of the stress

response becomes inherently linked to having the client accept responsibility and gain appropriate functional independence from the clinician.

The final three assumptions (5, 6, & 7) are perhaps more correctly thought of as "derived" holistic assumptions. By this we mean that, although not purely holistic from a systems perspective, they represent what holistic *treatment* has evolved to entail (see Ardell, 1977; Girdano & Everly, 1979).

A HOLISTIC TREATMENT MODEL

Having enumerated the basic assumptions on which a holistic approach to the treatment of excessive stress is based, we shall now describe a basic treatment design. This design is intended to serve as a basic structure within which the treatment strategies described earlier in this text may be meaningfully organized. With such a structure, the development of a comprehensive treatment paradigm is likely to be facilitated.

Table XVI presents the basic structural schema, which consists of three perspectives, or dimensions, from which to initiate intervention.

Preliminary Activities

Having the client undergo a *physical examination* should always be the first step in any treatment protocol which addresses itself to the problem of excessive stress. The results of this examination will entail valuable information concerning the client's general physical health. The most significant reason, however, for requiring a physical examination before treatment begins is to validate that the target problem is indeed stress-related and amenable to the proposed therapy. The stress response represents the epitome of mind/body interaction. For this reason, it is sometimes difficult to distinguish psychogenically induced clinical signs from signs which are organically induced. In some cases, clinical signs and symptoms which appear to be indicative of excessive stress may indeed be masking neurological pathologies, or even the presence of a tumor in the central nervous

Table XVI. A Holistic Treatment Model[a]

Preliminary activities
- Physical examination
- Psychological assessment

Holistic intervention (3 dimensional)

1. Helping the client develop and implement strategies for the avoidance/minimization/modification of exposure to stressors.
   - Client education (see Chapter 5)
     - Tutorial intervention
     - Bibliotherapy
     - Client self-assessment of stressors
     - Client self-awareness of manifestations of stress
   - Life-style modifications (see Chapter 5)
   - Counseling/psychotherapy (see Chapter 5)
   - Dietary alterations (see Chapter 6)
2. Helping the client develop and implement skills which reduce excessive psychophysiological functioning and reactivity.
   - Meditation (see Chapter 9)
   - Neuromuscular relaxation (see Chapter 10)
   - Controlled respiration (see Chapter 11)
   - Biofeedback (see Chapter 12)
   - Hypnosis (see Chapter 14)

   Skill development at this level may facilitate change at the first level.
3. Helping the client develop and implement techniques for the healthful expression of the stress response.
   - Physical exercise (see Chapter 13)
   - Catharsis (see Chapter 5)

[a] Pharmacotherapy may be useful at Levels 1 and 2 on a temporary basis during early stages of treatment (see Chapter 7).

system or in some organ innervated by the autonomic nervous system. Therefore, the nonmedical clinician should always integrate some form of physician-conducted physical examination into the treatment protocol for excessive stress.

In some instances, the clinician may opt to include the administration of a *psychological assessment battery* as part of the preliminary protocol. The main advantage of such an administration is that it yields information concerning the general psychological health of the client, and it does so in a rather efficient manner. Form R of the Minnesota Multiphasic Personality Inventory (MMPI) is often used for such purposes, in addition to scales which purport to measure coronary-prone behavior, locus of control, state and trait anxiety, and even hypnosuggestibility.

Holistic Intervention

On the basis of Table XVI, the therapeutic strategies overviewed on pages 8–9 and detailed throughout this text can be arranged in what appears to be a comprehensive treatment model for the problem of excessive stress arousal. By following the holistic principles of intervention as we have crudely formulated them in this chapter, a cogent rationale and format for clinical implementation are developed. Whether the utilization of such a program yields greater clinical efficacy remains to be seen. Research under way by the first author is currently attempting to determine whether adherence to holistic principles, as formulated in this chapter, does indeed yield increased therapeutic effect. In what may be one of the first empirical investigations into holistic intervention, Bhalla (1980) tested the utility of a "holistic" multidimensional intervention as described by the present authors. In this study, 52 "normal" college students were placed in varying intervention groups. Endocrine, cardiovascular, and electromyographic dependent variables were used. Results of the study indicate that multidimensional interventions are superior to unidimensional interventions for the reduction of those stress indicators. Conclusions based on the results of this initial study must be limited, however. Further research should be directed toward employing a combination of holistic principles to test for improved outcome in reducing psychophysiological stress levels.

The holistic model presented in this chapter is designed more to stimulate thought (and perhaps research) than to dictate conformity. All the treatment options detailed in this text have demonstrated their efficacy in the treatment of excessive psychophysiological stress arousal, individually and in combinations not considered "holistic." Therefore, the reader may simply view this final chapter as a theoretical extension of the treatment issues already presented. Similarly, the "holistic" principles that we have formulated may be perceived as a first attempt at operationalizing what holism means in a treatment paradigm, rather than a definitive statement.

SUMMARY

This, then, is the multidimensional and dynamic nature of a holistic approach to the treatment of excessive stress (see Girdano & Everly, 1979, for an earlier description). It is designed to match the truly holistic nature of the psychophysiological stress response itself. It is hoped, and initial evidence suggests, that additional therapeutic forces will be mobilized by the adoption of a holistic approach to treatment in lieu of a more traditional dualistic approach. Client motivation and self-esteem may ultimately increase when the client is given an active role in the determination and implementation of the treatment paradigm (see Everly, 1980a,b). The holistic approach described here is a dynamic and multidimensional treatment paradigm. Therefore it represents a highly flexible model—one that matches the nature of human personality and behavior. Greater client interest and self-dependence may ultimately emerge from such a model.

In the final analysis, it is hoped that the adoption of a holistic treatment approach will lead to an attitude of positive health consciousness on the part of the client. It is further hoped that this attitude will lead to the development of positive, health-promoting behaviors. Such health-promoting attitudes and behaviors may ultimately become intrinsically rewarding to the client (see Ardell, 1977; Glasser, 1976). Theoretically, at such a point one may expect the experienced level of health to increase: in effect, a higher level of health and wellness.

Although most of this chapter has pointed out the advantages of adopting a holistic treatment model, it is critical to emphasize that holistic intervention is no panacea.

While fostering self-responsibility in the client, the clinician must be aware of certain inherent problems. The client may develop a guilt reaction once he or she accepts the proposition that excessive stress is self-initiated and self-propagated (Shapiro & Shapiro, 1979). Similarly, self-responsibility for the alleviation of excessive stress becomes inappropriate when it discourages the client from seeking professional health care when it is clearly indicated (Halberstam, 1978).

In summary, holism represents a "new" and potentially rewarding model for the delivery of health-care services. However, the potential will be realized only if holistic principles are applied in a knowledgeable, a responsible, and an ethical manner.

EPILOGUE

In this text we have discussed numerous clinical interventions which will have utility in the treatment of excessive psychophysiological stress arousal. Certainly our list is not complete, for other techniques can be useful in treating excessive stress. We have chosen to omit several useful clinicial techniques, simply because we felt that their nature required far more extensive treatment than such a text as this would allow. We therefore refer the reader to the following sources in order to expand his or her therapeutic armamentarium even further.

Autogenic Therapy	Luthe, W. (Ed.). *Autogenic therapy* (Vols. 1–6. New York: Grune & Stratton, 1969.
Mental Imagery	Lazarus, A. *In the mind's eye.* New York: Rawson, 1977.
Behavior Therapy	Leitenberg, H. (Ed.). *Handbook of behavior modification and behavior change.* Englewood Cliffs, N.J.: Prentice-Hall, 1976.
Psychotherapy	Corsini, R. *Current psychotherapies.* Chicago: Peacock, 1973.

A major theme of this text has been that individual client differences play a major role in therapeutic outcome. In the final analysis, the clinician working with the client must decide which therapies to use and to what degree. Only then will therapeutic outcome be maximized.

APPENDIX A

Relaxation Training Report

Your Name________________Date________Time Started________Time Ended________
Where did you practice? ____
Relaxation technique used:
______Neuromuscular relaxation (specify type: ________________________)
______Meditation (specify type: ________________________________)
______Mental imagery (specify type: ____________________________)
______EMG biofeedback—uV level started______uV level ended______lowest uV level____
______Temperature biofeedback—temp started______temp ended______lowest temp____
______EEG biofeedback-type______starting level______ending level______most successful level______
______Other (describe ______________________________________)

Did you feel relaxed during the session? Yes No. If no, what seemed to prevent you from relaxing?

At that point where you felt the most relaxed, what were you thinking, imaging, etc.? Recall this as best as you can for you may use these same thoughts, images to foster deep relaxation in the future.

Describe any thoughts, emotions, fantasies, or dreamlike experiences that occurred.

Did your mind wander? Not at all Just slightly Moderately Very much so
Did you get drowsy? Yes No. Did you fall asleep? Yes No
During the session did you feel any:

Heaviness	Not at all	Just slightly	Moderately	Very much so. If so, where____
Floating or lightness	Not at all	Just slightly	Moderately	Very much so. If so, where____
Numbness	Not at all	Just slightly	Moderately	Very much so. If so, where____
Warmth	Not at all	Just slightly	Moderately	Very much so. If so, where____

Describe any other physical sensations that occurred.

Describe anything that you especially liked about the session.

List any clues or helpful strategies which may help you to relax next time.

Any other comments about this session which you feel are important. (Use back of sheet.)

Adapted from a training form used at the Menninger Foundation.

APPENDIX B

Physically Passive Neuromuscular Relaxation

Earlier in this text, we stated that "neuromuscular relaxation" was the term usually reserved for isotonic and isometric contractions of the striate musculature designed to teach the client to relax. The entire preceding discussion on neuromuscular relaxation has addressed that type of physically active procedure. By far the greater part of the literature has been generated on this active form of neuromuscular relaxation—hence our emphasis on reviewing that form. There does exist, however, what may be considered a physically passive form of neuromuscular relaxation. In this appendix we shall address that form of relaxation.

Physically passive neuromuscular relaxation fundamentally consists of having the client focus sensory awareness on a series of individual striate muscular groups, and then relax those muscles through a process of direct concentration. In the passive neuromuscular relaxation procedure described here, there is no actual muscular contraction initiated as part of the relaxation cycle—hence "passive" neuromuscular relaxation.

The procedure of physically passive neuromuscular relaxation may be considered a form of mental imagery and directed sensory awareness. Mental imagery as a therapeutic intervention has a long and effective history for a wide range of clinical problems (see Leuner, 1969; Sheehan, 1972). When applied to the reduction of muscle tension, the basic mechanism involved in passive neuromuscular relaxation appears to be useful in tension reduction. In a review of investigations into the role of neuromuscular relaxation in general tension reduction, Borkovec, Grayson, and Cooper (1978) conclude: "Apparently, frequent attempts to relax while focusing on internal sensations are sufficient to promote tension reduction" (p. 527). In our own clinical experience, we have found passive neuromuscular relaxation to be quite effective in reducing subjective as well as electromyographically measured muscle tension.

There do appear to be several distinct advantages and disadvantages when comparing passive neuromuscular relaxation with a physically active form of neuromuscular relaxation. Passive neuromuscular relaxation has the advantage of having no potential limitations based on physical handicaps, as compared with neuromuscular relaxation which involves actual muscle tensing. Another advantage is entailed in the fact that the client can execute a passive protocol without distracting others or drawing attention to him- or herself. Such is obviously not the case with a protocol that involves actual muscle contraction. A final advantage is that a passive protocol generally takes much less time to complete (usually half the time). The major disadvantage in using a passive form of neuromuscular relaxation resides in the fact that, like meditation or other forms of mental images, it leaves the client more vulnerable to distracting thoughts. This may be a significant drawback when using a passive protocol with obsessive-type clients, or clients who have a tendency to get bored easily.

Let us now examine one sample passive protocol.* The "preparation for implementation" phase will be fundamentally the same as for the physically active form of neuromuscular relaxation, except with a few alterations (refer to Chapter 10.) In Step 1 of the preparation for implementation (precautions), the precautions will be the same as described for general relaxation. However, the special precautions for meditation will prevail here, as opposed to those for the physically active neuromuscular relaxation. The physically passive component here is what dictates this alteration. Steps 2 through 4 may remain the same. Steps 5 through 8 may be omitted because of their reference to the actual tensing of muscles. The client should be instructed to breathe normally, in a relaxed manner.

*This protocol is written as if being spoken directly to the client.

BACKGROUND INFORMATION

It has long been known that muscle tension can lead to stress and anxiety—thus, if you can learn to reduce excessive muscle tension, you will reduce excessive stress and anxiety.

What you are about to do is relax the major muscle groups in your body. You can do this by simply focusing your attention on each set of muscles that I describe. Research has shown that, with *patience* and *practice*, you can learn to achieve a deeply relaxed state by simply concentrating on relaxing any of the various muscle groups in your body.

First, you should find a quiet place without interruptions or glaring lights. Find a comfortable chair or bed to support your weight. Feel free to loosen restrictive clothing and remove glasses and contact lens if you desire.

ACTUAL INSTRUCTIONS

OK, let's begin. I'd like you to close your eyes and get as comfortable as you can. Let the chair or bed support all your weight. Remember, your job is to concentrate on allowing the muscles that I describe to relax completely.

CHEST AND STOMACH

I'd like you to begin by taking a deep breath. Ready? Begin . . . (*pause three seconds*) and now exhale as you feel the tension leave your chest and stomach. Let's do that one more time. Ready? Begin . . . (*pause three seconds*) and now relax and exhale as the tension continues to leave and your chest and stomach are relaxed.

HEAD

I'd like you to focus your attention on the muscles in your head. Now begin to feel those muscles relax as a warm wave of relaxation begins to descend from the top of your head. Concentrate on the muscles in your forehead. Now begin to allow those muscles to become heavy and relaxed. Concentrate as your forehead becomes heavy and relaxed (*pause 10 seconds*). Now switch your focus to the muscles in your eyes and cheeks and begin to allow them to become heavy and relaxed. Concentrate as your eyes and cheeks become heavy and relaxed (*pause 10 seconds*). Now switch your focus to the muscles in your mouth and jaw. Allow those muscles to become heavy and relaxed. Concentrate as your mouth and jaw become heavy and relaxed (*pause 10 seconds*).

NECK

Now you can begin to feel that wave of relaxation descend into the muscles of your neck. Your head will remain relaxed as you now shift your attention to your neck muscles. Allow your neck muscles to become heavy and relaxed. Concentrate as your neck becomes heavy and relaxed (*pause 10 seconds*).

SHOULDERS

Now you can begin to feel that wave of relaxation descend into your shoulder muscles. Your head and neck muscles will remain relaxed as you now shift your attention to your shoulder muscles. Allow your shoulder muscles to become heavy and relaxed. Concentrate as your shoulders become heavy and relaxed (*pause 10 seconds*).

ARMS

Now you can begin to feel that wave of relaxation descend into your arms. Your head, your neck, and your shoulders will remain relaxed as you now shift your attention to the muscles in both your arms. Allow both your arms to become heavy and relaxed. Concentrate as your arms become heavy and relaxed (*pause 10 seconds*).

HANDS

Now you can begin to feel that wave of relaxation descend into your hands. Your head, your neck, your shoulders, and your arms will remain relaxed as you now shift your attention to the muscles in both your hands. Allow both your hands to become heavy and relaxed. Concentrate as your hands become heavy and relaxed (*pause 10 seconds*).

THIGHS

Now you can begin to feel that wave of relaxation descend into your thighs. Your head, your neck, your shoulders, your arms, and your hands will remain relaxed as you now shift your attention to the muscles in both your thighs. Allow both your thighs to become heavy and relaxed. Concentrate as your thighs become heavy and relaxed (*pause 10 seconds*).

CALVES

Now you can begin to feel that wave of relaxation descend into your calves. Your head, your neck, your shoulders, your arms, your hands, and your thighs will remain relaxed as you now shift your attention to the muscles in both your calves. Allow both your calves to become heavy and relaxed. Concentrate as your calves become heavy and relaxed (*pause 10 seconds*).

FEET

Now you can begin to feel that wave of relaxation finally descend into your feet. The entire rest of your body will remain relaxed as you now shift your attention to the muscles in both your feet. Allow both your feet to become heavy and relaxed. Concentrate as your feet become heavy and relaxed (*pause 10 seconds*).

CLOSURE

All the major muscles in your body are now relaxed. To help you remain relaxed, simply repeat to yourself each time you exhale, "I am relaxed." Take the next few minutes and continue to relax as you repeat to yourself, "I am relaxed" . . . "I am relaxed" (*pause about five minutes*).

REAWAKEN

Now I want to bring your attention back to yourself and the world around you. I shall count from 1 to 10. With each count, you will feel your mind become more and more awake, and your body become more and more responsive

> and refreshed. When I reach 10, open your eyes, and you will feel the *best* you've felt all day—you will feel alert, refreshed, full of energy, and eager to resume your activities. Let's begin: 1–2 You are beginning to feel more alert, 3–4–5 you are more and more awake, 6–7 now begin to stretch your hands and feet, 8– now begin to stretch your arms and legs, 9–10 open your eyes, *now*! You feel alert, awake, your mind is clear and your body refreshed.

On concluding the initial passive neuromuscular procedure, inform the client that he or she can use this procedure to relax once or preferably twice a day—before lunch and before dinner. Other times can also be useful as well, particularly when used as an aid for sleeping.

In summary, Appendix B has presented the clinician with a physically passive alternative form of neuromuscular relaxation, not as prescription, but as an example of how such a protocol could be created. This option is designed simply to expand the clinician's arsenal of stress-reduction interventions with which to meet the idiosyncratic needs of individual clients. The ultimate assessment of clinical suitability remains with the clinician, and should be made on an individual client basis.

APPENDIX C

Professional Associations and Journals as Resources on the Topic of Stress

PROFESSIONAL ASSOCIATIONS

Academy of Psychosomatic Medicine, Box 1053, Mountainside, New Jersey 07092

American Academy of Stress Disorders, Chicago, Illinois 60603

American Institute of Stress, New York, New York

American Physicians Society for Physiologic Tension Control, Portland, Oregon 97205

American Psychiatric Association, Washington, D.C. 20009

American Psychological Association, Washington, D.C. 20036

American Psychosomatic Society, 265 Nassau Road, Roosevelt, New York 11575

Biofeedback Society of America, 4301 Owens Street, Wheat Ridge, Colorado 80033

International Stress and Tension Control Association (formerly the American Association for the Advancement of Tension Control), P.O. Box 8005, Louisville, Kentucky 40208

Society of Behavioral Medicine, 600 N. Wolfe Street, Baltimore, Maryland 21205

PROFESSIONAL JOURNALS

Archives of General Psychiatry
Biofeedback and Self-Regulation
Brain/Mind Bulletin
Health Education
Journal of Clinical and Consulting Psychology
Journal of Human Stress
Journal of Psychosomatic Research
Psychophysiology
Psychosomatic Medicine
Psychosomatics

References

Adler, C., & Morrissey-Adler, S. Strategies in general psychiatry. In J. Basmajian (Ed.), *Biofeedback: Principles and practices for clinicians.* Baltimore: Williams & Wilkins, 1979.

Almy, T. P., Kern, F., & Tulin, M. Alterations in colonic function in man under stress. *Gastroenterology,* 1949, *12,* 425–436.

AMA Drug Evaluations. Acton, Mass.: Publishing Services Group, Inc. Latest edition.

Amkraut, A., & Solomon, G. From symbolic stimulus to the pathophysiologic response: Immune mechanisms. *International Journal of Psychiatry in Medicine,* 1974, *5,* 541–563.

Ardell, D. *High level wellness.* Emmaus, Pa: Rodale, 1977.

Arnarson, E., & Sheffield, B. *The generalization of the effects of EMG and temperature biofeedback.* Paper presented at the Annual Meeting of the Biofeedback Society of America, Colorado Springs, March 1980.

Backus, F., & Dudley, D. Observations of psychosocial factors and their relationship to organic disease. In Z. J. Kipowski, D. Lipsitt, & P. Whybrow (Eds.), *Psychosomatic medicine.* New York: Oxford, 1977.

Ballentine, R. *Science of breath.* Glenview, Ill.: Himalayan International Institute, 1976.

Balog, L. F. *The effects of exercise on muscle tension and subsequent muscle relaxation.* Unpublished doctoral dissertation, University of Maryland, 1978.

Barber, T. X. *Hypnosis: A scientific approach.* New York: Van Nostrand, 1969.

Bar-Or, O., & Buskirk, E. The cardiovascular system and exercise. In W. Johnson & E. Buskirk (Eds.), *Science and medicine of exercise and sport.* New York: Harper & Row, 1974.

Basmajian, J. Control and training of individual motor units. *Science,* 1963, *141,* 440–441.

Basmajian, J. (Ed.). *Biofeedback: Principles and practices for clinicians.* Baltimore: Williams & Wilkins, 1979.

Basmajian, J., & Hatch, J. Biofeedback and the modification of skeletal muscular dysfunctions. In R. Gathel & K. Price (Eds.), *Clinical applications of biofeedback.* Oxford: Pergamon, 1979.

Bassuck, E., & Schoonover, S. *The practitioner's guide to psychoactive drugs.* New York: Plenum, 1977.

Benjamin, L. Statistical treatment of the Law of the Initial Values in autonomic research. *Psychosomatic Medicine,* 1963, *25,* 556–566.

Benson, H. Yoga for drug abuse. *New England Journal of Medicine,* 1969, *281,* 1133.

Benson, H. Decreased blood pressure in borderline hypertensive subjects who practice meditation. *Journal of Chronic Diseases*, 1974, *17*, 163–169.

Benson, H. *The relaxation response*. New York: Morrow, 1975.

Benson, H., Beary, J., & Carol, M. The "relaxation response." *Psychiatry*, 1974, *37*, 37–46.

Bergin, A., & Garfield, S. (Eds.). *Handbook of psychotherapy and behavior change*. New York: Wiley, 1971.

Berkun, M. Experimental studies of psychological stress in man. *Psychological Monographs*, 1962, *76* (Whole no. 534).

Berstein, D., & Borkovec, T. *Progressive relaxation training*. Champaign, Ill.: Research Press, 1973.

Bhalla, V. *Neuroendocrine, cardiovascular, and musculoskeletal analyses of a holistic approach to stress reduction*. Unpublished doctoral dissertation, University of Maryland, 1980.

Blanchard, E., & Epstein, L. *A biofeedback primer*. Reading, Mass.: Addison-Wesley, 1978.

Borkovec, T., Grayson, J., & Cooper, K. Treatment of general tension: Subjective and physiological effects of progressive relaxation. *Journal of Consulting and Clinical Psychology*, 1978, *46*, 518–528.

Boudreau, L. TM and yoga as reciprocal inhibitors. *Journal of Behavior Therapy and Experimental Psychiatry*, 1972, *3*, 97–98.

Bowers, K. *Hypnosis for the seriously curious*. Monterey, Calif.: Brooks/Cole, 1976.

Bray, G. Lipogenesis in human adipose tissue: Some effects of nibbling and gorging. *Journal of Clinical Investigation*, 1972, *51*, 537–546.

Brod, J. Circulatory changes underlying blood pressure elevation during acute emotional stress in normotensive and hypertensive subjects. *Clinical Science*, 1959, *18*, 269–270.

Brod, J. The influence of higher nervous processes induced by psychosocial environment on the development of essential hypertension. In L. Levi (Ed.), *Society, stress, and diseases* (Vol. 1). New York: Oxford, 1971.

Brown, B. *Stress and the art of biofeedback*. New York: Harper & Row, 1977.

Brown, C. C. *Methods in psychophysiology*. Baltimore: Williams & Wilkins, 1967.

Brown, G. W. Life events and psychiatric illness. *Journal of Psychosomatic Research*, 1972, *16*, 311–320.

Budzynski, T. Biofeedback in the treatment of muscle contraction (tension) headache. *Biofeedback and Self-Regulation*, 1978, *3*, 409–434.

Budzynski, T. *Biofeedback and stress management*. Paper presented at the Johns Hopkins Conference on Clinical Biofeedback, Baltimore, November 2 & 3, 1979.

Campernolle, T., Kees, H., & Leen, J. Diagnosis and treatment of the hyperventilation syndrome. *Psychosomatics*, 1979, *20*, 612–625.

Cannistraci, A. *Voluntary stress release and behavior therapy in the treatment of clenching and bruxism* (Vol. 1). Cassette tape. New York: Biomonitoring Applications, 1975–1976.

Cannon, W. B. The emergency function of the adrenal medula in pain and in the major emotions. *American Journal of Physiology*, 1914, *33*, 356–372.

Cannon, W. B. *Bodily changes in pain, hunger, fear and rage*. Boston: C. T. Branford, 1953.

Cannon, W. B. & Paz, D. Emotional stimulation of adrenal secretion. *American Journal of Physiology*, 1911, *28*, 64–70.

Capra, F. *The tao of physics*. Boulder: Shambala, 1975.

Carrington, P. *Freedom in meditation*. New York: Anchor Press, 1977.

Carruthers, M., & Taggart, P. Vagotonicity of violence. *British Medical Journal*, 1973, *3*, 384–389.

Cattell, R. B. *The Sixteen Personality Factor*. Champaign, Ill., Institute for Personality and Ability Testing, IPAT, 1972.

Chavat, J., Dell, P., & Folkow, B. Mental factors and cardiovascular disorders. *Cardiologia*, 1964, *44*, 124–141.

Corson, S., & Corson, E. Psychosocial influences on renal function: Implications for human pathophysiology. In L. Levi (Ed.), *Society, stress, and disease* (Vol. 1). New York: Oxford University Press, 1971.

Cox, D., Freundlick, A., & Meyer, R. Differential effectiveness of EMG feedback, verbal relaxation instructions, and medication placebo with tension headaches. *Journal of Consulting and Clinical Psychology*, 1975, *43*, 892–898.

Crasilneck, N. B., & Hall, J. A. *Clinical hypnosis*. New York: Grune & Stratton, 1975.

Cuthbertson, D. Physical injury and its effects on protein metabolism. In H. Munro & J. Allison (Eds.), *Mammalian protein metabolism*. New York: Academic, 1964.

Cutting, W. *Handbook of pharmacology*. New York: Appleton-Century-Crofts, 1972.

Dahlstrom, W., Welsh, G., & Dahlstrom, L. *An MMPI handbook* (Vol. 2): *Research developments and applications*. Minneapolis: University of Minnesota Press, 1975.

Datey, K. A yogic exercise in the management of hypertension. *Angiology*, 1969, *20*, 325–333.

Davidson, J. The physiology of meditation and mystical states of consciousness. *Perspectives in Biology and Medicine*, 1976, *19*, 345–379.

Daebler, H. The use of relaxation and hypnosis in lowering high blood pressure. *American Journal of Clinical Hypnosis*, 1973, *16*, 75–83.

DeVries, H. *The effects of exercise upon residual neuromuscular tension*. Paper presented to the American Association of Health, Physical Education and Recreation National Convention, Minneapolis, May 1963.

DeVries, H. *Physiology of exercise*. Dubuque, Iowa: Wm. C. Brown, 1966.

DeVries, H. Physiological effects of exercise training regimen upon men aged 52 to 88. *Journal of Gerontology*, 1970, *25*, 325–336.

DeVries, H., & Adams, G. Electromyographic comparison of single doses of exercise and meprobamate as to effects on muscular relaxation. *American Journal of Physical Medicine*, 1972, *52*, 130–141.

Dodson, L., & Mullens, W. Some effects of jogging on psychiatric hospital patients. *American Corrective Therapy Journal*, 1969, Sept.-Oct., 130–134.

Dorpat, T. L., & Holmes, T. H. Mechanisms of skeletal muscle pain and fatigue. *Archives of Neurology and Psychiatry*, 1955, *74*, 628–640.

Duffy, E. *Activation and behavior*. New York: Wiley, 1962.

Dunbar, H. F. *Emotions and bodily changes*. New York: Columbia University Press, 1935.

Duncan, C. H., Stevenson, I., & Ripley, H. Life situations emotions and paroxysmal acuicular arrhythmias. *Psychosomatic Medicine*, 1950, *12*, 23–27.

Edelberg, R. Electrical activity of the skin. In N. Greenfield & R. Sternbach (Eds.), *Handbook of psychophysiology*. New York: Holt, Rinehart & Winston, 1972.

Eisler, R., & Polak, P. Social stress and psychiatric disorder. *Journal of Nervous and Mental Disease*, 1971, *153*, 227–233.

Eliot, R. *Stress and the major cardiovascular disorders*. Mount Kisco, N.Y.: Futura, 1979.

Ellis, A. Emotional disturbance and its treatment in a nutshell. *Canadian Counselor*, 1971, *5*, 168–171.

Ellis, A. *Humanistic psychology: The rational-emotive approach*. New York: Julian, 1973.

Emmons, M. *The inner source: A guide to meditative therapy*. San Luis Obispo, Calif.: Impact, 1978.

Engel, B. T. Operant conditioning of cardiac function: A status report. *Psychophysiology*, 1972, *9*, 161–177.

Engle, G. Sudden and rapid death during psychological stress. *Annals of Internal Medicine*, 1971, *74*, 771–782.

Epstein, S., & Coleman, M. Drive theories of schizophrenia. *Psychosomatic Medicine*, 1970, *32*, 114–141.

Erickson, M., Rossi, E., & Rossi, S. *Hypnotic realities*. New York: Irvington, 1976.
Espagnat, B. d'. The quantum theory and reality. *Scientific American*, 1979, *241*, 158–181.
Everly, G. S. *The Organ Specificity Score as a measure of psychophysiological stress reactivity*. Unpublished doctoral dissertation, University of Maryland, 1978. (a)
Everly, G. S. *Contraindications and negative side-effects of biofeedback and relaxation training*. Paper presented at the Annual Meeting of the Washington, D.C./Maryland Biofeedback Society, Baltimore, June 1978. (b)
Everly, G. S. A technique for the immediate reduction of psychophysiologic stress reactivity. *Health Education*, 1979, *10*, 44. (a)
Everly, G. S. A psychophysiologic technique for the rapid onset of a trophotropic state. *IRCS Journal of Medical Science*, 1979, *7*, 423. (b)
Everly, G. S. *The development of less stressful personality traits in adult learners: Preliminary findings*. Proceedings of the Lifelong Learning Research Conference, College Park, Maryland: U. S. Adult Education Association and the University of Maryland, 1980. (a)
Everly, G. S. The development of less stressful personality traits in adults through educational intervention. *Maryland Adult Education*, 1980, *2*, 63–66. (b)
Everly, G. S. *Stress in adults: Educational and clinical issues*. Paper presented to the Federal Interagency Panel for Research and Development on Adulthood, Washington, D.C., May 28, 1980. (c)
Everly, G. S. *Teacher burnout: Cause and treatment*. Paper presented to the Annual Conference of the Maryland Association for Publically Supported Continuing Education, College Park, May 2–3, 1980. (d)
Everson, G. Bases for concern about teenagers' diets. *Journal of the American Dietetic Association*, 1960, *36*, 17–21.
Fair, P. Biofeedback strategies in psychotherapy. In. J. Basmajian (Ed.), *Biofeedback: Principles and practice for clinicians*. Baltimore: William & Wilkins, 1979.
Fernando, C., & Basmajian, J. V. Biofeedback in physical medicine and rehabilitation. *Biofeedback and Self-Regulation*, 1978, *3*, 435–456.
Folkow, B., & Neil, E. *Circulation*. London: Oxford University Press, 1971.
Frazier, T. Avoidance conditioning of heart rate in humans. *Psychophysiology*, 1966, *3*, 188–202.
Freedman, R., & Papsdorf, J. *Generalization of frontal EMG biofeedback training to other muscles*. Paper presented at the 7th Annual Meeting of the Biofeedback Society, Colorado Springs, February 1976.
Freeman, G. L. Toward a psychiatric Plimsoll Mark. *Journal of Psychology*, 1939, *8*, 247–252.
Friedman, M., & Rosenman, R. *Type A behavior and your heart*. New York: Knopf, 1974.
Fröberg, J., Karlsson, C., Levi, L., & Lidberg, L. Physiological and biochemical stress reactions induced by psychosocial stimuli. In L. Levi (Ed.), *Society, stress, and disease* (Vol. 1). New York: Oxford University Press, 1971.
Fromm, E., & Shor, R. (Eds.). *Hypnosis: Research developments and perspectives*. Chicago: Aldine-Atherton, 1972.
Fuller, G. *Biofeedback: Methods and procedures in clinical practice*. San Francisco: Biofeedback Institute of San Francisco, 1972.
Gaarder, K., & Montgomery, P. *Clinical biofeedback: A procedural manual*. Baltimore: Williams & Wilkins, 1977.
Gallwey, T. *Inner tennis*. New York: Random House, 1976.
Gatchel, R., & Price, K. Biofeedback: An introduction and historical overview. In R. Gatchel & K. Price (Eds.), *Clinical applications of biofeedback: Appraisal and status*. New York: Pergamon, 1979.
Gellhorn, E. *Principles of autonomic somatic integrations*. Minneapolis: University of Minnesota Press, 1967.

Gellhorn, E. Central nervous system tuning and its implications for neuropsychiatry. *Journal of Nervous and Mental Disorders*, 1968, *147*, 148–162.

Gellhorn, E. Further studies on the physiology and pathophysiology of the tuning of the central nervous system. *Psychosomatics*, 1969, *10*, 94–104.

Gellhorn, E., & Kiely, W. Mystical states of consciousness: Neurophysiological and clinical aspects. *Journal of Nervous and Mental Disease*, 1972, *154*, 399–405.

Gevarter, W. *Psychotherapy and the brain*. Unpublished paper. Washington, D.C.: NASA, 1978.

Gifford, S., & Gunderson, J. G. Cushing's disease as a psychosomatic disorder: A selective review. *Perspectives in Biology and Medicine*, 1970, *13*, 169–221.

Girdano, D. A. Performanced based evaluation. *Health Education*, 1977, **8**, 13–15.

Girdano, D., & Everly, G. *Controlling stress and tension: A holistic approach*. Englewood Cliffs, N.J.: Prentice-Hall, 1979.

Girodo, M. Yoga meditation and flooding in the treatment of anxiety neurosis. *Journal of Behavior Therapy and Experimental Psychiatry*, 1974, *5*, 157–160.

Glass, D. C. *Behavior patterns, stress, and coronary disease*. Hillsdale, N.J.: Erlbaum, 1977.

Glasser, W. *Positive addiction*. New York: Harper & Row, 1976.

Glaus, K., & Kotses, H. *Generalization of frontalis muscle tension*. Paper presented at the 8th Annual Meeting of the Biofeedback Society, Orlando Florida, March 1977.

Glaus, K., & Kotses, H. *Generalization of conditioned frontalis tension: A closer look*. Paper presented at the 9th Annual Meeting of the Biofeedback Society, Albuquerque, New Mexico, March 1978.

Glueck, B., & Stroebel, C. Biofeedback and meditation in the treatment of psychiatric illness. *Comprehensive Psychiatry*, 1975, *16*, 309.

Glueck, B., & Stroebel, C. Psychophysiological correlates of relaxation. In A. Sugarman & R. Tarter (Eds.), *Expanding dimensions of consciousness*. New York: Springer, 1978.

Graham, D. T. Caffeine: Its identity, dietary sources, intake and biological effects. *Nutrition Reviews*, 1978, *36*, 97–102.

Graham, D. T. Psychosomatic medicine. In N. Greenfield & R. Sternbach (Eds.), *Handbook of psychophysiology*, New York: Holt, Rinehart & Winston, 1972.

Grace, W., Seton, P., Wolf, S., & Wolff, H. G. Studies of the human colon: I. *American Journal of Medical Science*, 1949, *217*, 241–251.

Grace, W., Wolf, S., & Wolff, H. Life situations, emotions and chronic ulcerative colitis. *Journal of the American Medical Association*, 1950, *142*, 1044–1048.

Greden, J. F. Anxiety or caffeinism: A diagnostic dilemma. *American Journal of Psychiatry*, 1974, *131*, 1089–1092.

Green, E., & Green, A. General and specific application of thermal biofeedback. In J. Basmajian (Ed.), *Biofeedback: Principles and practice for clinicians*. Baltimore: Williams & Wilkins, 1979.

Greenberg, I. M. *A general systems theory of trance state*. Unpublished manuscript, 1977.

Greenfield, N., & Sternbach, R. *Handbook of psychophysiology*. New York: Holt, Rinehart & Winston, 1972.

Greenspan, K. Biological feedback: Some conceptual bridges with analytically oriented psychotherapy. *Psychiatric Opinion*, 1979, 17–20.

Guyton, A. C. *Textbook of medical physiology*. Philadelphia: Saunders, 1976.

Halberstam, M. Holistic healing: Limits of the new medicine. *Psychology Today*, 1978, 26–28.

Harlem, O. *Communication in medicine*, New York: S. Karger, 1977.

Harvey, J. Diaphragmatic breathing: A practical technique for breath control. *The Behavior Therapist*, 1978, *1*, 13–14.

Haskell, W., & Fox, S. Physical activity in the prevention and therapy of cardiovascular disease. In W. Johnson & E. Burskirk (Eds.), *Science and medicine of exercise and sport.* New York: Harper & Row, 1974.

Hassett, J. *A primer of psychophysiology.* San Francisco: W. H. Freeman, 1978.

Hathaway, S., & McKinley, J. *Manual for the MMPI.* New York: The Psychological Corporation, 1967.

Heisel, J. S. Life changes as etiologic factors in juvenile rheumatoid arthritis. *Journal of Psychosomatic Research*, 1972, *17*, 411–420.

Henry, J. P., & Ely, D. Biologic correlates of psychosomatic illness. In R. Grenell & S. Galay (Eds.), *Biological foundations of psychiatry*, New York: Raven Press, 1976.

Henry, J. P., & Stephens, P. *Stress, health and the social environment.* New York. Springer, 1977.

Hess, W. *The functional organization of the diencephalon.* New York: Grune & Stratton, 1957.

Hewitt, J. *The complete yoga book.* New York: Schocken, 1977.

Higdon, H. Can running cure mental illness? *Runner's World*, 1978, *13*, 36–43.

Hilgard, E. R. A neo-dissociation theory of pain reduction in hypnosis. *Psychological Review*, 1973, *80*, 396–411.

Hodges, R. E. The effects of stress on ascorbic acid metabolism in man. *Nutrition Today*, 1970, *5*, 11–12.

Holmes, T. H., Trenting, T., & Wolff, H. Life situations, emotions, and nasal disease. *Psychosomatic Medicine*, 1951, *13*, 71–82.

Holmes, T. H., & Wolff, H. G. Lift situations, emotions and backache. *Psychosomatic Medicine*, 1952, *14*, 18–33.

Humphrey, J., & Everly, G. Perceived dimensions of stress responsiveness in males and females. *Health Education*, in press.

Hymes, A. Diaphragmatic breath control and post surgical care. *Research Bulletin of the Himalayan International Institute*, 1980, *1*, 9–10.

Jacobson, E. *Progressive relaxation.* Chicago: University of Chicago Press, 1938.

Jacobson, E. *Modern treatment of tense patients.* Springfield, Ill.: Charles C Thomas, 1970.

Jacobson, E. *You must relax.* New York: McGraw-Hill, 1978.

Jencks, B. *Your body: Biofeedback at its best.* Chicago: Nelson-Hall, 1977.

Johns Hopkins Hospital Dietary Manual. Baltimore: Johns Hopkins Hospital, 1973.

Johnson, R., & Spalding, J. *Disorders of the autonomic nervous system.* Philadelphia: F. A. Davis, 1974.

Jones, R. A. *Self-fulfilling prophecies.* New York: Erlbaum, 1977.

Kamiya, J. Operant control of the EEG alpha rhythm and some of its reported effects on consciousness. In C. Tart (Ed.), *Altered states of consciousness.* New York: Wiley, 1969.

Karvasarsky, B. *Golovnye boli pri nevrozakh i pogranichniykh sostoyaniyskh.* Leningrad: 1969.

Kendall, B. Clinical relaxation for neuroses and psychoneuroses. In E. Jacobson (Ed.), *Tension in medicine.* Springfield, Ill.: Charles C Thomas, 1967.

Kirtz, S., & Moos, R. H. Physiological effects of social environments. *Psychosomatic Medicine*, 1974, *36*, 96–114.

Kraus, H., & Raab, W. *Hypokinetic disease.* Springfield, Ill.: Charles C Thomas, 1961.

Kroger, W. *Clinical and experimental hypnosis.* Philadelphia: Lippincott, 1977.

Kroger, W., & Fezler, W. Hypnosis and behavior modification. Philadelphia: Lippincott, 1976.

Kuhl, W., Wilson, H., & Ralli, E. Measurements of adrenal cortical activity in young men subjected to acute stress. *Journal of Clinical Endocrinology and Metabolism*, 1952, *12*, 393–406.

Lacey, J., & Lacey, B. Verification and extension of the principle of autonomic response-stereotypy. *American Journal of Psychology*, 1958, *71*, 50–73.

Lacey, J., & Lacey, B. The law of initial value in the longitudinal study of autonomic constitution. *Annals of the New York Academy of Sciences*, 1962, *98*, 1257–1290; 1322–1326.

Lachman, S. *Psychosomatic disorders: A behavioristic interpretation*. New York: Wiley, 1972.

Lader, M. H. Psychophysiological aspects of anxiety. In M. H. Lader (Ed.), *Studies of anxiety*. Ashford, Kent, England: Headly Brothers, 1969.

Lang, I. M. *Limbic involvement in the vagosympathetic arterial pressor response of the rat*. Unpublished master's thesis, Temple University, 1975.

Lang, P. J. The application of psychophysiological methods to the study of psychotherapy and behavior modification. In A. Bergin & S. Garfield (Eds.), *Handbook of psychotherapy and behavior change*. New York: Wiley, 1971.

Lang, P., Rice, D., & Sternbach, R. The psychophysiology of emotion. In N. Greenfield & R. Sternbach (Eds.), *The handbook of psychophysiology*. New York: Holt, Rinehart & Winston, 1972.

Lazar, A. The effects of the TM program on anxiety, drug abuse, cigarette smoking, and alcohol consumption. In D. Orme-Johnson, L. Domash, & J. Farrow (Eds.), *Scientific research on the TM program*. Geneva: Maharishi International University Press, 1975.

Lazarus, R. S. *Psychological stress and the coping process*. New York: McGraw-Hill, 1966.

Lazarus, R. S. *Patterns for adjustment*. New York: McGraw-Hill, 1976.

LeBlanc, J. *The role of catecholamines in adaptation to chronic and acute stress*. Paper presented at the proceedings of the International Symposium on Cathecholamines and Stress, Bratislava, Czechoslovakia, July 1976.

Leuner, H. Guided affective imagery. *American Journal of Psychotherapy*, 1969, *23*, 4–21.

Levi, L. Psychosocial stimuli, psychophysiological reactions and disease. *Acta Medica Scandinavica*, 1972 (Entire Supplement 528).

Levi, L. *Emotions: Their parameters and measurement*. New York: Raven Press, 1975.

Levi, L. The effect of coffee on the function of the sympathoadrenomedullary system in man. *Acta Medica Scandinavica*, 1967, *181*, 431–438.

Lindsley, D. B. Emotion. In S. S. Stevens (Ed.), *Handbook of experimental psychology*. New York: John Wiley, 1951.

Lindsley, D., & Sassaman, W. Autonomic activity and brain potentials associated with "voluntary" control of pilomotors. *Journal of Neurophysiology*, 1938, *1*, 342–349.

Lipowski, Z. J. Psychophysiological cardiovascular disorders. In A. Freedman, H. Kaplan, & B. Sadock (Eds.), *Comprehensive textbook of psychiatry*. Baltimore: Williams & Wilkins, 1974.

Lum, L. C. Hyperventilation: The tip of the iceberg. *Journal of Psychosomatic Research*, 1975, *19*, 375–383.

Luria, A. R. The mind of a mnemonist (L. Solotaroff, trans.). New York: Basic Books, 1958.

Luthe, W. (Ed.). *Autogenic therapy* (Vols. I–VI). New York: Grune & Stratton, 1969.

Luthe, W., & Blumberger, S. Autogenic therapy. In E. Wittkower & H. Warnes (Eds.), *Psychosomatic medicine*. New York: Harper & Row, 1977.

Maas, J., Gleser, G., & Gottschalk, L. Schizophrenia, anxiety, and biochemical factors. *Archives of General Psychiatry*, 1961, *4*, 109–118.

MacLean, P. D. On the evolution of three mentalities. *Man–Environment System*, 1975, *5*, 213–224.

Mahl, G. F., & Brody, E. Chronic anxiety symptomatology, experimental stress and HCI secretion. *Archives of Neurological Psychiatry*, 1954, *71*, 314–325.

Malmo, R. B. Studies of anxiety. In C. Spielberger (Ed.), *Anxiety and behavior*. New York: Academic, 1966.

Malmo, R. B. Overview. In N. Greenfield & R. Sternbach (Eds.), *Handbook of psychophysiology*. New York: Holt, Rinehart & Winston, 1972.

Malmo, R., & Shagass, C. Physiologic study of symptom mechanisms in psychiatric patients under stress. *Psychosomatic Medicine*, 1949, *11*, 25–29.

Malmo, R., Shagass, C., & Davis, J. A method for the investigation of somatic response mechanisms in psychoneurosis. *Science*, 1950, *112*, 325–328.

Marañon, G. Contribution á l'etude de l'action émotive de l'adémaline. *Revue Français d'Endrocrinologie*, 1924, *2*, 301–325.

Mason, J. B. A re-evaluation of the concept of non-specificity in stress theory. *Journal of Psychiatric Research*, 1971, *8*, 323–333.

Mason, J. B. Organization of psychoendocrine mechanisms: A review and reconsideration of research. In N. Greenfield & R. Sternbach (Eds.), *Handbook of psychophysiology*. New York: Holt, Rinehart & Winston, 1972.

Mason, J. W. A Review of psychoendocrine research on the sympathetic-adrenal medullary system. *Psychosomatic Medicine*, 1968, *30*, 631–653. (a)

Mason, J. W. Organization of psychoendocrine mechanisms. *Psychosomatic Medicine*, *1968*, *30* (Entire Part II). (b)

Mason, J. W. A review of psychoendocrine research on the pituitary-adrenal cortical system. *Psychosomatic Medicine*, 1968, 30, 576–607. (c)

Mason, J. W., Maher, J., Hartley, L., Mougey, E., Perlow, M., & Jones, L. Selectivity of corticosteroid and catecholamine responses to various natural stimuli. In G. Serban (Ed.), *Psychopathology of human adaptation*. New York: Plenum, 1976.

Massachusetts General Hospital Dietary Manual. Boston: Little, Brown, 1976.

McClure, C. Cardiac arrest through volition. *California Medicine*, 1959, *90*, 440–448.

McNair, D., Lorr, M., & Droppleman, L. *Profile of mood states manual*. San Diego: Educational and Industrial Testing Service, 1971.

Meichenbaum, D., & Novaco, R. Stress inoculation: A preventive approach. In C. Spielberger & I. Sarason (Eds.), *Stress and anxiety* (Vol. 5). New York: Wiley, 1978.

Meltzoff, J., & Kornreich, M. *Research in psychotherapy*. Chicago: Aldine, 1970.

Miller, N. E. Biofeedback and visceral learning. *Annual Review of Psychology*, 1978, *29*, 373–404.

Miller, N. E. General discussion and a review of recent results with paralyzed patients. In R. Gatchel & K. Price (Eds.), *Clinical applications of biofeedback*. Oxford: Pergamon, 1979.

Miller, N., & Dworkin, B. Critical issues in therapeutic applications of biofeedback. In G. Schwartz & J. Beatty (Eds.), *Biofeedback: Theory and research*. Chicago: Aldine, 1977.

Mittelman, B., & Wolff, H. Emotions and gastroduodenal function. *Psychosomatic Medicine*, 1942, *4*, 5–61.

Moos, R., & Engel, B. T. Psychophysiological reactions in hypertensive and arthritic patients. *Journal of Psychosomatic Research*, 1962, *6*, 227–241.

Mountcastle, V. B. *Medical physiology*. St. Louis: Mosby, 1974.

Musaph, H. Itching and other dermatoses. In E. Wittower & H. Warnes (Eds.), *Psychosomatic medicine*. New York: Harper & Row, 1977.

Naranjo, C., & Ornstein, R. *On the psychology of meditation*. New York: Viking, 1971.

Nicassio, P., & Bootzin, R. A comparison of progressive relaxation and autogenic training as a treatment for insomnia. *Journal of Abnormal Psychology*, 1974, *83*, 253–260.

Nidich, S. Influence of TM on a measure of self actualization: A replication. *Journal of Counseling Psychology*, 1973, *20*, 565–566.

Ogden, E., Shock, N. Voluntary hypercirculation. *American Journal of the Medical Sciences*, 1939, *198*, 329--342.

Ohlsen, M. A. Protein nutrition in aged man. *Annals of the New York Academy of Sciences*, 1958, *69*, 913–915.

Orme-Johnson, D., Farrow, J. *Scientific research on the Transcendental Meditation program.* Collected paper, New York: Mararishi International University Press, 1978.

Ornstein, R. *The psychology of consciousness.* San Francisco: Freeman, 1972.

Pagano, R., & Frumkin, L. The effect of Transcendental Meditation on right hemisphere functioning. *Biofeedback and Self-Regulation*, 1977, *2*, 407–415.

Paul, G. Strategy of outcome research in psychotherapy. *Journal of Consulting and Clinical Psychology*, 1967, *31*, 109–118.

Paul, G. Physiological effects of relaxation training and hypnotic suggestion. *Journal of Abnormal Psychology*, 1969, *74*, 425–437. (a)

Paul, G. Inhibition of physiological response to stressful imagery by relaxation training and hypnotically suggested relaxation. *Behavior Research and Therapy*, 1969, *7*, 249–256. (b)

Paykel, E., Myers, J., Dienelt, M., Klerman, G., Lindenthal, J., & Pepper, J. Life events and depression: A controlled study. *Archives of General Psychiatry*, 1969, *21*, 753–760.

Penfield, W. *The mystery of the mind.* Princeton: Princeton University Press, 1975.

Peper, E. Problems in biofeedback training. *Perspectives in Biology and Medicine*, 1976, *19*, 404–412.

Pfeiffer, C. C. Mental and elemental nutrients. New Canaan, Conn.: Keats, 1975.

Pollock, M. L. The quantification of endurance training programs. *Exercise and Sport Science Reviews* (Vol. 1). New York: Academic, 1973.

Pratap, V., Berrettini, W., & Smith, C. Arterial blood gases in pranayama practice. *Perceptual and Motor Skills*, 1978, *46*, 171–174.

Robinson, C. H. *Normal and therapeutic nutrition.* New York: Macmillan, 1972.

Rochefort, G. J. *et al.* Depletion of pituitary corticotropin by various stresses and by neurohypophyseal preparations. *Journal of Physiology*, 1959, *146*, 105–116.

Roessler, R., & Greenfield, M. (Eds.). *Physiological correlates of psychological disorders.* Madison: University of Wisconsin Press, 1962.

Roldán, E., Alvarez-Pelaez, P., & deMolina, F. Electrographic study of the amygdaloid defense response. *Physiology and Behavior*, 1974, *13*, 779–787.

Ryan, A. History of sports medicine. In A. Ryan & F. Allman, *Sports medicine.* New York: Academic, 1974.

Sabbot, I., McNew, J., Hoshizaki, T., Sedgwick, C., & Adey, W. Effect of a 30 day isolation stress on calcium phosphorous and other excretory products in the unrestrained chimpanzee. *Aerospace Medicine*, 1972, *43*, 142–148.

Sarbin, T., & Coe, W. *Hypnosis: A social psychological analysis of influence communication*. New York: Holt, Rinehart & Winston, 1972.

Sartre, J. P. *Being and nothingness* (H. Barnes, trans.). New York: Philosophical Library, 1956.

Schnore, M. M. Individual patterns of physiological activity as a function of task differences and degree of arousal. *Journal of Experimental Psychology*, 1959, *58*, 117–128.

Scrimshaw, N. The effect of stress on nutrition in adolescents and young adults. In F. Heald (Ed.), *Adolescent nutrition and growth.* New York: Appleton-Century-Crofts, 1969.

Select Committee on Nutrition and Human Needs, U.S. Senate Dietary Goals for the United States (2nd ed.). Washington, D.C.: U.S. Government Printing Office, 1977.

Selye, H. The General Adaptation Syndrome and the gastrointestinal diseases of adaptation. *American Journal of Proctology*, 1951, *2*, 167–184.

Selye, H. *The stress of life.* New York: McGraw-Hill, 1956.

Selye, H. *Stress without distress.* Philadelphia: Lippincott, 1974.

Selye, H. *Stress in health and disease.* Reading, Mass.: Butterworth's, 1976.

Serban, G. Stress in schizophrenics and normals. *British Journal of Psychiatry*, 1975, *126*, 397–407.

Shader, R. (Ed.). *Manual of psychiatric therapeutics*. Boston: Little, Brown, 1975.

Shagass, C., & Malmo, R. Psychodynamic themes and localized muscular tension during psychotherapy. *Psychosomatic Medicine*, 1954, *16*, 295–313.

Shapiro, D. *Precision nirvana*. Englewood Cliffs, N.J.: Prentice-Hall, 1978.

Shapiro, D., & Giber, D. Meditation and psychotherapeutic effects. *Archives of General Psychiatry*, 1978, *35*, 294–302.

Shapiro, J., & Shapiro, D. The psychology of responsibility: Some second thoughts on holistic medicine. *New England Journal of Medicine*, 1979, *301*, 211–212.

Shearn, D. Operant conditioning of heart rate. *Science*, 1962, *137*, 530–531.

Sheehan, P. *The function and nature of imagery*. New York: Academic, 1972.

Shoemaker, J., & Tasto, D. Effects of muscle relaxation on blood pressure of essential hypertensives. *Behavior Research and Therapy*, 1975, *13*, 29–43.

Shontz, F. *The Psychological aspects of physical illness and disability*. New York: MacMillan, 1975.

Simons, D. J., Day, E., Goodell, H., & Wolff, H. Experimental studies on headache. *Research Publication of the Association of Nervous and Mental Disorders*, 1943, *23*, 228–244.

Spiegel, H., & Spiegel, D. *Trance and treatment*. New York: Basic Books, 1978.

Spielberger, C., Gorsuch, R., & Lushene, R. *The STAI Manual*. Palo Alto, Calif.: Consulting Psychologists Press, 1970.

Stein, L., Wise, C., & Berger, B. An Antianxiety action of benzodiazepines. In S. Garattini, E. Mussini, & L. Randall (Eds.), *The benzodiazepines*. New York: Raven Press, 1973.

Steinmark, S. & Borkovec, T. *Assessment of active and placebo treatment of moderate insomnia*. Paper presented at the Midwestern Psychological Association, Chicago, 1973.

Stephenson, P. Physiologic and psychotropic effects of caffeine on man. *Journal of the American Dietetic Association*, 1977, *71*, 240–247.

Sterman, M. B. Neurophysiological and clinical studies of sensorimotor EEG biofeedback training: Some effects on epilepsy. In L. Birk (Ed.), *Biofeedback: Behavioral medicine*. New York: Grune & Stratton, 1973.

Sterman, M. B., & Friar, L. Suppression of seizures in an epileptic following sensorimotor EEG feedback training. *Electroencephalography and Clinical Neurophysiology*, 1972, *33*, 89–95.

Stern, R., Ray, W., & Davis, C. *Psychophysiological recording*. New York: Oxford University Press, 1980.

Sternbach, R. *Principles of psychophysiology*. New York: Academic, 1966.

Stoyva, J. Self-regulation and stress-related disorders: A perspective on biofeedback. In D. I. Mostofsky (Ed.), *Behavior control and modification of physiological activity*. Englewood Cliffs, N.J.: Prentice-Hall, 1976.

Stoyva, J. Why should muscular relaxation be clinically useful? In J. Beatty (Ed.), *NATO Symposium on biofeedback and behavior*. New York: Plenum, 1977.

Stoyva, J. Guidelines in the training of general relaxation. In J. Basmajian (Ed.), *Biofeedback: Principles and practices for clinicians*. Baltimore: Williams & Wilkins, 1979.

Stoyva, J., & Budzynski, T. Cultivated low-arousal: An anti-stress response? In L. DiCara (Ed.), *Recent advances in limbic and autonomic nervous systems research*. New York: Plenum, 1974.

Stroebel, C. F. *Non-specific effects and psychodynamic issues in self-regulatory techniques*. Paper presented at the Johns Hopkins Conference on Clinical Biofeedback, Baltimore, November 1979.

Swonger, A., & Constantine, L. *Drugs and therapy: A psychotherapist's handbook of psychotropic drugs.* Boston: Little, Brown, 1976.

Tart, C. *States of consciousness.* New York: Dutton, 1975.

Taub, E., & Stroebel, C. Biofeedback in the treatment of vasonconstrictive syndromes. *Biofeedback and Self-Regulation*, 1978, *3*, 363–374.

Taylor, J. A scale for manifest anxiety. *Journal of Abnormal and Social Psychology*, 1953, *48*, 285–290.

Townsend, R. *et al.* A comparison of biofeedback-mediated relaxation and group therapy in the treatment of anxiety. *American Journal of Psychiatry*, 1975, *132*, 598–601.

USDA/HEW Dietary Guidelines for Americans. Washington, D.C.: U.S. Government Printing Office, 1980.

Usdin, E., Kretnansky, R., & Kopin, I. *Catecholamines and stress.* Oxford: Pergamon, 1976.

Vahia, N. Psychophysiologic therapy based on the concepts of Pantanjali. *American Journal of Psychotherapy*, 1972, *27*, 557–565.

Vanderhoof, L. *The effects of a simple relaxation technique on stress during pelvic examinations.* Unpublished master's thesis, University of Maryland School of Nursing, 1980.

Wain, H. Hypnosis in consultation-liaison psychiatry. *Psychosomatics*, 1979, *20*, 678–689.

Wain, H. (Ed.), *Clinical hypnosis in medicine.* Chicago: Yearbook Medical Publishers, 1980.

Weil, J. L. *A neurophysiological model of emotional and intentional behavior.* Springfield, Ill. Charles C Thomas, 1974.

Weiner, H. *Psychobiology and human disease.* New York: Elsevier, 1977.

Weiner, H., Thaler, M., Reiser, M., & Mirsky, I. Etiology of duodenal ulcer. *Psychosomatic Medicine*, 1957, *19*, 1–10.

Wenger, M. A., Clemens, T., Coleman, D., Cullen, T., & Engel, B. Autonomic response patterns during intravenous infusion of epinephrine and norepinephrine. *Psychosomatic Medicine*, 1960, *22*, 294–307.

White, J. *What is meditation?* New York: Doubleday Anchor, 1974.

Whitehead, W. Biofeedback in the treatment of gastrointestinal disorders. *Biofeedback and Self-Regulation*, 1978, *3*, 375–384.

Wilder, J. The Law of Initial Values. *Psychosomatic Medicine*, 1950, *12*, 392–401.

Wilmore, J. Individualized exercise prescription. In *Exercise in cardiovascular health and disease.* New York: Yorke Medical Books, 1977.

Wittkower, E. D. & Warnes, H. (Eds.) *Psychomatic medicine.* New York: Harper and Row, 1977.

Wolf, S., & Glass, G. B. Correlation of conscious and unconscious conflicts with changes in gastric function and structure. In H. G. Wolff, S. Wolf, et.al. (Eds.), *Life stress and bodily disease.* Baltimore: Williams & Wilkins, 1950.

Wolff, H. G. *Headache and other head pain.* New York: Oxford University Press, 1963.

Wolpe, J. *Psychotherapy by reciprocal inhibition.* Stanford: Stanford University Press, 1958.

Yates, F., & Maran, J. Stimulation and inhibition of ACTH release. In W. Sawyer & E. Knobil (Eds.), *Handbook of physiology*, 1972.

Yuwiler, A. Stress, anxiety and endocrine function. In R. Grenell and S. Galay (Eds.), *Biological foundations of psychiatry.* New York: Raven Press, 1976.

Zuckerman, M. The development of an affect adjective checklist for the measurement of anxiety. *Journal of Consulting Psychology*, 1960, *24*, 457–462.

Zuckerman, M., & Lubin, B. *Manual for the Multiple Affect Adjective Checklist.* San Diego: Educational and Industrial Testing Service, 1965.

About the Authors

George S. Everly, Jr., Ph.D. is Associate Professor of Psychology, Loyola College, Baltimore, Maryland; Associate Professor of Health Education, University of Maryland, University College; and also a Lecturer, Counseling and Personnel Services, University of Maryland, College Park, Maryland.

Robert Rosenfeld, M.D. is Assistant Chief of Consultation-Liaison Psychiatry Service, Department of Psychiatry, Walter Reed Army Medical Center, Washington, D.C.

WITH CONTRIBUTIONS BY

Roger J. Allen, Ph.D. is Director of Research and Graduate Studies, Director of the Psychophysiologic Research and Biofeedback Learning Laboratories, Department of Health Education, University of Maryland, College Park.

Lora C. Brown, M.S., R.D. is a Nutritionist at the Johns Hopkins Hospital, Baltimore, Maryland.

Steven A. Sobelman, Ph.D. is Associate Professor of Psychology and Director of Graduate Studies at Loyola College, Baltimore, Maryland.

Harold J. Wain, Ph.D., F.A.P.M. is Director of Consultation-Liaison Service, Department of Psychiatry, Walter Reed Army Medical Center, Washington, D.C.

Index